S0-BSJ-253

WITHDRAWN

PRINCE METTERNICH

Prince Metternich

PRINCE METTERNICH

Statesman and Lover

BY

RAOUL AUERNHEIMER

ALLIANCE BOOK CORPORATION

NEW YORK

Lenoir Rhyne College
LIBRARY

940.28
Au 3P

18356
Dec. 1941

COPYRIGHT 1940 BY RAOUL AUERNHEIMER

Translated by James A. Galston

PRINTED IN THE UNITED STATES OF AMERICA
BY THE VAIL-BALLOU PRESS, INC., BINGHAMTON, N. Y.

Introduction

We live in an Age of biography. This literary development has now become most evident, and the reasons for it
cannot be attributed solely to a sudden preference of publishers and their authors. That form of biography, which
is so bold as to wish to be more than merely an aid to
drawing-room conversation, is actually a veiled response of
our generation to a materialistic historical perspective which
has grown tedious.

If the world consisted merely of mud and logic, as the
materialists would have us believe, there would be little
reason to write biographies, much less to read them. On the
contrary, if the lives of certain individuals, who somewhere
in the course of history have taken the helm, fascinate us,
the cause can only be that we have an unconscious desire
to substitute history in a deeper, truer meaning, or if this
is already the case, to probe its significance. The proof lies
in the fact that men have been writing history for several
thousand years. What sense would there be in the mere recording of a senseless series of events? It is for this reason that
writers from Thucydides to Charles Beard have felt themselves drawn to this field of endeavor and have devoted their
lives to it.

These ideas are not new, but in these propagandistic days

they have an air of novelty. A century ago, in the time of Metternich, an Austrian historiographer, Hormayr, resolved this problem soundly. In writing of biography, he said, "Biography is not history. Biographies form the ingredients, and spices of history. For history flows out of the lives of men, and each era revolves about its great men, and should we doubt it, we may learn how through the strength or weakness of individuals, nations come into being, flourish and decay; how, often, a single man may decree to the present its course, and to posterity, what it may record. Hormayr closes his paragraph with the pious hope that "his book would be read with the heart, since it had come from the heart."

The Metternich era was that of Napoleon. The flames which still beat about the world today, were kindled by that fiery son of revolution. Then as now, an entire continent was involved, and in the end the destiny of nearly the entire world was caught up, and there was created a fateful division between might and right, which split the nations into two belligerent camps.

A man of titanic, and in the end, boundless ambition, strove for supreme power, first in his own land, then over adjacent nations, and finally over Europe. No continental country whose national spirit did not spring out of the revolutionary flame of an inspired people was able to impede his progress, be it Austria, Prussia, Russia, Spain, or the German States.

Only Great Britain, protected by its geographical position, continued the struggle with varying success, during Napoleon's entire career. To crush England, the Autocrat of the Continent devised the so-called Continental System in order to freeze Britain's imports and exports, and deal a death blow to the trade of the country, and therefore to the nation itself. For a time he planned a direct invasion of the island kingdom. He had a vast fleet of rafts built at Boulogne, in order to ferry a great army across the Channel. After Trafalgar, he changed his plans, and transferred his troops elsewhere on the continent, where their triumphal march could not be halted.

The similarity between Napoleon and Hitler is a favorite topic in the nations not yet overwhelmed by Fascism. In the other countries, there is little left to say. But to speak seriously we must state at once, that the resemblance is one of events, far more than of personality. The parallelism of historical development cannot be denied. We can speak already of the Napoleonic successes of Hitler, and almost (here we antici- pate) of the Hitlerian success of Napoleon. The path in life taken by both creators of such astonishing sequences of events, show a striking similarity. Both are entirely self-made men. In times of world-chaos, they rose out of the depths, Na- poleon from obscure bourgeois beginnings, Hitler out of even more obscure proletarian origins. Both strove grimly and determinedly for the highest power in the state, and appro- priated it, after proclaiming themselves "leaders" of their people. Strange paradox of history that in both cases it was, strictly speaking, not even their own people they rose to govern. Napoleon was of Italian parentage, and became Emperor of the French, while Hitler is an Austrian and be- came the Overlord of a Greater Germany, and the restorer of Prussian imperialism. One went from Ajaccio to Paris, the other from Braunau to Berlin. Notwithstanding all the remarkable historical similarities in the lives of the two men, we can hardly speak of a similarity in their char- acters. Napoleon was a Plutarchic personality while Hitler stems from Wagner's music dramas, and German mythology. Nothing is more absurd than to attempt to see in him a disciple of Nietzsche, the philosopher of "the hammer." Mussolini can with greater justice claim Nietzsche as a spiritual ancestor. "The hammer" of which Nietzsche wrote was the hammer of antiquity, the other which Hitler swings is the hammer of Thor, the ancient German war god. The atmosphere in which he breathes so stormily is the air of "Der Götterdämmerung." Finally, as men the two autocrats are totally dissimilar.

Napoleon, despite the dazzling light in which he lived, had many strongly human characteristics. He was a devoted husband, a tender father, a lover and a son. Hitler has no mother to share his glory, and to stand above or even behind him. Even if he had one, she would not dare admire him, and even wonder in the same breath as did Madame Letizia, *"Pourvu que ça dure!"* Above all, we must not overlook the cardinal difference stemming from the use and abuse of power. Napoleon ordered the execution of the royalist Duc d'Enghien, whose blood thereafter stained the imperial mantle. What is that compared with Hitler? In the German concentration camps thousands of political prisoners are brutally tortured and executed year after year. If Hitler is indeed a Napoleon, he must be one without concentration camps. But if these are removed, the departure is so far from the reality that hardly anything remains.

The resemblance of the historical background goes even further. Then as now, the gigantic conflict narrowed down to single combat between the conqueror of Europe and Great Britain. In this duel, Metternich played the rôle of an ambiguous second until he was able to become a crippling opponent. He stayed in the background as long as he could. Finally the refusal of Russia to enjoy without envy the Napoleonic successes in western and central Europe led to a shattering of the Continental System. Napoleon forsook his plan of an alliance against England, and turned Russia-wards. He forged a coalition such as the world had never seen. Austria, Prussia, all the other German States, and the Lowlands marched under the eagles to Moscow.

There at last he was beaten. To put it in another way, his victory proved his own undoing. The artful Russian strategy lured him ever deeper into the endless steppes, and the Russian winter did the rest. A year later, shortly before "The Battle of the Nations," at Leipsic, Metternich wrote to his father, "Europe can still be saved." In the meantime, in a diplomatic flanking movement without parallel, Metternich had transformed himself from an ally of Napoleon's into his most formidable opponent, and the creator of a coalition against the French Emperor.

Metternich had foretold the downfall of the Empire six years before, in a Paris dispatch to the Austrian Foreign Office. He had arrived at his remarkable prophecy less through observation, than from a firm conviction, which he maintained all his life: the certainty that in the end, every revolution swallows its own offspring. He had correctly recognized that Napoleon was no isolated genius, no white-hot meteor newly fallen to earth, but the hero of a great mass movement unleashed by the Revolution, French Nationalism. Napoleon was a child of revolution. Metternich was the child of counter-revolution, his action was reaction, and as the great reactionary, who earnestly tried to force the flow of the 19th century back into the channels of the 18th, he lives in history which has been so unfavorable to him until now. It is true that Napoleon was the dynamic modern, while Metternich personified the static 18th century, and

this stubborn immutability cost him the sympathy of posterity. But there followed after the wise and progressive 19th
century, the self-despairing 20th century, which in a large
part of Europe, and particularly in the region where Metternich lived, has been pushed back into the 17th century
to the time of the guilds, of fallacious racial concepts and
hatreds, serfdom, religious persecutions, devilish Machiavel-
lianism, and witch hunts.

What was reaction in the 19th century may seem, at least
in this sphere of Europe, progress, and at the same time, a
heavy burden is added in that the destiny of the continent
and the fate of the entire world now are endangered by European Nationalism.

With the *"allons enfants de la patrie,"* of the French,
Nationalism began its march. Spreading over all frontiers
in the first explosion, French Nationalism kindled the German "Wars of Independence," produced the German Reich
fifty years later, and led to the unification of Italy; the states
which direct today the nationalist movement, and spread
far and wide the new articles of faith.

Then, towards the end of the 19th century, the smaller
European states followed the example set by the great
powers, and observed that they were nations also. For if
a nation qua nation is sacred, it matters little to the collective egoism of its people whether the population numbers
five, ten, or one hundred millions. The liquidation of the
Austro-Hungarian monarchy, the last international union
of nationalities in Europe, was the logical and historical result. Out of the wrecked Habsburg empire, that part which
became Czecho-Slovakia endured the same fate twenty years
later. Poland and Rumania followed. They had the bitter
choice between dismemberment or disappearance. Before

they had been told that Nationalism and Imperialism were incompatible. Now, however, after they had become thoroughly convinced of that, a new form of Nationalism stalks the stage, Nationalist Imperialism, far more brutal in nature, which is no longer applicable to all nations, but is valid merely for the favored few. Nations may be equal before God—that much Fascism admits—but on earth the master-race is God. The wheel of time having made a complete revolution, Europe turns back to witch-hunting, and reactionary Metternich who condemning nationalist principles, fought the European hegemony of the "Grande Nation," stands suddenly revealed as a revolutionary. He, who declared not once but a thousand times that Nationalism meant Jacobinism, would have been the least surprised man in Europe at the Hitler-Stalin alliance.

In this far-reaching foresight lies the significance of Metternich while his task lay in the direction of thwarting Napoleonic imperialism. He conceived the plan, and carried it through, in which he pitted the art of diplomacy against military genius. The first step was the marriage of the Austrian Emperor's daughter to the "usurper." The second was the consequent split between France and Russia, and the third, the formation of a European coalition, which in the end was to prove stronger than the single man who felt himself called "to restore order" in Europe. Even then a nationalist order might have resulted in the sense of a master race such as the French were in those days. Metternich was well aware of this danger, and he planned methodically the creation of an international European order which would preserve the balance of power and be in the nature of a European confederation. The fruit of his endeavors lasted, after all, until the tragedy of 1914, just as the lengthening shadow of Metternich spread over Austria until the golden twilight of the Francisco-Josephinian epoch. His example and his spirit remained a model for Austria to follow.

Until very recently, Metternich's portrait presided quietly in the white-walled palace of the seemingly unchanged Austrian State Chancellery, and three generations of young attachés and older diplomats admired, *en passant,* the handsome pleasure-loving face. All these Ballhaus princelings lived and loved in the Metternich style, while his smoothly refined and metaphorical manner of writing set an example for the leading editorials of Vienna newspapers to follow. His imitators may have lacked his industry, his talent, and his spirit, but at least they aped his fashions, and smiled philosophically over the course of events, as he had done. Only in March 1938 did they cease smiling and recall Metternich's teaching. The best thing about Metternich was that he was a true European, "The Knight of Europe," and as such recognized the demagogic nature of nationalist instincts. Europe can exist as a group of nations, but never as a set of warring nationalisms.

Metternich had understood this problem sooner than any other statesman in Europe, because he had to administer a multi-national state. Who can deny that the course of events he warned against have dismally come true. Nationalist imperialism is today a world-wide peril, while a United States of Europe would mean world-wide hope.

Seen from this angle, the Austria of Metternich was the first experiment towards a European solution. He did not limit, at least in theory, the national application of the principle of autonomy, thereby preserving political unity. Unfortunately this principle of maintaining the stability of the government by federation and decentralization, which is the cornerstone of the American Constitution, was departed from radically by Metternich's successors. Austria was short-sighted enough to yield to the aspirations of the German-ophiles, and because of it, Austria and the rest of Europe fell apart. But the solution of force has at least this comfort-ing character: it is a transitory solution. In the end, reason will conquer, although perhaps not altogether without our co-operation.

"Trust in God but keep your camel securely tethered," is a sagacious Arab proverb. Metternich, philosopher that he was, probably knew the maxim, and acted accordingly.

"Principles are the formulae of truth," was one of his favorite sayings, and so he was all his life, with regard to Europe, a faithful anti-nationalist. When the European solu-tion for which he strove is found, without imperialism, and not limited to Central Europe alone, then Metternich's mem-ory, and all of Europe will be re-established. This work has been written to point out this course. The author can only hope for what his countrymen of a century ago prayed: that his book may be read with the heart, out of which it has come.

R. A.

Petersham, Mass.
August 20, 1940.

The author wishes to express his warm appreciation of the editorial aid rendered him by Mr. S. R. Shapiro. Mr. Shapiro also translated the introduction and compiled the biographical table and the index.

Contents

BOOK THREE

THE DICTATOR OF EUROPE

BOOK FOUR

THE WISE MAN WITH THE THOUSAND RECOLLECTIONS

BOOK ONE

A Personality in the Making

A Young Cavalier Grows Up

The importance of a man may as little be revealed from his lineage as the final effect of a mixture of red and violet pigments, as they lie freshly squeezed on the artist's palette. Not even if the palette be that of a Titian or a Tintoretto, is the revelation a significant one. All the significance lies in the application of the oils to the canvas.

There are, nevertheless, three illuminating facts to be stated in the case of Clemens Metternich, who was born on May 15, 1773, at Metternich Court, Koblenz on the Rhine, because these three facts fit so well in the picture to be painted: He saw the light of day on the banks of the Rhine, his father was of the German nobility, and his mother was a devout Catholic.* These three elements, nobility, Catholicism, and the drop of Burgundy wine which seems to flow through the veins of every Rhinelander, are unquestionably substantiated in his character through his ancestry. What he made of them, however, was of his own doing.

In ancient days, the Rhine formed the Roman boundary line: the vertical one, be it understood, for the horizontal boundary was the Main which flows into the Rhine, and there are those who read a deeper meaning in the fact that in German, Rhine and Main rhyme. In either case, the Romans who were realistic politicians, knew what they were doing when they fixed these boundaries and adhered to them. They believed, though they did not adhere rigidly to it, that politically, and socially, Germany could only be trusted and associated with, as far as the wine grew. The Rhinelanders, themselves, being wine-loving Catholics, were well aware of that fact. The wine in the chalice and the wine in the goblet quite patently influenced their character. This fact applies also in the case of Metternich's parents, with the distinction that his father's tastes were rather in the direction of the goblet, while his pious mother inclined towards the chalice.

Metternich's father, whose surnames were Franz Georg, was a German of the old school, conscious and proud of his Teutonic origin. Glorying in the fact that in the course of centuries his family had produced a number of both ecclesiastical and secular dignitaries within the German-speaking realm, he conscientiously insisted upon his son's familiarity with the German language, a fact with which no fault can be found. Metternich remained true to this teaching throughout his life, writing the beautiful German of the classical epoch in sturdy Gothic characters.

On the other hand, his mother, who lived to a very old age, insisted upon conducting her correspondence with him in French. This may be considered nonessential, but the fact remains that Metternich, early accustomed to express himself in French, was able to do so very aptly throughout his long life, so that half of his innumerable letters were penned in that language. He never was a good Teuton in the national sense of the term. There is a question, of course, whether or not the national Germans are the good ones. Perhaps it may be said of Metternich that, though he was not a good German, he was a better one.

It can at any rate be assumed from Metternich's early attitude that, as far as his character and his personality were concerned, he was more his mother's child than his father's: his mother's son, but by no means mother's boy. This was true also of Napoleon, whom fate had decreed to be Metternich's great antagonist. Who was Napoleon's father? A pettifogging lawyer in the small Corsican town of Ajaccio. All-important was his mother, Laetitia.

Marie Beatrice Metternich, née Kageneck, was a lady whose nose, tongue, and intellect, were all sharp characteristics which she passed on to her son, Clemens. Physically, too, they resembled each other, and the resemblance grew with the years. As an old lady Madame Metternich looked exactly as her son did twenty-five years later, in one of his last portraits. From this it may be inversely deduced that in her youth the mother must have been very good-looking.

The handsome mother brought up her favorite son well, although she proceeded intuitively rather than deliberately when she encouraged his natural impulses towards maturity. Thus she once wrote to the immature fledgling who, somewhere in Germany, had expressed himself disparagingly about German music as compared to French music, because —and that was undoubtedly her opinion, too—he considered the latter infinitely more charming than the former. Her gentle motherly reprimand was to the effect that it was proper to praise the music of the country in which one happened to be living: in Germany the German, in France the French, and so on. A golden rule this, containing the seeds of the secret of the future Pied-Piper's consummate charm. On another occasion she commissioned the 17-year-old student to procure for her some piece of finery, a little lace cap possibly, in Strasbourg, because the latest Paris fashions were more readily obtainable there than at home. Clemens showed so much taste in executing the commission that, upon receipt of the package, he got a letter of praise from his mother, saying that he was *"le meillieur commissionaire que je connaisse."*

While thus his mother determined with a few feminine touches the characteristic fundamentals of the future ladies' man, whose adaptability (*vide,* music) and whose good taste (*vide,* lace cap) were to be praised by many, there can be no doubt that the future man of the world, into which the Strasbourg student was slowly growing, was strongly influenced by the blunter nature of his father. Count Franz Georg not only insisted upon his son's speaking a decent German but, worldly wise, he also advised him to keep socially on good terms with the old ladies. The latter advice was dictated as little by reasons of humanity as the former insistence had its foundation in German patriotism, a feeling still foreign to Franz Georg Metternich, the German noble, and never to be recognizable in the make-up of his son. The elder Metternich, with the fleshy wine-lover's nose in his epicurean face, was as far from being a man of deep feeling as he was from being a fiery patriot. Thoroughly familiar, however, with his ancestral history, which to an aristocrat frequently represents history itself, he was aware of the fact that for centuries the Counts Metternich as German nobles had made a living principally because they *were* German nobles, and thus it was obviously essential to be German. Family experience likewise had taught him that while substantial posts were mostly striven for because of young women, they were usually handed out by or at least arranged for through the agency of old ladies. That is why the elder Metternich advocated a show of attention to them and a display of complaisance. His art of living was directed towards practical goals and borne by a robust egoism. These characteristics, too, were to be among his son's heritage, with the sole difference, perhaps, that the somewhat uncouth hand of the older man felt slenderer and moved more lithely in the diplomat's glove. All in all it may be said of Clemens Metternich that his father's rather ignoble character-complex represented that part of the intellectual heritage of the son which the latter had to overcome. Emperor Franz, who knew character, confidentially called the elder Metternich a "phlegmaticus." It is also reported that one of his utterances was maliciously circulated among his own set. When faced once with a perplexing confusion of facts he was said to have put certain documents to one side and remarked with the utmost placidity: "This matter, like all other matters, will sometime and somehow reach its conclusion." Silly as the saying is, the dash of fatalistic philosophy it contains may have had a slight share in young Metternich's character mixture. We are told that he always remained unruffled, forever the "master of the next step."

The general education of the adolescent Metternich was the usual one accorded those of his sphere of life at the end of the 18th century. His parents being Catholic, he was, to begin with, sent to the Jesuit school which quite fitted in with the fact that in her later years his mother was generally referred to as a "great friend of the Jesuits." Young Clemens likely learned early from the disciples of Loyola how to talk to everyone, to every class, to every profession, and to either of the sexes, in their respective language. In this art the Jesuits were past masters. Perhaps it was also due to their teaching that he established his own autocratic formula governing veracity: if someone asks you what he has no right to ask, it is permissible to lie. This is a rather convenient simplification of morals, especially suitable to blue-eyed diplomats of Metternich's caliber. He was presently to embark upon his future profession, when he became a student at the Diplomatic College in Strasbourg where, some years before, Talleyrand had studied. There he was taught by Koch how to write long notes in a dainty handwriting, cleverly putting others in the wrong by frivolously citing international laws which those in power were ever able to twist and mould according to their fancy. On the other hand, he also learned from his private tutor, who went by the unaristocratic name of Simon, how to walk about openly without a wig, an undertaking which at that time would almost stamp a youth of his class as a revolutionary. It was the only revolutionary action of which Metternich was ever guilty. Among the other things he learned in Strasbourg were swimming and playing the fiddle, accomplishments of some importance to a society man of whom sportsmanship was expected and to a frequent guest at house parties where versatility was at a premium. His attractive "Attic" exterior was praised even then by his tutor, although not in these words. Finally, there were theater parties from time to time, the worldly minded Strasbourgers being rather fond of going "to the comedy," as they called it. It is a fact that the future State-Chancellor retained a liking for this form of diversion throughout his life.

Koch and Simon: Koch was the systematizer who taught the young Metternich to arrange his ideas pedantically before putting them to actual use and not to compose any piece of writing without careful previous construction. Simon, however, the daring foe of wigs, surprisingly turned into a revolutionary when the towering waves of the French Revolution surged as far as Strasbourg, where the Town Hall was carried by force. It is to be assumed that at heart he had always been a revolutionary. At any rate, he was from that moment decidedly affiliated with the Left, while Metternich's face was resolutely turned towards the Right. Naturally, the storming of the Strasbourg Town Hall was not at all to the liking of Metternich's progenitor, the wine-addicted Rhenish nobleman who firmly insisted upon his inherited privileges. He immediately ordered his son to remove himself to Mainz, the residence of the Prince-Archbishop, where courtly and gallant life in the French taste continued as if nothing had happened. His former tutor had to turn to writing text-books for use in the schools of Paris. When, years later, thoroughly impoverished, he knocked at Metternich's door, he was turned away. In the long run, Mainz proved to be stronger than Strasbourg.

Another reason why Mainz was stronger in Metternich's life was his liaison with a charming young woman. It was there that the Count, scarcely twenty years old, first was initiated into the mysteries of love. It was of decisive and lasting importance to the young man's love-life that the first object of his affection was a married woman, although she was a belle of but eighteen years; she had many admirers, and he himself retained his fondness for her for more than thirty years. She was a Madame Constance de Caumont-La Force, whose husband was in the diplomatic service of France. It seems that Monsieur Caumont was kept busy by his duties throughout the day, giving Metternich ample time to devote himself to the bored young woman. He had matriculated as a student at the University of Mainz but spent most of his time with Constance. Twenty-five years later, in a kind of general confession to Princess Lieven, he wrote:

"We were in each other's company all day long and yet had not the courage to ask of each other what we both desired." If the self-complacent remark has its deeper meaning in the fact that Metternich *knew* what Constance desired, this knowledge may at any rate lead one to assume a rather far-reaching intimacy. This is further substantiated by the fact that the mature State-Chancellor, in speaking of his sweetheart of former days, says that the young woman's thoughts may have been of him rather than of her husband, even during the nights which followed their daily meetings.

That was the nature of Metternich's first love and of his very first sweetheart, whom a rapturous contemporary described as the perfect model of a Hebe or Psyche. It is of importance that she was Psyche, too, which is to say that the sensual-social connection was not without its admixture of a psychical element which ennobled it. In Metternich's life the charming Constance played about the same part as the worldly Lilly in the life of Goethe, the one in Mainz, the other in the not-far-distant Frankfort. The soulfully romantic Kates and Claires, however, who in Goethe's life came before and after, were conspicuously absent in the case of Metternich. It may be said that he started at once with a Madame von Stein. There is in Metternich a total lack of any contact with the middle classes, not only in the conference-room, but in his love-making as well. Social activities were his forte as they were his weakness, his fortune and his danger, his blessing and his curse. Almost without exception he loved married women—among whom his own wife was not included. No maiden, as far as is now ascertainable, ever played a part in his love-life; and the women were all members of the upper class. They all attracted him as gen-

tlewomen, before they were able to captivate him as women.
In spite of the pretended innocence of their affair, the
charming Constance, too, captivated him as a woman and
kept him captive for three years. This period was followed
by years of an intimate and pleasant friendship which
largely lived on the memories of delightful experiences.

In the meantime, however, Metternich, the student in
Mainz, had another and more serious first experience which
also was destined greatly to influence his intellectual development. It was the meeting with Herr Professor Vogt,
the "well-founded historian in a conservative sense," as
Metternich described him later. Vogt was the propagator of
the "Metternich System" and of that conception of Europe
which was at the bottom of all subsequent theories of Metternich. In his principal work Vogt developed the fundamental principles of a "European Republic," without himself being a republican. Quite in the spirit of his century,
the learned man explained mechanically how such a condition was to come about: attraction and repulsion, love
and hatred of two historical-political principles. "Two
masses keep clashing in Europe. The democratic party aims
at liberty and equality and, if it degenerates, at disbelief
and anarchy; while the monarchistic party strives for order
and belief and, if it degenerates, for despotism and super-
stition. The aristocratic party must constantly keep to the
middle, preaching moderation and the maintenance of the
status quo." In this complicated mystic formula of the two
parties—there being, as a matter of fact, three, for the aristocratic one bobs up all of a sudden—we see all of the black
magic of the political wizard to come: of two make three; of
three make one; and the one is absolutism, of which, to be-

gin with, good old Vogt had not thought, perhaps because, being a well-brought-up German professor, he had taken it for granted.

Vogt was a theorist of the academical variety whose abstract speculations unwittingly smooth the way for the dictators. What he visualized in his academical dreams was a "Christian Republic" on German soil which, in the meantime, he conscientiously plowed with foot-notes and fertilized with learned toil. In his last will, which presumably was his first, Professor Vogt stipulated that his heart and brain, enclosed in a box, be lowered to the bottom of the Rhine where, it may be supposed, they have been resting to this day. Metternich, who called himself Vogt's "grateful pupil," had his teacher's coffin buried at the foot of the wall enclosing his Castle Johannisberg, which even today haughtily dominates the valley of the Rhine.

Metternich, the student and man-in-the-making, lived in Strasbourg and Mainz as a young cavalier, accompanied and watched over by his father-confessor and tutor. His younger brother, Joseph, familiarly called Pepe, shared the little establishment which was a miniature Court. But in contrast to Pepe who, as aristocratic circles put it, was and remained to be a "simple-minded thinker," the talented Clemens never missed an opportunity for gathering solid knowledge. He did not mind loading up his school-satchel, and at the same time he laid a firm foundation for his general views of life. His character, too, began to make itself felt, a fact which is made apparent by the judgment of his fellow-pupils who tagged him with the stigma of a triple "F." *Fin, faux, fanfaron,* they labeled their dashing companion, the English meaning of which is: subtle, false, and braggardly. It was nothing but a spiteful boyish prank. Nevertheless Metternich was never quite able to outgrow the insidiously tacked-on three "F" 's. Like every adolescent pupil, he experienced the world at school; but the world, as nobody can deny, had already had its experience of him, too.

The French Revolution

THE rococo idyll of Mainz was not entirely idyllic. To begin with, young Metternich, nineteen years old, at the time, had to interrupt the idyll in order to journey to Brussels, as his father suddenly had been appointed to the post of Governor of the Austrian Netherlands. But even before his departure he had become aware of certain undercurrents below the surface of the gracious and mannerly life at the Electoral Court of Mainz. Curiosity prompted Clemens, the student, to investigate, although prudence cautioned him against becoming implicated. There was, for instance, the bookseller, Georg Forster, an interesting man who years before had accompanied James Cook, the explorer, on his voyages and was now dealing in forbidden books and revolutionary writings; there was Kotzebue, a dissolute writer of comedies, who was considered to be a Jacobin; there were the "illuminati" and the political visionaries, and all of them fireflies of the French Revolution, perhaps even live sparks, which had been wafted over from the scene of the Paris conflagration. Whenever the youth felt impelled to withdraw his inflammable imagination from their influence, he found himself surrounded by refugees, whose loose morals and fantastic frivolity furnished him with a distorted image of the French Revolution. Life itself saw to it that there was

14

no danger of the student Metternich's becoming one-sided. Moreover, he was by natural inclination a student who pursued his studies beyond the lecture-room.

Meanwhile another Imperial Coronation took place. Leopold, a Habsburg of considerable importance, the worthy brother of Emperor Joseph and Marie Antoinette, was dead; his nephew Franz, whom Metternich had met at Strasbourg, became his successor at the age of twenty-four, still quite insufficiently prepared for his exalted task. It was barely two years since Metternich had first gazed in wonderment at the medieval pomp of the Frankfort coronation, and now he was again privileged to witness the splendid spectacle. This time, he even took an active part, and he was able to adorn the beautiful picture. As president of the Young Men's League of Catholic Noblemen, he opened the ball, a slender Cherubino in pale-green silk with silver facings, while his partner was a lovely girl in pink satin whose grace and charm were greatly commented upon. She was the future Queen Louise of Prussia, then still a Mecklenburg princess. At the very moment when the handsome couple floated past the dull gaze of the young Emperor, Louis XVI was being seized and imprisoned in Paris. Here we have a simultaneity the significance of which only became apparent in historical retrospect, and remained long a secret to the gaily dancing couple. Thus we see juxtaposed the gray Parisian scene, and the brilliant glitter of the countless candles which illuminated the great chamber of the Romer, the Town Hall of the city of Frankfort.

The entire coronation party was invited by the Elector to Mainz where the feverish festivities continued. But soon, young Metternich journeyed to his native city of Koblenz where a more serious atmosphere prevailed. There, under the command of the Duke of Brunswick, an Austro-Prussian army was being raised which, it was announced boastfully, was to deal a death blow to the French Revolution. In that army, there was Goethe, who accompanied the Duke of Saxe-Weimar into battle, and who a few weeks later, after the battle of Valmy had been won by the revolutionary forces, wrote this prophetic sentence: "From here, and to-day a new era takes its beginning, and we are privileged to say that we were present." Metternich, too, was present, even if he did view the proceedings from the safe quarters of the diplomatic corps.

The threats barked forth before the battle, by the Duke of Brunswick, in his orders to the German army turned out to be nothing but empty shouting and bluster, as was to be the case on many a subsequent occasion. Valmy was followed in rapid succession by Jemappes and the taking of Mainz— all lost battles for Brunswick. First it was Dumouriez who was victorious, then Custine who entered Mainz; and finally came Carnot and Moreau. The French Revolution boasted of a galaxy of fine generals. Napoleon, who came later, was but one of them. Unquestionably, there are times which in themselves are uplifted and form, as it were, a pedestal for future monuments. Young Metternich, too, wherever he found himself, was privileged to stand upon such a pedestal. Out of a stormy background of world change his youthful figure steps forth expectantly.

After Jemappes there was no remaining in Brussels for Metternich's father. The Governor retreated hastily to Koblenz, accompanied by his son and secretary. The "Metternich Court" at Koblenz, as shown on a little picture of that period, was a rather unprepossessing old box. There the family rallied, presumably in an atmosphere of gloomy depression, for their possessions on the left bank of the Rhine were already in danger. Once more the fortunes of war turned, and the Governor was able to return to Brussels with his staff. But the city was not to be held long; either by making concessions, as the elder Metternich tried to do, or by an unyielding attitude, as the reactionary Vienna Government ordered. Finally the Governor, who found himself in a corner, made a desperate suggestion to the central government. He would arm the peasantry of Southern Belgium against the onrushing revolution, would form a kind of "home guard," as the Austrian Fascists did in the 1920's. But that suggestion met with a rude reception when submitted to his superior, Minister Thugut, who was as dull a fellow as his name indicated. To put arms in the people's hands! Why, that would be the height of folly.

The ardent zeal with which young Clemens seized upon his father's idea of a home guard, and the fact that he later even issued a pamphlet on the subject, may be an indication that the original idea was partly his own. Not much later he penned his first political pronouncement. Marie Antoinette had "sneezed into the basket," as the sans-culottes called the beheading of a person. An outraged coalition was formed among Austria, Prussia, England, Holland, and Spain to avenge this monstrous deed. It was the Governor's task to issue a manifesto to the Belgian army, and the indolent man had no objection to his son's attending to the matter. Clemens did it with the requisite *élan* in which his natural indignation eloquently manifested itself. "The blood of Maria Theresa, the blood of Austria, has stained the scaffold! Its voice cries out for revenge! Heaven and earth demand it! Onward, soldiers . . . !!" It is significant that it was a woman who drew from the embryo statesman Metternich this first political outcry.

The fact that Brussels was a forlorn hope slowly broke upon Metternich *père,* and he made the necessary arrangements to leave. He lost no time in having his young son appointed attaché at The Hague legation and, at the same time, sent him on a visit to England, whither he journeyed in the company of a Count Desaudrouin who was to negotiate a Belgian loan in London. There Clemens remained for almost half a year. He made the acquaintance of Pitt, and was presented to the King and to the Prince of Wales. He became acquainted with the king of fashion, Beau Brummell, attended the trial of Warren Hastings, and watched the naval parades which made a lasting impression upon him. He was quite delighted with England and even had something to say in favor of English parliamentarianism. His approval was subsequently modified by the Austrian reactionaries who regrettably claimed that it was not suitable for Austria.

Finally, as things were again in utter confusion on the Continent, Clemens had to take his reluctant departure. But where was he to go? The Hague legation to which he was attached no longer existed; Brussels was occupied and had long since been left by the elder Metternich; the family possessions on the left bank of the Rhine, which had yielded a yearly income of 50,000 gulden, were definitely lost; Koblenz, too, was in the hands of the victorious French army; and "Metternich Court," which had served as the family's last retreat, was quite inaccessible. There was nothing left but to arrange a meeting in Düsseldorf, presumably at some inn. Imagine the reunion with his father, his mother, and the intellectually inferior brother Pepe! It surely was the most dismal moment in the young man's life. More than half a century was to elapse before he, then a man of almost eighty, found himself in a similarly desperate situation.

Now, to be sure, he was young and handsome. It seems that his mother took these two facts duly into account when in a family council she proposed to have the Metternich head-quarters moved to Vienna. The thought that he was now a man may have passed through her mind as she sat facing him across the bare table of the inn and gauged the effect of his newly acquired semi-English manners: "He is pleasing to women . . . , he will make his way in Vienna. On to Vienna!" she urged the others, while her husband, per-plexed but phlegmatic as usual and twiddling his thumbs, once more put his reliance in the likelihood that "this matter, like all other matters, will somehow reach its conclusion."

When they were all squeezed into the coach, emblazoned with the Metternich arms, and were rolling along from Düs-seldorf to Vienna, it was the specter of the great event of the French Revolution which, invisible to all but Clemens, sat opposite him in the carriage, pointing the way into the fu-ture. Like himself, the shipwrecked Governor had lost his position. He had also lost his possessions, almost his name, and, at least for the time being, whatever influence he had. As for Clemens, he had had to flee from Mainz to Koblenz, from Koblenz to Brussels, from Brussels to London, and from London to Düsseldorf—always and everywhere treach-erously threatened by the wolf's jaws of the French Revolu-tion. This new political fact of the revolution was the foe of all his friends, for so far he had found friends only among the refugees; it had cheated him out of love's happiness; and it had even cost his Emperor's aunt her pretty head. It finally had made him a fugitive from his own country and pursued him relentlessly by evoking in his memory a series of ineradicable pictures of horror and devastation. It is understandable therefore, and almost a matter of course, that he considered this detestable development the basic fact of his life and made its obstruction his mission.

It is infinitely enlightening of Metternich's character and of the fate which was to develop from it that his first movement was a counter-movement. Not that he wanted something, but that he did *not* want it, made him productive. Not with an affirmative, but with a negative, did he enter upon the great career that was to be his. Such was the political program which, without giving it much thought and quite intuitively at first, he adopted as his own. The supporting ideology he provided only at a later date, a procedure adopted by many a dictator after him.

On to Vienna!

Wrecked by the French Revolution, the Metternich family were washed ashore on the banks of the Danube. The journey's main purpose, as determined at the Düsseldorf family council, was to appease the irate Emperor. He was irate because Count Metternich, whom he had made Governor of the Netherlands, had returned minus the Netherlands. But unfortunately no invitation to appear at Court and offer a justification was received. Neither the Emperor, his two State-Ministers, Thugut and Kobenzl, nor Count Trautmannsdorff who was particularly hostile towards him, seemed at all anxious to hear what he had to say for himself. A seemly pretext therefore had to be looked for to make plausible the journey to Vienna where everything else would follow in good time. The pretext was found in the Metternichs' neglected Bohemian estate of Königswart which, after the loss of the possessions on the left bank of the Rhine, had as a matter of fact assumed considerable economic importance. The estate was about half-way between Düsseldorf and Vienna so that it seemed quite natural for young Clemens to stop off at Königswart, while the shipwrecked Governor and his wife continued their journey with suitable speed. Thus the forms were observed, at any rate, and the Metternichs were able to make their initial arrangements in

Vienna before their son, who occupied more of his mother's heart than her husband, came to join them about a fortnight later.

It was late in November of the year 1794, when the Metternich family, despondent and gloomy, were fully assembled in Vienna. November was not a month calculated to make Vienna look its best. Moreover, it had not yet attained the rank of a beautiful city, like Paris or London. Its beauties it had, but it was not beautiful. Its chief charm, its surroundings and the large gardens of its suburban districts, did not show up to advantage in winter. The "Inner City," where the socially elect lived and where it may be assumed the Metternichs, too, took lodging, boasted no gardens, and the thoroughfares were narrow and unclean. It consisted of a labyrinthine maze of streets and alleys, the pavements were bumpy, and covered with filth. The fine people—they called them the "better people" in Vienna—never set foot on the dirty streets, not all of which were even paved. They floated above the filth in their coaches or in sedan chairs. At night torch-bearing servants ran ahead of their vehicles, the only street lighting there was at that time. If nobody happened to drive past, or if a lantern-bearing wanderer did not stumble by, it was pitch dark.

It is questionable whether at that time the Metternichs had any torch bearers. But they had a son who in due course of time would be likely to provide those torch bearers—and all else they required. In those days Countess Marie Beatrice may have looked into his clever blue eyes even oftener and more fondly than was her wont and speculated upon the meaning of the mysterious smile which lately had come to play upon the lips of the young voluptuary. He had brought that man-of-the-world smile from London where some beautiful lady may have implanted it with her kisses. At any rate, Constance was no longer the sole object of his love. His doting mother knew all about Constance, as she knew of his other amours, and she probably thought it best that there were others besides Constance. "How fortunate," she thought, "that the mischief done by women in the plural, can always be made up for by woman in the singular." She may have looked sorrowfully and somewhat bitterly across at her husband who, when he went for his glass of wine, was known to be rather susceptible to passing belles.

In that respect, father and son had no difficulty in making friends in Vienna. But when it came to finding an entrée into Vienna society, it was a different story. Society, which to Countess Metternich meant the aristocracy, kept aloof, and was entrenched behind its bastions like the Inner City. The city was surrounded by walls, pierced only by small loopholes. Society was quite similar. A good knowledge of strategy was needed to storm either citadel. In addition, the aristocracy was never too gracious to strangers coming from Germany. They acted very much like Metternich was to act fifty years later; while most cordial towards French and English visitors, they were glacial to those who were proud of being good Germans. They had not yet gotten over the loss of Silesia, and society was filled with a great rage against all that was Prussian. To be sure, the Metternichs were Rhinelanders and Catholic Counts, but that was all that was known of them. After all they were nothing but *émigrés*. That status is not looked on with favor anywhere, especially in circles which pride themselves on their exclusiveness.

As a matter of fact the Metternichs were not connected with any of the great houses of the Austrian aristocracy. A favorite game indulged in during the early stages of an acquaintanceship in Vienna, was the so-called "climbing of the family tree." It meant a genealogical conversation, in the course of which families in all their ramifications were gone over with meticulous detail until to mutual joy it could be ascertained that a cousin many times removed had married into the family of an aunt of equally distant relationship. Unfortunately, in the case of the Metternichs, this game was not productive of any positive results.

However, it was ascertained, or perhaps it had been known all the time, that they had a few sovereign bishops in the family and that their sixteen quarters were in order. But not even that made a very deep impression. So the family of the "has-been" governor "in disgrace" was snubbed and was at first the recipients of very few invitations.

But while this attitude of aloofness was generally adopted, it was not taken into consideration that the has-been governor in disgrace had a wife. She took up the fight and stood on the offensive. Without making any number of unnecessary calls or waiting for invitations which never came, Countess Marie Beatrice recalled, during those first weeks in Vienna, what she probably had had in mind already in Düsseldorf: that she had gone to school with a daughter-in-law of State-Chancellor Kaunitz. No doubt it had been a convent school and the fact formed a strong tie. Here, at last, was something that was binding, here was a foundation upon which one could build; and Countess Marie Beatrice began to build. Her school friend had a daughter who was then nineteen years of age. She was not a beauty, but had a good figure, was excellently brought up, was not at all dull and—most important—the only grand-daughter of the recently deceased Prince Kaunitz. Clemens had just reached the age of twenty-two, was well born, extremely handsome, and gifted beyond the average. His mother conducted him to the house of her school friend who looked the young man over carefully. Then the Princess sent for her daughter Eleonore. The girl dropped a deep curtsy to the Countess, before blushing prettily, she extended her hand to the young man. Needless to say, there were a few difficulties to overcome. Eleonore's father, the Prince, thought the young man had had rather an abundance of experience with women. Then, too, he was poor, while Eleonore was rich. What did it all matter? She could thank her stars for having so gallant and handsome a suitor. Prince Ernst Kaunitz gave his consent reluctantly. When he finally yielded it appeared that his daughter had anticipated him. She probably would have eloped with Clemens. They subsequently lived at the Kaunitz Palace, which later became the famous State-Chancellery on the Ballhausplatz in Vienna.

While this bargaining took place—for on the part of Metternich it was a bargaining, a prudential match, as he himself admitted years later—the social position of the Rhineland immigrants changed for the better at once. The hostile Ministers Trautmannsdorff and Kobenzl became reconciled with Count Franz Georg; Thugut became friendly again; the Emperor granted him first an audience, then a grant of 40,000 gulden to indemnify him for the loss of the Rhenish possessions, and finally even an annual retiring allowance of 8000 gulden until his services would again be required. The Emperor was known for his niggardliness; and if he refrained from exercising it in this instance, the high esteem in which the Kaunitz family was held can be measured by it.

Countess Marie Beatrice had calculated correctly, and a

single move had won her game of chess. It may be assumed that she lost no time in consulting her *Almanach de Gotha* and making a list of the people who had hesitated to invite her, so that she, in turn, could retaliate.

The Apprenticeship of Alcibiades

THE wedding took place in September, 1795, at Austerlitz, which was a village dominated by a castle. Both village
and castle were hereditary possessions of the Kaunitz family.
At Austerlitz, twelve years later, Napoleon defeated the
Austrians. Following the battle, he slept, surrounded by
captured flags and trophies, in the very room that witnessed
the union of Metternich with the young Princess Kaunitz.
A recent French biographer of Metternich, Grunwald, seized
upon this contrast by wittily and dramatically setting the
"Sun of Austerlitz" against the Metternich wedding night.
Disregarding the irony inherent in the situation, it is fascinating enough to warrant a moment's reflection on the
fact that two great careers unsuspectingly and prophetically
crossed each other's path at this historically significant
point.

Clemens Metternich was a young cavalier who married
in order to continue his aristocratic lineage and to replenish
the family exchequer through a fortunate match. It may
be assumed that young Clemens was fully aware of his family
obligations when taking the sacramental vows. That his
parents were in no doubt about the significance of the match
is quite obvious. His mother had made the choice for him,
and his father had every reason to approve of it. "I married

27

neither of nor against my will," the State-Chancellor later wrote to the Princess Lieven. Aristocracy did not, and still does not, regard such things sentimentally; no more do the peasants, between whom and the country nobility there exists a certain affinity. In this connection it is significant that at the noble wedding at Austerlitz prevailing custom demanded that six peasant lads and girls be married at the same time. They united dutifully and, if all went well, prospered. All this was not an affair of the heart, but rather a question of deliberate and natural selective breeding. Viewed from that angle, Metternich's marriage at the age of twenty-three was both an exercise in natural selection and an aristocratic union.

These facts characterized the young couple's first years of married life. The young paterfamilias, having no definite occupation or professional ties, spent his time more pleasantly than usefully. He had married as a cavalier and proposed to live as such. It seems that the gay, if empty, existence he led between the ages of twenty-three and twenty-eight and which was manifestly paid for by his wife's money suited him more completely than his biographers like to record. At any rate, he made no serious effort whatsoever to change his mode of living, except that at one time he was touched by a desire to run off to America—he felt his life was so purposeless. He suppressed his impulse, he admits, out of consideration for his family. The adventurous idea was born no doubt out of a desire to find some kind of use for his dormant gifts, and his intentions were frustrated by his father-in-law, Prince Kaunitz, who, for reasons which can only be conjectured, was opposed to any sort of diplomatic activity. He was probably of the opinion that one great diplomatist in the family was quite enough.

So the idle Clemens and his young wife—who soon became a mother—frequented social gatherings, played hosts to others, and accepted whatever invitations came their way. In between, boredom and a craving for knowledge induced him to dabble in botany and medicine, of which latter science a trace may be found in one of his feuilletonistic comparisons. The statesman, he said at the height of his power, is like a physician. If the cure is successful, Nature has asserted itself; if the patient dies, the physician is blamed.

Political activity being out of the question for the time being, the young Count lived much like Shakespeare's Prince Hal quaffing wine with Falstaff, or like Plutarch's young Alcibiades whose alcoholic exuberance made him turn over the statues and cut off the tails of the dogs of Athens. The type of the frivolous, though gifted, young nobleman is by no means restricted to Greece and, due probably to the example set by Metternich, the Vienna Ballhausplatz became quite an Alcibiadean stamping ground and remained so for fully a century. These young men were fired by ambition, yet like true sophisticates they claimed to have no ambition whatever. Metternich, too, was fond of making such claims for his own person, although there were in his character unmistakable indications of an ambition striving for an extensive education. In this he differed notably from the light-footed and light-hearted little Ballhaus-blades.

Socially, Metternich sought the company of the clever Princess Liechtenstein and even talked philosophy at times with his elders. While Vienna could not, of course, afford him the luxury of sitting at the feet of a Socrates, as Alcibiades did in Athens, he could at least enjoy the company of old Prince de Ligne to whose influence can be traced Metternich's cleverly pointed speech and his grand manner.

Also he must have found time for a good deal of reading in his days of storm and stress; else it would be impossible to explain his later wide knowledge of literature. One of the great features of reading is that one has to be alone to do it; and so Clemens learned the art of being solitary—the best possible schooling for a future premier.

There were at first no chances for diplomatic advancement for the husband of Princess Kaunitz, beyond having himself attached to his father's staff when the latter was appointed to the time-wasting but prestige-bearing post of representing the German Empire at the Congress of Rastatt. The death of Prince Ernst Kaunitz, who had opposed a diplomatic career for Clemens, facilitated the appointment, while on the other hand, the connection with the house of Kaunitz may have been instrumental in bringing about the re-enlistment of the elder Metternich's services. As a matter of fact, the latter seems to have been the perfect man to bring the Congress of Rastatt to its fruitless conclusion. The solemn assembly continued its sessions for a year and a half, and the deliberations led to less than nothing, except that they ended with the assassination of two of the three French delegates—the so-called "Rastatt Envoy Murders." The third member of the French delegation escaped with his life. Clemens could not entirely avoid associating with the three representatives of the young French Republic, though his dislike of these "Bolsheviks" was not lessened by their slovenly dress and their uncouth manner of wearing their hair. He wrote contemptuously about them to his wife, who had been unable to accompany him to Rastatt because she already had to attend to maternal duties and was in rather delicate health.

Without finding the task unduly irksome and without

pretending to suffer from a broken heart, the young husband adjusted himself to a temporary bachelorhood. Courtesy made him complain a little in his letters to Eleonore about boredom and lack of stimulation; he did not disdain, however, to look for and find the latter at the gaming tables and at little suppers in the company of complaisant ladies. Spiteful observers accused him at the time of giving himself too many airs, of being seen in questionable company, and of disdaining that of his equals. Again he resembled Alcibiades.

The French delegates, true radicals that they were, ridiculed the elder Metternich's punctiliousness, which went so far that he actually counted the steps which according to the rank of the various delegates he descended to meet them, and his pompousness in conducting the sessions while sitting enthroned under a canopy. On the whole, however, both he and his young hopeful seem to have had quite a gay time in Rastatt, as proved by the fact that after no more than three months of "strenuous activity" he applied for and received an Imperial grant of 40,000 gulden.

Unless official duties brought them together, father and son went their separate ways. There were times, however, when they surprisingly came across each other, because they happened to be in pursuit of the same belle. This was meat for the slanderous Kotzebue who, as he had done in Mainz, was standing watchfully at the edge of events. He fashioned one of his most capital comedies, which he called "The Two Klingsbergs" and which for generations provided amusement for audiences of the Vienna Burgtheater who chuckled at the obvious portrayal of Metternich *père et fils*. That both of them did not take their conjugal fidelity too seriously in Rastatt is beyond any doubt—as is the fact that women always occupied a good deal of time in their lives. There was, however, one difference. While the tastes of the father were those of a gourmand, his son's were distinctly gourmet. The former was a Casanova at best, the latter a Don Juan at times. A sensual yet spiritual wooer, Clemens drew a sharp line between being in love and loving. He readily permitted himself to be in love, taking whatever offered itself; when it came to loving his demands were high, even superlative. But in order to be able to make so fine a distinction it was necessary that he first gather undistinguished experience, for which there was ample opportunity in Rastatt. Alcibiades' years of apprenticeship thoroughly enlightened him as to the limits of his personality.

The Congress of Rastatt was opened by Napoleon. It seems, however, that Clemens Metternich was not yet present on that occasion; and as Napoleon, detained by his Egyptian venture, failed to appear at the Congress' final session, Metternich was to his chagrin unable to make his great antagonist's acquaintance then. The historic meeting did not take place until much later.

His experiences in Rastatt did not finish the apprenticeship of Alcibiades. The most remarkable event, perhaps, was the farewell breakfast given by the ultra-reactionary Garnsbach Hussars, a celebration which was followed with embarrassing quickness by the assassination of the two French envoys.

Upon his return to Vienna, Clemens breathed again the soft, amorous, and gossipy air of the Vienna salons. His social relations with Princess Eleonore Liechtenstein became closer. Her salon was a hotbed of politics, and had been for the ten or fifteen years that the beautiful Princess had been the intimate friend of the since-deceased Emperor Joseph. At present she was in opposition to Minister Thugut's foreign policy, which was so strongly and unalterably reactionary that it was too much even for Metternich. Thugut clung to the traditional basic formula of Kaunitz: friendship with France, irreconcilable enmity towards Prussia. With the stubbornness of the subordinate, Thugut insisted upon clinging to this policy at a time when Austria, conquered by France and humiliated at the Peace of Campoformio, naturally should have sought a rapprochement with the equally threatened Prussia. Returning from Rastatt, Metternich, at the salon of Princess Liechtenstein, may have used his oratorical ability in support of the latter view all the more vigorously since Thugut had never proved himself a friend of the House of Metternich. It was not that Clemens intrigued against Thugut, but he undermined his position. The still beautiful Princess listened to him with a gentle smile. She was a few years older than he, a fact which did not prevent her from finding the young man devilishly handsome. Thugut was soon ousted, and his successor, Trautmannsdorff, lost no time in appointing Metternich Minister to Dresden. It is not unlikely that Princess Eleonore Liechtenstein had used some of her magic.

The appointment of the twenty-nine-year-old young man as Minister Plenipotentiary to the not overly important Duchy of Saxony did not end the apprenticeship of Alcibiades. On the contrary, it may be said to have received a new impetus. Life in Dresden still flowed on in the gallant rococo style that had prevailed in Mainz ten years earlier. It was a style that suited Metternich, and his extraordinary ability enabled him quickly to adjust himself to his new surroundings and to the path he was to travel.

Before embarking upon it, he wrote a remarkably clever and mature letter to the Emperor who had confirmed his appointment. It was the letter of a statesman who knows his value, knows what he has to give, and knows also what he may demand. He began by doubting his competency—a doubt that showed that he was eminently competent—and, in a highly immodest manner, played the part of the meekly modest. He said he had accepted the appointment only to avoid the necessity of being disobedient to His Imperial Majesty. At the same time he requested permission to resign as soon as he became conscious of his insufficiency. In other words, the young man threatened to resign even before he had assumed his portfolio. That is something only elderly prime ministers at the height of their power have the audacity to do. As a matter of fact, fully forty-seven years passed before, for the first and last time, he handed in his threatened resignation; from which it may inversely be assumed he had during that period no occasion to be dissatisfied with his conduct of affairs.

It is also remarkable that Clemens Metternich, prior to the assumption of his new post, did a good deal of research in the Vienna archives. The result of his search was a voluminous memorandum on the recent inglorious Austrian policy, and its relationship to Saxony in the past decade. The essential thought of the memorandum was a conscientious outlining of his own tasks in Dresden. There can be no doubt that this was done with the approval of Thugut. At any rate, in a manner, the young man gave himself his own instructions.

This memorandum is proof of a remarkable assiduity, a quality which distinguished Metternich throughout his life, but which manifested itself seriously now for the first time.

An assiduous Alcibiades is no longer an Alcibiades, and it would therefore seem as if a full stop were to be made here; provided, of course, that there had been a real need in Dresden for an industrious Austrian Plenipotentiary. That this was not the case was in part due to the fact that an anti-Prussian policy had been officially dictated to Metternich, while in his own heart and for reasons of expediency he inclined towards a pro-Prussian attitude. So there was not much he could do. He went about a good deal in society, made the acquaintance of the beautiful Bagration, an eighteen-year-old Russian who, in a Russian way, may have reminded him of the charming Constance. She was the wife of a Russian general, and society called her *"le bel ange nu,"* for she manifested a remarkable sense of economy when it came to buying material for her evening gowns. A year later she presented the general with a little daughter and suggested the child be given the name of Clementine. As the general did not object she was actually baptized in that name. Clemens, ever in favor of a closer relationship with Russia, was radiant.

At about the same time Madame Metternich, née Kaunitz, gave birth to a child. It was her fourth, two having died. Slanderous tongues asserted that Metternich was no more the father of the latest-born than the Russian general was Clementine's father. Certain it is that Countess Metternich, somewhat tired of her husband's affairs after but six years of married life, had on her own account instituted a policy of reprisals. Theirs not being a marriage of love, the Metternich ménage remained almost untouched by these events, and there never was a break in their relations.

Like most travelers Metternich soon went from Dresden to Berlin. There he became the successor to Count Stadion who advanced to St. Petersburg. This succession alone proved that Vienna had already begun duly to appreciate Metternich's gifts and meant to make use of them.

The young Minister stood high in favor in Berlin because he was well acquainted with the exceedingly beautiful Queen Louise. He had made her acquaintance in Frankfort where she had been his partner in opening the Coronation Ball. She was a woman of unimpeachable reputation, a fact which made it possible for her to receive Metternich within her closest circle of friends without any danger of compromising herself. There was no constraint, however, in the development of his relations with the Duchess of Sagan, another scantily clad angel *à la* Bagration. She soon became the latter's successor, just as Metternich had become the successor of Stadion. Later Metternich, in referring to her, remarked somewhat acidly that she was a woman *"qui aime comme l'on dine."* There can be no doubt that he did dine with her on any number of occasions. Their relations, repeatedly interrupted, continued a long time and were not terminated until 1816. Madame de Staël, on the other hand, never made any impression upon him. He had no desire to embrace a book, nor did he wish to be embraced by one. This must by no means be taken to imply that he was faithful to the Duchess for any length of time. The sharp-tongued Berliners, in referring to the Ambassador whose duties took him away from his office so much, averred that he was always in love and always absent-minded: a fact, they said acidly, which was harmful to him in politics, but more so in love.

Among the achievements of Metternich's years in Berlin must be counted his friendship with Gentz, who later became his associate of many years in the State-Chancellory. He was the most corruptible among all the gifted journalists, and the most gifted among all the corruptible ones of his age. Gentz was a romanticist, a man of the world, and a snob. Whenever he was routed out from one of these poses, he escaped into another; and if nothing else would do, he propitiated everyone, even posterity, by the wonderful Goethe-esque style of his writing. A romantic man of the world, also was the fascinating Prince Louis Ferdinand whom the aesthetes of the Berlin tea-tables liked to call the "Prussian Alcibiades." In his play "The Prince of Homburg," Heinrich von Kleist has immortalized the enchanting young man with the wind-swept shock of dark hair. All Berlin was in love with the Prince. He resembled Canova's conception of Death—a dashing death in a Prussian uniform—and it may be assumed that he did not fail to impress Metternich, who probably felt himself attracted to him as to a heroic variation of himself. For even if they were both young, were both Alcibiadeses, they were as different as a ballad is from a diplomatic note penned on vellum-paper. Their fates, too, were utterly different. Louis Ferdinand was a romantic firebrand, while Metternich, with all of his seeming recklessness, was fundamentally a prosy fellow. The one died young, the other reached a great age. While Louis Ferdinand, in despair over the fate of his fatherland, rode to a heroic death at Saalfeld at the inception of a lost war, Metternich, in "controlled despair," permitted himself to be pushed up a rung of the ladder. He was transferred to Paris.

When Metternich was sent to Paris, the Emperor made him a Privy Councillor, with the title of "Excellency." More attractive, unquestionably, than the most heroic death on the battle field, particularly when one is only thirty-four and the youngest Privy Councillor in the oldest monarchy in Europe.

Bel Ami Comes to Paris

LIKE Maupassant's Bel Ami in the well-known novel of Paris, Metternich owed to women all of the successes he had hitherto enjoyed. Even beyond that he had much in common with Bel Ami, gay Lothario and careerist, with perhaps the notable difference that Metternich began where Bel Ami had left off: at marrying for money. In the case of Metternich the money was moreover fittingly supplemented by the noble name of Kaunitz. The splendor of that name continued to shed its luster long after the death of Austria's greatest statesman, and now it surrounded Metternich with waves of reflected glory. At that point in his career Princess Liechtenstein had begun to take notice of him, had given him some thought, and had practised some of her magic. With her assistance he had received an appointment to Dresden and was later transferred to Berlin, where again the friendship of Queen Louise quickly created a position for him. But now after Berlin, where his policy to force Prussia into an alliance against Napoleon had practically been shipwrecked, a man for the first time interested himself in his advancement. It was the French Minister, Monsieur La Forest, who recommended him to Napoleon, and the latter, in turn, found the young man interesting because of his connection with the house of Kaunitz. With the approval of Emperor Franz, therefore, Metternich became the Ambassador of a country which at Austerlitz again had suffered a decisive defeat and was still quite stunned by the blow.

"The gentlemen with the white cuffs," as Rahel Varnhagen once called the diplomats, thrive largely on the art of finding the right word at the right moment and—this too is an art—of launching it effectively. (When Metternich, newly appointed Ambassador of Austria, stood for the first time in the presence of Napoleon in September, 1806, the Emperor said after an introductory question concerning Metternich's youthful years: "You are very young to be the representative of the oldest dynasty in Europe." "As old as Your Majesty on the day of Austerlitz!" was Metternich's quick but well-considered rejoinder, a bull's-eye at the very first shot. In it were compliment and impudence, duplicity and sincerity, parry and lunge—model of a diplomat's reply. Metternich made it at the moment when he was handing his credentials to Napoleon. But the answer itself was a credential.) There can be no doubt that Napoleon considered it in that light; he was himself a master of the Plutarchic word and duly appreciated it in others.

Two years later the relations between France and Austria and, by the same token, between Emperor and Ambassador, had changed for the worse to such and extent that Napoleon, in passing Metternich at some reception, would stop but for a moment, having nothing else to ask but: "And how is Madame Metternich?" To which Metternich, in turn, invariably replied: "Always the same, Your Majesty!"

Between these two phrases Metternich's ambassadorial career glided along. He could never make much headway with the Emperor, and at the peace negotiations following upon the unfortunate military campaign the only thing he was able to squeeze out of him was Trieste, which he gained for Austria in 1808 and which, with one brief interruption, remained with that country for 110 years. Nevertheless, his relations with Napoleon were rather amicable—especially in the beginning. The tension came later; it found expression in Napoleon's pointed remark: "Metternich is in a fair way to become a statesman. He already lies quite nicely."

It was late in the summer of 1806 when Metternich made his entry into Paris. At first he made only temporary arrangements for bachelor quarters. Madame Metternich and the children joined him later when they moved into the ambassadorial palace. In the meantime he wrote a letter to the love of his youth, Madame Constance Caumont, in which there were still traces of gallantry. The lady had been in Paris a short time before, having been installed in his immediate neighborhood. Then she had retired to her Castle Chanday, in Brittany—or rather, had buried herself there. In vain did he try to persuade her in his letter to return to Paris as he could "not possibly" visit her at Chanday: "*Je ne devrais bien ne pas aller vous y voir.*" The letters written by Metternich, the lover, are of inestimable advantage to posterity in their indiscretions. Everything may be read between the lines. No doubt the young woman with the "dark hair and blue eyes," who might have posed as a model for Hebe, was still quite pretty; yet, she remained at Chanday—a fact which presumably also suited Monsieur Caumont. However, he sent Constance some rare plants from the Imperial Conservatory of Schönbrunn which she wished to plant at Chanday. Metternich and his wife then took up their quarters at the Embassy.

A picture of that period, painted by Gérard, immortalized

Metternich's outward appearance. The apple-green Cherubino of 1792, dancing the minuet at the Coronation Ball
at Frankfort, has changed into an already slightly statuesque
and somberly clad gentleman. All that is left is the blue
gaze in the somewhat impudently smiling voluptuary's face
which still retains traces of a childlike expression. The dress,
as far as it is revealed, is gaudily overtrimmed in the Empire
style. We behold a young buccaneer of love with a profusion
of cloths and decorations round his neck. That is what Metternich looked like at the time, unless he happened to wear
the Maltese uniform—red with black facings—which made
him appear decidedly interesting.

But there is also a second picture of him, a word-picture
from the pen of Madame de Rémusat, who in her memoirs
of the Empire's days of glory assigned a modest little place
to the new Austrian Ambassador, Count Metternich. Quite
casually she mentioned that in the year 1806 a new figure
made its appearance at the Court of Napoleon. It was a
certain Metternich who had played a rather important part
in Europe and who in the end had proved brazenly lucky,
although it was alleged that his gifts did not go beyond the
level of a second-rate political intrigue. At that time he was
young, and had a good figure. *"Il obtint des succès auprès
des femmes. Un peu plus tard il parut s'attacher à Madame
Murat."* "His feelings for her seemed to have lasted long
enough to keep her husband on the throne of Naples for a
considerable time and possibly served also to protect her in
the exile of her choice. . . ."

It cannot be said that this is a very flattering picture; nor
was such to be expected of Madame de Rémusat. She was
an acrimonious noblewoman who had seen better days and
who for the sake of a living was forced to endure a rather

precarious position at the Court of Napoleon. As is so often the case in similar circumstances, the compulsion turned into downright venom by whose discharge she revenged herself with a sort of emigrant's spite on those with whom she had to associate. She knew how to wield the pen and how to turn slander into classical forms. In this she was immeasurably aided by the resources of French grammar. How instructive, for instance, is the *passé defini: "Il obtint des succès. . . ."* This is no mere gossip, it is an historical fact. *"Un peu plus tard il parut s'attacher à Madame Murat"* is also quite significant. It shows that Caroline was at best the second, if not just one out of many. Furthermore: *"il parut"* —it seemed; whether it was actually so may be considered an open question. One thing, however, is certain: Caroline owed to him the tiny throne of Naples and her ultimate sanctuary in Austria, chosen by her because she wished to be near him. To be near? And to whom? Madame de Rémusat has already told us: to the handsome face of a mediocre diplomat with a certain gift of intrigue. Every little sentence is steeped in vinegar. At any rate, though, the comprehensive judgment of the experienced lady at Court clearly shows us how the young Ambassador was thought of in the influential circles of Paris society. He was successful but not popular. His unpopularity was due to the same reason everywhere: his "brazen" luck. There is a price to be paid for it.

For the second time Austria had been vanquished on the field of battle and humbled at the conference table. A reactionary army of hirelings, drummed up according to a rusty recruiting system and led by fossilized generals—of whom Mack was the most petrified—had proved themselves incapable of resisting an army recruited from the people and fired by a genius for war. Archduke Karl alone held out some hope, although for the time being he represented but a promise not yet fulfilled. In the meantime Napoleon had slept in the Imperial Apartments at Schönbrunn. The French officers, who attracted many a gaze from the eyes of the pretty women of Vienna, had hailed with enthusiasm the "Fidelio" of a certain Beethoven, while the Viennese, who had not yet got beyond their Gluck, coldly refused to acknowledge the young composer. Emperor Franz, beaten on the battle-field, had lost no time in leaving Vienna, as he was to do again in the year 1809. He had a natural aversion to Napoleon and was loath to meet him. It was only after the Battle of Austerlitz, in 1806, that armistice negotiations compelled him to make Napoleon's personal acquaintance. After that first meeting he summed up his impressions in the famous sentence: "Now I can stomach him less than ever!"

What Napoleon had done to Austria in the first ten years of his unparalleled career was nothing short of taking it by the scruff of its neck and standing it in the corner of Europe, its face turned to the East. Not more than ten years before, the long arm of the Habsburgs had reached beyond Germany into the Netherlands, a fact sufficiently well known to Metternich. That arm, holding the Imperial German Crown and the Burgundian lands on the left bank of the Rhine, was seen to end in a clenched fist whenever anybody dared to cast a covetous eye upon German possessions. All that, however, was now buried in the past. Austria had relinquished its claims upon Belgium and Holland, dropped the Imperial Crown, and lost Burgundy. As a compensation it had received Venice, a city more venerably illustrious even than the Habsburgs themselves, although they were somewhat at a loss as to what to do with it. Galicia, too, which was added a little later, was insufficient to compensate Austria for the West of Europe, which seemed to be definitely lost as a legitimate sphere of interest.

A vanquished and superannuated State, shrunk to four-fifths of its former size; an army which had lost confidence in itself; an incompetent and somnolent administration; finances on the verge of bankruptcy; a dejected Emperor who, in spite of his readiness to attend to the round of daily duties at his writing-desk, seemed to have given up his Empire and only now and then, in the manner of cynical weaklings who cover up their impotence by laughter, poked fun at world-history: that was the background against which the scarlet Maltese uniform of Metternich stood out in bold relief. Impossible to imagine a more thankless task than that which faced Metternich at the beginning of his ambassadorial career! To make matters worse there was his youthful appearance. It is said that Metternich was at that time in the habit of powdering his strikingly blond hair in an effort to make himself look a little older than he actually was.

While a thankless task is apt to repel a mediocre actor, it sometimes fascinates a great one. Metternich was a great actor. Not only had he accepted his appointment to Paris as a matter of course (for, as a Berlin journalist said on the occasion of Kaiser Wilhelm's abdication: "a corner-store like that is not to be found every day"), but he also endeavored to get out of the position the highest reward it could yield: diplomatic compensation for the lost military campaign. Was he successful in that direction during his Paris years, from 1806 to 1809? If the question is limited to that very space of time, it must be answered in the negative. If, on the other hand, it is extended beyond Metternich's am-

bassadorial incumbency in Paris, to 1814, the answer may
be boldly affirmative. Whatever successes he achieved during those early years in Paris and what they contributed to
the portrait of the man, they bore no marks of greatness yet;
but they were the forerunners of greatness to come.

In order to hold his own with Napoleon, Metternich
first had to become acquainted with his incommensurable
opponent; more than that, he had to study him. There was
opportunity for that in Paris, and he knew how to make the
most of it. To know a man! What does it mean? It means to
set him against one's own self. Insight into human character
presupposes a knowledge of one's own. Even when he wrote
that first letter to Emperor Franz thanking him for his appointment, Metternich was already a personage, as he was
in Dresden and Berlin when in Alcibiadean boyishness he
accepted glory as little more than a plaything. His conscious
personality, however, came to the fore only in Paris. The
Paris period was significant not so much because he mastered
his task, but rather because inwardly he came ever closer to
its mastery; not that he triumphed over Napoleon, but that
he developed faculties which would enable him to triumph
over him eventually. The greatest success of Metternich's
days in Paris was that on leaving that city he was Metternich. Up to that point we may observe a continuous growth
and a building up of his personality by means of a persistent
questing after his own soul. Thereafter the personality was
an established quantity.

Personality is one thing; the will which inspires it is another. Only out of the fruitful combination of these two
elements is the historical deed born.

And what was Metternich's will? A diplomat of average
capacity would answer: to serve his Emperor, to leave his

post with marks of honor, and, if possible, finally to become foreign minister in order that he might guide other ambassadors as he himself had been guided.

That was not Metternich's will in Paris. Although a monarchist, he was not a princely servitor in that sense; not an ambitious officer yearning to mount from rank to rank; and not a collector of decorations. Neither was he a patriot according to the text-book definition of the word; not a German patriot, and not an Austrian one either, but rather a European one. He wanted to safeguard Europe against revolution; he wanted to realize an idea and as the protagonist of that idea to reestablish fallen Austria in its former glory. That was his will in Paris and in the days following Paris, and in a shadowy mental vision it had been his will even before. But now in Paris and in the overawing presence of Napoleon the great statesman-in-the-making possessed himself of the substance to be moulded. To master it is the mission of his life: of that he is now convinced. And he would master it!

Beyond that, Paris was Paris, and Metternich was himself—a personality within whose mental structure the master of statecraft was forever counterbalanced by the master of the art of living. He lost no time in starting an affair with Caroline Murat and, a little later, with Madame Junot whose husband, after his Spanish victories, had been made Duke of Abrantès by Napoleon. While the second of these was a duchess, the first, who stood sponsor for Clemens in the Parisian way, was Napoleon's own sister. *"Une tête de Cromwell sur les épaules d'une jolie femme,"* are the words with which, in two strokes, Talleyrand wittily sketched her outward appearance.

As for Cromwell, Metternich surely had considerably less use for him than for what remained: wasn't he a counter-revolutionary and Cromwell a rebel? But it is by no means impossible that in the very fact lay a certain fascination for Metternich, the arch-conservative, just as in her turn the Cromwell-head may have been intrigued by the reactionary in Metternich's make-up, although at first she discarded him contemptuously as a *tête de crème*. In love, opposite political views are not infrequently the cause of an erotic attraction, while on the other hand party-affiliation is no reason why even the most highly principled politician should fall in love.

Caroline was a tremendously ambitious woman. Just as Madame Bovary, according to the famous words of Flaubert, wanted at once to be dead and to live in Paris, so Caroline wanted to be Queen of Poland and of Spain at the same time. She finally became Queen of Naples and incidentally the mistress of Metternich. Possibly her ambitious nature had something to do with that, too! At the Court of the upstart Napoleon, who was still secretly held up to ridicule by his well-trained courtiers, Metternich embodied the world of former days, the sovereign 18th century. He was a young cavalier of the old school and he represented conservative power at the Court of the "Son of the Revolution." Dangerous premises, these, for a woman who, dissatisfied as most ambitious women are, gets on the wrong road erotically because she is looking for the right road politically!

It was Napoleon himself who recommended Metternich to her care and, as it were, set them together by the ears, even if he did not actually bring them together. *"Amuse ce niais,"* he said to his little sister, to get Metternich in his clutches. Caroline took his words literally and soon, as Napo-

leon had desired, he actually had a spy. The trouble was that
the spying was not done in his behalf but rather in that of
Metternich. Through Caroline the latter learned and was
able to report to Vienna that Napoleon was once more thinking of adorning his head with a crown—that of Lombardy,
presumably—simply because Josephine had ordered a new
coronation robe. At the same time he learned that Napoleon
was contemplating divorce—years before he actually made
the thought come true; or that things were turning out decidedly badly in Spain; and other matters of this kind, all
highly important first-hand news. He was always excellently
informed—a rarity among Austrian diplomatic representatives.

The case of the beautiful and voluptuous Laure Junot,
Duchess of Abrantès, with whom principally for the sake of
his pleasure Metternich soon deceived Caroline, was altogether different. Here was a romantic woman who insisted
upon having her romance. Women of her kind, if they love,
do so to talk about it—first to the lover; then to a woman
friend; and finally, perchance, to posterity. Laure Junot
did all that in the most conscientious manner and without
any undue amount of consideration for her boorish husband
whom she deceived while at the same time she trembled at
the thought of him. She finally went so far as to write her
memoirs, in which she once more recreated her great experience, much bedecked with sweet exaggerations and, in the
romantic style, extravagantly garlanded with lachrymose effusions.

According to her, the handsome Ambassador with the
eyes of a child and the smile of a Mephistopheles sought her
out in the country, at Folie St. James, in Neuilly, near Paris.
They were alone; he threw himself at her feet; she bowed

down towards him, and their lips met. Then he jumped up and in his arms carried her to a nearby grotto where, so she asserts, she later shed "tears of blood" because of her evil deed. It reads indeed like a society novel by Eugène Sue, who possibly may have supplied her with the tears at a reduced price.

All the same, that first stormy meeting with its fiery declarations of love amidst thunder and lightning did not remain a solitary experience. Tenderer and more serene hours of companionship followed, and brightened the long solitudes of the Duchess whose husband was busy capturing flags in Spain. "Every evening," she pretends to remember —although this is probably an exaggeration—every evening at ten o'clock "he," meaning Metternich, came in his carriage which he dismissed at once. At three in the morning, when he left his beautiful Calypso in her "grotto," he cautiously took another carriage which, hidden in a side-street, had awaited him. Only if he had affairs of State, which, after all, happens to an ambassador, he remained away, and it may be assumed that among those "affairs of State" were certain invitations from Caroline Murat. In that event he made his excuses to Laurette and drove on to Caroline, not because the little Cromwell-head held more allure for him, but because the sister of Napoleon brought him in contact with Talleyrand and Fouché, both of whom were already plotting against Napoleon. Laure and Caroline never caused Metternich of the Paris days to lose sight of his goal, which under all circumstances remained more important to him than either or both of the ladies.

That goal was the overthrow of Napoleon. For its attainment Austria needed an army which was a match for the French and a leadership which recognized that "a victorious

battle is won only on the day after the battle, and a lost
battle lost only four days after it was lost." No great strategist
could have formulated this truth more concisely than the
statesman Metternich did in one of his diligent reports from
Paris. And no prophet in the year 1807 could have predicted
more accurately what actually *did* happen in 1813. Six years
ahead of time Metternich prophesied in a dispatch to Vienna
the inevitable end of the French Empire and the ultimate
downfall of Napoleon.

For the time being, to be sure, that was a long way off.
Napoleon's successes continued and surpassed one another,
not deterred one whit by the merely moral conviction of
Metternich that any despotism was ultimately doomed to
failure. The French were inherently a peace-loving people,
finding themselves compelled against their will to wage war
continuously. This was duly realized by the young Austrian
Ambassador at the time of his peaceful conquests in the
drawing-rooms of Paris. His realization, however, did not
alter the fact that these very Frenchmen were wallowing in
seas of blood in Spain, and that Murat, Caroline's husband
cuckolded by Metternich, captured Madrid while Napoleon
ordered the royal family taken to Bayonne as a first step
towards dethroning them. Bayonne, in 1808, was no more
than Munich, 130 years later: a sham solution which deceived no one. Napoleon made his brother Joseph King of
Spain, quite as Hitler made Herr Bürckel, Governor of
Austria, or Baron Neurath, Protector of Bohemia-Moravia.
The war went on. Spain struggled as Poland did in our day
and, like Poland, was trampled under foot rather than conquered. In the meantime the great accounting with England, which was back of the war with Spain as some years
later it was to be back of the Russian campaign, was still

unsettled and was to remain unsettled until the day of Waterloo. Napoleon's chief aim—to seal the Continent hermetically against England—had not been attained either in Portugal where he first attempted it or in Spain; and, England remained unconquered and unconquerable. All this was quite evident to Metternich, although as a German philosopher would have expressed it, idea and experience were not at first in accord. There was something of a German philosopher in the statesman Metternich, and it was not the worst part of him either. "I was born a thinker," he was heard to say of himself in retrospect, years later.

Thoroughly convinced of the eventual collapse of the Napoleonic regime—a conviction greatly strengthened by the close Caroline-engineered contact with Talleyrand and Fouché—Metternich tried to stir up war in Vienna. Upon his return to Paris, at a reception, he was addressed by Napoleon: "Does your Emperor wish me to pay him a visit in Vienna?" Angrily he upbraided the Ambassador because Austria was arming. "You may be convinced, Sire, that just as you count the heads of our soldiers, we shall know how to count yours," was Metternich's bland and impertinent reply. Experience demonstrates that when questions and answers of that kind are exchanged between Ambassador and potentate, the former is justified in feeling shaky, be his name Henderson or Metternich. Before long the Austrian envoy knew he was being watched closely. In fear of his life, he wrote to his illustrious colleague, Prince Schwarzenberg, in Petersburg, that if it came to the worst he would know how to die and would see to it that all incriminating documents were burned in good time. It was not long before the war of 1809 actually broke out, the third war in ten years between Austria and France. On the occasion of

the very last reception, Napoleon, who had borne his an-
noyance with Metternich long enough, announced to him
with dictatorial bluntness that he would march upon Vienna
by way of Rastatt and Munich. He then mounted his horse
and after a brief address permitted himself to become the
center of a martial ovation by his guards, with the assembled
Court and the Austrian Ambassador as silent witnesses. A
few moments later the French Foreign Minister, Monsieur
Champagny, approached Metternich and assured him in the
name of the Emperor that Napoleon bore him no personal
grudge, even if at times it had looked that way. Metternich
bowed courteously: "Tell His Majesty that I have never
taken his remarks quite seriously." The aristocrat versus the
upstart, beginning and end of Metternich's stay in Paris.
For the time being, to be sure, a defenseless aristocrat whose
only weapons were pointed words.

In the end, things did not run quite smoothly. At the outbreak of the war Metternich was arrested and interned in
Paris. Even the customary exchange at the frontier for the
French *chargé d'affaires* in Vienna was accompanied by considerable difficulty because the Austrians had unreasonably
detained the Frenchman.

At last everything was ready and Count Metternich was
permitted to proceed in a mail coach across Southern Germany towards home. Before the gates of Vienna a big battle
was being waged, the Battle of Wagram. Metternich alighted
from his coach and watched it. With the aid of a telescope
which he is said to have bought for the very purpose, the
returned Ambassador stood behind his Emperor and followed with intense interest the magnificent but unfortunately vain assaults of Austrian regiments in the face of the

murderous artillery fire from the French. Then, quite composed, he stepped back and folded up his telescope again.

The frivolity of the "gentlemen with the white cuffs" playing their game of chess on the backs of the peoples at times has caused posterity to shake their heads in wonderment. We may draw what consolation we can from the fact that the frivolity of those chessboard artists of the last century was no jot less than that shown in the past twenty years of European history.

BOOK TWO

How to Defeat Napoleon?

Austria Is at Stake

A FOREIGN SECRETARY is responsible for the foreign policy of his country while the Ambassador is but his instrument. After the lost campaign of 1809, it was therefore the logical and correct thing for Emperor Franz to dismiss his Foreign Secretary, Count Stadion. It is strange, however, that on the very day following the disastrous Battle of Wagram, the Emperor should have entrusted to Metternich the further conduct of his ousted minister's affairs and, two months later, after the conclusion of peace, formally placed in his hands the portfolio of foreign affairs. After all, Metternich, the Alcibiades in diplomat's dress, had shown himself so far to be anything but lucky and had managed to run the Ship of State aground twice. In 1805 he had sounded the call to arms and had lost the war. In 1809 he had again stirred up the fires of war, and again Austria had suffered a crushing defeat. That it was he who had urged Austria into war is not denied by Metternich himself. The memoranda he elaborated while spending a brief summer holiday in Vienna, in 1808, had gone far to stiffen the vacillating Emperor's warlike attitude. Nevertheless, the Emperor did not punish his counsellor for the disastrous advice given him. On the contrary, far from having lost confidence in him, he appointed the shipwrecked mate to captain the badly battered vessel.

57

It is true that in doing this His Majesty came to what was to prove a historically correct decision. But, granting that Emperor Franz had a good deal of insight into human character, one should greatly overrate him were one to assume that his appointment of Metternich was a matter of striking far-sightedness. It was not the Monarch's perceptive power nor his political judgment that was responsible for the choice; rather it was the Emperor's character, the Habsburg character, which kept Austria together for many centuries, and concerning which a few remarks may be apropos in this connection.

In one of the secondary scenes of his *"Don Carlos,"* Schiller put into the foreground this Habsburg characteristic, which is to be found in the mediocre Habsburgs as well as in the great ones. It occurs in the audience scene, when Admiral Medina faces Philip II for the first time after the loss of the Spanish Armada and, kneeling, admits his defeat. The King bids him rise and makes him welcome in Madrid: "I sent you to contend with mortal men, and not with rocks and tempests!" He takes him back into favor and holds out the hope of a further use of his services. Nothing would be more absurd, however, than to draw conclusions as to Philip's kindness of heart from this truly imperial attitude towards the vanquished admiral. He will remain to be known in history for his cruelty and gloomy severity. By dealing so magnanimously with his admiral he was actuated by two motives, both of which were Habsburg characteristics. First, there was a certain chivalry towards a man so humiliated that he was quite without defense. That is a Christian quality, and the Habsburgs were always good Christians. The other motive was an autocratic impulse. Whatever a subordinate does, no matter if he is an admiral or even a state minister, is not of prime importance. If he is successful, the Habsburgs have a new achievement to their credit; if he fails, the Habsburgs have lost a battle. In any event, the faithful servant has done his duty. Even if it should have been his advice which led to the battle that was lost, that does not weigh heavily. For to admit that the subordinate's counsel was decisive would be to admit that a Habsburg does not make his own decisions. Under no circumstances must an autocrat make so fatal an admission. That is why the Emperors forgave what had happened and, both in the case of Medina and in that of Metternich, in the 17th century as well as in the 19th, reserved to themselves the right to make further use of their services. Not out of leniency, but out of haughtiness. The minister is a tool, nothing else; and for a blow that goes amiss, not the hammer is to be held responsible but he who wields it. That is the way of princes, the way of the Habsburgs.

Viewed from that angle it is rather less astonishing that Franz did not blame his Ambassador for his failure, than that the latter forgave the Minister his great successes; for success almost makes one a compeer. . . . That Franz actually took the attitude he did is to his credit and shows that, with all of his narrowness of mind, there was, after all, something of the master in him.

In October of the year 1809 the curious burghers of Vienna were fond of driving out to the suburb of Brigittenau on a fine Sunday to have a look at the French soldiers peacefully encamped before the city's gates. It is even said that now and then some beautiful lady would alight from her carriage to pay a visit to one of the handsome enemy officers. Peace was on the way and was finally concluded in November. Shortly after, Metternich was appointed to the post of Austria's Foreign Secretary. Gentz, his friend and political accomplice, marveled at the light-heartedness with which the man of failure accepted the new appointment. To his mother, Metternich said in a letter, how difficult he found it to accept, but that he considered it his duty. The former may have been a slight exaggeration, but his sense of duty was certainly a fact.

In the meantime the peace negotiations, which turned out so disadvantageously to Austria, were conducted; first, by Metternich himself, and then by the inefficient Prince Liechtenstein, a choice which did not fail to enrage the former. In the course of these negotiations, which placed the burden of an unbearable war indemnity upon a weakened and shrunk Habsburg Empire, Metternich clearly perceived what was at stake. Austria itself was at stake.

Metternich was not an Austrian. According to his origin he was a Rhinelander and, in view of his upbringing, a European. But at that time, in those fateful days, and after the hotly fought and lost battle, he found a way, *his way,* to Austria. It was not a way of love. It may be that Metternich loved Europe, but he certainly did not love Austria. In the written utterances of a tireless pen there is hardly an instance when he praises the Austrian landscape or the beauties of Vienna, although, when in exile, he expressed a fleeting longing for his villa in Vienna. When he was a very old man and lived at his Castle Johannisberg on the Rhine, he wrote to his daughter that the Rhine flowed through his blood. As for the Danube, he never made a similar assertion.

And yet, after this lost war, he learned to have faith in

Austria. Faith without love—a strange faith, indeed. But it was a strange country, too, that inspired that faith.

In order to understand this strangeness one has to go back quite a long way. What was so strange, above all, was the fact that Austria was not so much a country as a problem—a problem which not only brought the country and the Empire into existence, but finally even outlived it. This, in a roundabout way, borders upon immortality.

Pre-eminently, the problem lay in the fact that, while there was in Europe a country named Austria which had existed for 500 years, there was virtually no such being as an Austrian. Austria never was a national entity; neither was it a super-national one, like the Roman World Empire which, at any rate, was ruled by the Romans. But who and where were the Austrians who ruled Austria? The Germans, no matter whether they lived this side or beyond the former black-and-yellow boundary-posts, were loath to admit they did the ruling. And the others? Were the Hungarians, Austrians? The Czechs? The Poles? The Italians? The Croats? They were all resigned to live in Austria for a few centuries, but they would not have thanked anyone, not even at that time, for calling them Austrians. The centuries-old strange fact about Austria was that it was an Empire without a people.

That was the European concept, too. Occasionally at castles in Southern Germany or at old inns, one meets with 17th-century Tables of Nations, listing the European peoples and faithfully enumerating their predominant characteristics in old spelling and Gothic letters: the Spaniards —who were then at the head of world affairs—the English, the French, the Italians, and even the Sarmatians were all depicted in their national costumes and suitably described. Each of these nations had its own heraldic animal, each had its predominant characteristic; each lived and died in its own peculiar way. Of the "Englanders," for instance, it was said that they died "in the sea"; of the French "at war"; of the Germans "in the wine." One was like a lion, another like a fox, and still another like a bear.

In vain will one look among this European family of nations for the "Austrian." He had no heraldic animal, neither had he any outstanding characteristic; he had neither pride nor craftiness; he did not live, nor did he die. Only in 1919, after the destruction of the Austro-Hungarian Monarchy, the Austrian, as a character, made his independent appearance—without standing the test particularly well. It may be said paradoxically of the Austrian that he began to exist only when he had ceased to exist. *Quand on est mort, c'est pour longtemps!* From which it possibly may be deduced that he will continue to exist for a long time.

It would nevertheless be wrong to assume that it was only the Habsburg Crown which held together the peoples living in the Danube basin. That was possibly so in the beginning. Later it was still something else, some common characteristic that was, and still is, left of Austria: the human species, the Austrian form of living. The latter had its political significance, too, a fact which mainly interested the European politician, Metternich. For him Austria was the Europe of Central Europe; the European idea confined to a spatially determinable and determined cultural area. As soon as this recognition had come to Metternich he clearly saw his mission. At the age of thirty-six he had come to the conclusion that he had a life-task to fulfill. Up to that time his life and work had been little more than an official employment.

"*Ce niais,*" this clown, Napoleon had said of him; "*tête de crème*" Caroline had disdainfully called him at the beginning of their acquaintance. Well, he had proved to her that his head was not made only of "*crème,*" and she had been nothing loath to let him prove it. He still wore on his wrist the bracelet she had given him, a circlet woven out of her own hair. At times, after the unfortunate conclusion of peace, when stroking it absent-mindedly the thought may have flashed through Metternich's mind that he would prove also to Napoleon that he was neither a clown nor a puppet. The very fact of Napoleon's invincibility led him to the conclusion that it was necessary to vanquish him. Austria was at stake! The realization of that fact formed the main-spring of his future life.

Samson and Delilah

"I stepped on to an abyss covered with flowers."
Napoleon. St. Helena. April 28, 1816.

NAPOLEON is invincible, but he is only invincible on the battlefield. This brilliant idea may have flashed through Metternich's head in the hot summer weeks after Wagram. The rest of the plan was a matter of logic, as was always the case with Metternich. If not on the field of battle, Napoleon would have to be mastered in some other sphere; if not by the hand of man, perhaps by the hand of woman. That was an expedient which would readily suggest itself to Clemens, the ladies' man. That he was a ladies' man now worked to his historical advantage. Only a man who realized the tremendous power of women, and to whom they meant so much could have conceived the idea of letting a woman strike down the new Caesar.

Like every Caesar, Napoleon had had many affairs with women, but he was the opposite of a ladies' man. He was not indifferent to women but he had never had the time to devote himself to them properly. He breathed world history, and only between breaths was he able to enjoy a woman. Affairs of the heart to him were intermezzos between the five acts of his heroic existence. Between the first and second acts, Italian campaign and 18th Brumaire, Josephine, the delightful Creole, was the first to possess his heart and to share his glory. Between the second and third acts in snow-covered Poland, Walewska, his sweetest love; while between the third and fourth acts there was the childlike Marie Louise. In the fifth act before the actor left the stage, there was the seventeen-year-old daughter of his one-time host on St. Helena, Betsy Balcom; a young hoyden, she played many pranks on Napoleon, which he cheerfully endured. Twenty-five years later she made a book of her experiences on St. Helena and her friendship with the fallen hero. The others hardly counted. They were nothing but incidents in his heroic life. He loved between battles, kissed between peace treaties, and while snatching a kingdom, or deposing a monarch embraced a beautiful woman. Never let pleasure interfere with your work, was his constant principle in matters of this kind. His life was a magnificent tragedy, charged with action and tension, a purple thunderstorm, pierced only by the light of the eternal stars shining forth between wind-driven clouds. Was not Venus, too, one of the stars that stood on his firmament? Well, perhaps so. And why not? A star among stars.

Metternich's life, far from being a tragedy, was rather a novel in several volumes, and he himself its hero. As for the stars, the ceiling of some drawing-room usually extended between them and his head. Epical as his character was, so was the course of his life; up and down and changeable as the nature of women, whom he knew as well as they knew him. And that is why he had come to know what Napoleon did not know: that there is always a Delilah to trim the locks of the all-too-impetuous and over-confident Samson, thus robbing him of his best strength. Now, after the conclusion of peace, in the year 1809, he put his knowledge to use.

He was aided by the fact that he had known for some time, and rather intimately, the circumstances leading up to Napoleon's divorce, although they transpired generally only now. He had at his fingers' tips what others still had to learn. As early as 1806 the "Emperor by his own grace" had contemplated a separation from Josephine. Napoleon's own little sister, Caroline, had brought Metternich the news, and it is probable that they had discussed exhaustively the compelling reasons which drove Napoleon to a divorce. Now all Europe knew these reasons—or at least thought they knew them. It was said that the Emperor desired off-spring, that he was longing for a crown prince. To be sure, Napoleon was a man of the people, an Italian. The Italians are almost as fond of children as the Americans, although they do not surrender so completely to them as do the latter. But there was something else, too, that prompted Napoleon to seek a divorce; that something, although Napoleon himself was hardly more than half conscious of it, was woman herself. So far, he who had transformed France and all of Europe, had only known experienced women. Josephine was a widow when he married her. It was the same story with all the others that came after her: the actress Mars, Walewska, or whatever their names might have been. They were all widows, more or less; while he, the greatest man of the century, was permitted merely to continue their amatory life. Now that he was approaching his forties, he felt inclined not only to take over a woman as one takes over an estate heavily encumbered with mortgages and tax-arrears, but to possess a woman independently of others and to educate her up to his standard. To establish in the virgin heart of a girl, a legitimate kingdom of his own and, without antecedents, to live happily in it, was now a temptation for the

formative power of the man who had made Europe sub-
servient to his will. Perhaps Metternich knew that, too, although he did not share Napoleon's creative taste in that
point. But he was willing to accommodate him and to provide for the Emperor of France what he desired in his in-
most heart: *une jeune fille.*

Metternich set to work immediately, hardly waiting for
the ink on the disgraceful peace-treaty of Schönbrunn to
dry. It may safely be assumed that he had known from the
beginning the name of the charming Delilah whom he
thought to procure for the victor, although he carefully kept
the name to himself. For this was another thing he had
learned in the school of love: act, but do not talk about it.

To begin with, he followed his usual custom by compos-
ing a memorandum which, as the newly fledged Foreign
Secretary, he dutifully submitted to his Emperor. He explained in his usual circumstantial way that, for the time being, there was nothing to do for Austria but to flatter and
wait. With time, comes counsel.

As a next step, he summoned into his presence a Monsieur
Laborde. The man was a French Count with commercial
ambitions who had made rather a good thing in Austria out
of contracts for the Napoleonic army, and had therefore remained in Vienna for some time. Metternich desired to see
him immediately before his return to Paris. He received
him at the State-Chancellory; in the conversation which
ensued, conducted in a purely social tone, he quite followed
the outlines of his own memorandum. Above all, he assured
Monsieur Laborde (as though that were any of his business!)
of Austria's honest intention to behave peacefully in the
future, and to eat gently out of the victor's hand. Thus, he

hoped, according to ancient traditions, the relations between France and Austria would become progressively
friendly and cordial. In between he even said—or was it possible that Monsieur Laborde who was listening with both
ears could have misunderstood?—why, he actually said something about an *"alliance de famille."* Without of course
mentioning any names. With a seeming attempt to take back
his own words and with an apologetic smile, Metternich
added: *"Cette idée est de moi!"* Then he rose and dismissed
his astonished caller. Like a clever nerve specialist, he had
given him a little injection; now his grateful patient, who
could not get over his surprise at being so confidentially
treated by His Excellency, found himself dismissed with a
cordial: *"Au revoir!"*

"Alliance de famille?" thought Monsieur Laborde, as he
proceeded by post-stages to Paris. What had been his meaning, and how was he, Laborde, to let Napoleon know about
it? Well, no matter how, he would see that Napoleon heard
of it. Monsieur Laborde felt naturally highly honored to
be the bearer of a message from His Excellency who had
deigned to chat with him so confidentially—one might even
say, without restraint. "A charming man, indeed!" thought
Laborde, rocking in the mail-coach. For the hundredth time
the words recurred to his mind: *"Alliance de famille!"* He
rubbed his hands and felt very important.

But before this emissary even reached Paris, the Austrian
embassy, strange to say, knew all about his message. As there
was no telegraph yet in those days one would have been inclined to think of magic; but, as in every conjuring trick,
the explanation turned out to be an extremely simple one.
The fact was that Madame Metternich had remained in
Paris with the children. Why? Very simple: when the war

broke out, she did not leave Paris, preferring to await there the decisions of the battle field. It was but natural that, through her husband, she always knew a little more than the Embassy, and she did not fail to communicate to the Ambassador the greater degree of her knowledge.

She also continued to correspond with her husband about this "European affair," as she called it in one of her letters still extant. At the same time, Floret, the First Secretary of the Embassy, reported to Metternich along the lines indicated by her. The Ambassador himself, Prince Schwarzenberg, remained in the background. There were reasons. Floret's first report in the matter showed, however, that Schwarzenberg was informed. As for Floret himself, he reported to Metternich that he had got in touch with Senator Semonville and spoken to him about the Archduchess. "And your chief?"—by which he meant Schwarzenberg—Semonville had asked at once. "What does he think about it?" "I can vouch for him," Floret replied with a smile, whereupon Semonville continued to make conscientious inquiries: "And Monsieur Metternich? And Emperor Franz?" Floret was able to give more or less satisfactory answers to these questions, too.

The Senator now felt firm ground under his feet and followed the matter up immediately. It seems that the intermediary had been well chosen, presumably by Metternich himself. It was not long before Madame Metternich received an invitation from the deposed Empress Josephine who wished to have a talk with her. Obviously informed by Semonville, Josephine began to show an unfeigned and surprising interest in Napoleon's remarriage. She said quite bluntly to her visitor, who of course lost no time in forwarding the news to her husband, that she desired an Austrian Archduchess for him. Thus the connection was established and had already reached Napoleon's immediate *entourage;* for, although divorced, the ex-Empress still belonged to the inner circle.

It was but natural that Josephine should be desirous of maintaining that position with Napoleon and it is probably because of that desire of hers that, in the manner of discarded favorites, she was keen on being the one to procure her successor. But conceivably she had also another, a more womanly, reason. Napoleon had turned away from her because he urgently required an heir to his throne to perpetuate his dynasty and because she, being six years his senior, was no longer likely to become a mother. In taking the matter of Napoleon's remarriage into her own hands, Josephine emphasized that reason. That is to say, she wanted all the world to know: "I am, and I shall remain, the Empress. For nursery purposes he now needs someone else. I am going to do the selecting!" In the matter of fertility, moreover, the Habsburgs enjoyed an enviable reputation. Maria Theresa had had seventeen children, and the wife of Emperor Leopold II, nineteen.

Whatever the reason, it was quite obvious that Empress Josephine favored the project, and there is little doubt that Napoleon secretly did, too. But he was not yet ready to admit it. On the contrary, the great strategist set in motion a tactical maneuver, concerning which Floret sent a report to Vienna at Christmas. Napoleon had sent a courier to St. Petersburg, instructing the French Ambassador there to sound out Czar Alexander. The Czar had a sister, Grand Duchess Anna, a girl of but sixteen, and Napoleon would not have been averse to making her Empress of the French. In addition to the fact that, after all, the Romanovs were

people with whom one need not be ashamed to show oneself in public, Napoleon rather liked Alexander personally.
He once paid the Russian ruler a doubtful compliment by
saying that if he were a woman he'd make him his mistress.
Politically, too, the connection would be desirable, for Russia had not yet joined the Continental System, and there
seemed to be no other way of getting at England, a most
obstinate foe who, in the end, was to prove his downfall.

Metternich, on the other hand, was anxious to prevent
the very thing that tempted Napoleon: an alliance between
France and Russia, through which Austria, lying between
them, would be dangerously hemmed in. For these and
other reasons Metternich, beginning in January, 1810, pursued his plan with an almost fanatical obstinacy. Originally
it had been but an idea like any other; now it turned into a
truly important affair of State, a parallel to the great work of
Kaunitz, forty years before, when Marie Antoinette became
the wife of the French dauphin. Well, was not Metternich
the grandson-son-in-law of the great Kaunitz? Was he not
his successor at the Vienna Ballhausplatz? Was not his wife
a Kaunitz by birth? A little Kaunitz, she was now rushing
about in Paris, busy either with Empress Josephine or at the
Austrian Embassy, doing her best to bring about the consummation of the great work. In the early days of February,
after the acts had duly been signed at the Embassy, she was
able to report to her lord and master with a sigh of relief:
"At last it is done, may the saints be praised!" As though she
were begging for a bit of praise for her own efforts in the
matter, she added charmingly: *"Je n'y ai pas peu contribué!"*

The conclusion of this all-important match had been
preceded by a little farce, of which Metternich knew nothing, and which throws a glaring light upon Napoleon's true

character. As a matter of course the Emperor was thoroughly informed from the very beginning, or at least since the early days of December, 1809, of the intentions of the Imperial Court of Vienna. Not without reason did he keep a hell-hound like Fouché, his Minister of Public Safety; not without reason did the Paris police keep in touch with people like Monsieur Laborde.

Napoleon's own attitude during the weeks that followed plainly showed that he neither disapproved nor was indifferent to Metternich's intentions. When shortly before New Year's, Countess Metternich very pointedly took leave of her Paris acquaintances and asked to be received in audience by Napoleon before starting on her long-delayed return to Vienna, the Emperor showed a sudden concern by insisting that it was now too cold for traveling and requesting that she stay in Paris a little longer. The lady from the House of Kaunitz knew that the request was really a command, and she lost no time in assuring His Majesty that she would comply with pleasure if her husband would grant her permission. She at once informed the latter, who at last saw his goal in sight; he determined to proceed all the more firmly in Paris since there was still some danger that, in the end, Russia would snatch away the bridegroom from under his nose.

Napoleon himself would not have minded such a development and actually would have preferred the Russian girl of sixteen to the Austrian one of seventeen—only for political reasons, of course, for he did not know either of them personally. What he did was to assume an attitude of watchful waiting, not moving a finger, permitting the Metternich project to proceed apace. That he probably chuckled to himself at the haste shown by the Court of Vienna, is another matter. In the meantime, the Russian decision, which was in the hands of Czar Alexander but subject also to the influence of the Empress Dowager, was rather long in coming. Little by little, the delay became rather awkward, and the courtiers began to shake their heads dubiously. Emperor Napoleon's message to St. Petersburg had gone forward on November 21st, 1809, but when the letter arrived the Czar unfortunately was not in town. He had left his capital shortly before and only returned a fortnight later, to take part in the Russian New Year's festivities. It seems it had not been convenient to forward his mail. But even now the Romanovs' joyful consent was longer in coming than was to the liking of Paris. When finally, on January 21st, exactly two months after the first inquiry had been sent, the answer came, it contained any number of evasive excuses but amounted to nothing less than a sugar-coated and diplomatically phrased refusal.

Now even Napoleon could not have entertained any further doubts that he was considered not good enough for the Romanovs, and from that moment he was quite sure in his mind that the Habsburgs would do. He lost no time in sending his stepson, Eugène Beauharnais, to the Austrian Embassy to see Prince Schwarzenberg and officially submit his suit. His wooing was truly Napoleonic. He demanded the immediate signing of a prepared document, threatening that, unless his demand were complied with, he would place his order somewhere else; he was quite well aware that there were any number of pretty girls in Russia, or in Saxony. At least that is how Prince Schwarzenberg somewhat meekly reported the matter to his Chief in Vienna after having duly signed his name on the dotted line. Napoleon's wooing in the form of an ultimatum—it was nothing less than that—was a complete success.

But, as a matter of fact, it was now more a success of Napoleon's than one of Metternich's. From that moment everything proceeded at a Napoleonic tempo. The Duc de Neufchâtel was sent to Vienna, and the Imperial daughter was married to the French Emperor's representative by proxy. The marriage agreement was solemnly signed at the same time, and no sooner was the writing-sand blown off the still damp signatures than Marie Louise was bundled into one of the Habsburgs' high-slung traveling coaches—which may still be seen in the Imperial collection of vehicles at Schönbrunn. Relays of horses drew her through the snow-clad Austrian lands into her fabulous new Empire. Her way took her through Southern Germany and Eastern France to the outskirts of Compiègne, near Paris. There the night was to be spent and horses changed for the last time.

Night was falling and rain was coming down in torrents when the Imperial coach made a brief halt at the last posting house before Compiègne. There, leaning against the church-portal, his arms crossed on his chest, and wrapped in a great-coat, stood a short, stout man; and another figure, one who had kept a close watch, loomed up close beside him. Now the latter whispered a few words to the stout one, who immediately rushed towards the coach, making it difficult for the other man to precede him by half a step, flung open the coach-door, and uttered the announcing, but also warning, cry: *"L'Empereur!"* Napoleon quickly vaulted into the coach, pushed the frightened lady-in-waiting to one side, and, making himself comfortable at the side of his pretty Viennese wife, continued the journey to Compiègne in the company of Marie Louise. There Caroline was waiting, the one with the little Cromwell head; the three of them had supper together, and the whole party spent the night there. On the following morning Napoleon had his breakfast served in his young wife's bedroom and sipped his chocolate in utter contentment. In Paris, a few formalities had to be observed, like the official wedding ceremony at the Cathedral of Notre Dame to the ringing of many church-bells, and the congratulatory levee for 1500 invited guests. As if she had been wakened out of a dream, the young girl overnight had become Empress of the French. Poor child! She had not even been asked if she wanted to—a monstrous proceeding that even went beyond what was customary at the 18th-century courts.

This arbitrary procedure was not without its material significance either, a fact well known to the gentlemen in Paris; for it did not even give Austria time to stipulate its conditions, although that must have been uppermost in the country's calculations. This was possibly the reason why Metternich, though he had ostensibly gained his object, wrote a letter to Prince Schwarzenberg in which he did not conceal His Majesty's dissatisfaction. He went so far as to speak of a *"manque de forme,"* a rather strong expression in a communication addressed to an Ambassador. Luckily for Napoleon—though his luck was not to be of long duration—the young bride who was primarily concerned in the matter failed entirely to notice the rather insulting informality, or even to wonder about it. A few weeks after the dictate of Paris, when she was conversing at table with the French Ambassador in Vienna, she did not show the least sign of resentment. She put a few questions—charmingly curious and girlish questions—which were forwarded to

Paris with an amused smile. Thus they were preserved for posterity. Her first question was whether or not there might be in Paris a *"musée Napoléon"* with which she would greatly wish to become acquainted. Well, that question probably had been suggested to her by one of the ladies-in-waiting and was really nothing but an *"attention,"* as they called it at the Court of the Habsburgs, a courtesy which cost nothing and was likely to give pleasure. The second question, however, in which she asked about music in Paris, came from the very heart of a daughter of Vienna who would prefer even her wooing to proceed in waltz-time. Being an Austrian, she did not fail to think of the country-side, inquired about the surroundings of Paris, and confessed that she vastly preferred living in the country. One of the next questions was disarming in its charming naïveté. She asked whether the Emperor would be angry at her inability to dance the quadrille. She would gladly start at once to learn it and take lessons from a dancing-master, if Napoleon should wish it. Finally she ventured to mention a wish of her own: a harp and a teacher with whom she could twang its strings; for she liked nothing better than to play the harp. . . .

From all this, we get the charming portrait of a girl in an empire setting, quite unable to disguise her Viennese origin. Only a Viennese girl could chatter so ingenuously and wish so modestly. Only a Viennese girl, even if she was the daughter of an Emperor, taught to be submissive, could unite so charmingly, humbleness and gentle animation.

But scarcely had the bells of Notre Dame ceased to ring and the daughter of the Habsburgs, now Empress of the French, ventured to raise her pale blue eyes, when something happened that nobody could have expected. Two days after the wedding, and one day after the levee, Metternich suddenly turned up among the gradually dispersing wedding guests, although nobody had invited him to come. Nevertheless, he considered it necessary to undertake the journey. He felt drawn to Paris as an artist feels drawn to his work, or a capitalist who has invested a great deal of money is drawn to the opening of a new industrial plant. He also had a number of other reasons why he wished to make the City on the Seine his abode for some time—reasons both of a political and a private nature. The private ones were closely connected with gallant memories of his ambassadorial days. At any rate, there was his wife in Paris, the good Eleonore, whom he had not seen for a year and to whom it was about time he paid a visit.

Metternich was a statesman and an expert in the art of living who, in his Paris days, actually was a *"viveur."* The actuality came close to causing him a good deal of unpleasantness so that his first stay in Paris came near ruling out his second one, after Napoleon's wedding. The fact of the matter was that his affairs with Laure and Caroline were attended with consequences; not the kind of consequences found in old-fashioned novels, but others which were not so very pleasant either and went to prove that there is a final retribution both in politics and in love.

While Napoleon was wooing and finally leading Marie Louise to the altar, something had happened during the Paris carnival which cannot be called an unusual occurrence at a time when masked balls were the order of the day: a masker had slipped a note into the hand of a jealous husband. The man who seized it with surprise and a moment later stared at it in utter discomfiture was Junot, whom Na-

poleon had made Duke of Abrantès after the bloody Spanish war. It was said that the person who handed over the
slip of paper and immediately disappeared again in the
throng was Caroline Murat.

Junot was advised by the solicitous guardian of his honor
to have a look at his wife's escritoire. He would find a little
package tied round with a pink silk ribbon—the love letters from Count Metternich.

The Duke hastened home, did as he was told, and found
the letters. He called his wife to account, and she confessed
what would have been difficult for her to deny. The deceived husband raged and fumed. He wrote a letter to Metternich, proposing Mainz as the meeting-place for the unavoidable duel. It is rather questionable that Metternich
ever received the letter. Its dispatch may have been prevented by Napoleon's command. The fact that he was
known in those days to have called Junot a *"butor,"* a blockhead, justifies the assumption that he had caused himself to
be well informed as to his Marshal's affair.

At any rate, on the following day Junot was seen to adopt
a different method—one infinitely more convenient. Instead
of proceeding to Mainz he called upon Madame Metternich
and bitterly complained about her husband. It probably was
not the first visit of a similar kind the Countess had received
and, having long since renounced all feelings of jealousy (if
she had ever been jealous at all), she listened to her caller
quietly. Then, firmly, she gave him a piece of her mind: a
man like he should be the last to play the part of Othello.
Here was, probably, an allusion to Caroline, with whom the
Duke was rumored to have entertained tender relations.
Moreover, she continued, what was done could not be un-

done. It was advisable to set things straight without making a furore about them.

Without losing any time, the Countess had herself driven to Laure's house and made a strong practical appeal to her. What success she had may be learned from the Duchess' memoirs which were published later. Being fond of reliving the part she was in the habit of writing down everything conscientiously. The reader is told that the beautiful Laure, tied to the stake of love, had to endure a second, and even more horrible, scene from the infuriated *"butor"* who, having abandoned his journey to Mainz, demanded nothing less than that she, "a bleeding and torn woman," as she expressed it, once more recognize and confirm his conjugal rights. The Duchess, a sensuous beauty and fond of tragical upheavals, actually made the sacrifice demanded of her. Memories of the "grotto" and of the "tears of blood" she had then shed because of her evil deed may have assailed her. Having again become a dutiful wife, Countess Metternich later called her with a fine smile an "ingenious woman" which, in spite of the fact that she wrote memoirs, the naughty little Laure certainly was not.

The interesting figure in this somewhat cheap, sentimental intrigue was not the romantically swayed and finally "torn" Duchess, nor her husband, the blockhead in a Marshal's uniform, but Countess Metternich who with consummate skill and cleverness managed the affair. It was enacted simultaneously and entirely parallel with Napoleon's wooing of a bride, so that the main action of that theatrically stirred winter in Paris did not fail to be accompanied by a satyric game. The diplomatic Countess Metternich, in attending to both matters, certainly had her hands full in

keeping them properly apart and yet managing them well.
Being a conscientious ambassadress in retirement, she knew
how to convey the distinct impression that the two affairs
were of entirely different importance. She obviously made
light of the private one, both with respect to tone and date.
The tone was the same which a well-schooled cabinet secretary would use in reporting to His Excellency, with appropriate preciseness, happenings which really are none of the
writer's personal concern. The date was February 7th, the
very day on which Napoleon's marriage agreement was
signed at Prince Schwarzenberg's palace. In a letter sent to
her husband a day before, she had called the impending
marriage an affair of European importance. Now that that
was settled, she sent in her report about the other concurrent matter which, in weeks of correspondence, she had
never even mentioned, although she must have known
about it for some time. In a cool matter-of-fact tone, she explained all the developments, the matter of the anonymous
letter at the masked ball at the Marescalchi Palace, and what
followed.

But she also mentioned another version without deciding
which was the correct one. According to one, Junot had
shadowed his wife to the ball and had overheard Laure arranging a rendezvous with Monsieur de L., *"pour lequel
s'interessent beaucoup de personnes."* In order to divert the
jealous Junot's attention from Monsieur de L., he had been
put on the track of Metternich, and so the matter of the old
letters suddenly had been unearthed. *"On vous savait absent
et dans l'impossibilité de vous aboucher avec la barbe bleu."*
"La barbe bleu" is of course Monsieur de L., Metternich's
successor, and *"on"* is the naughty Laure, at whose door a
piece of treachery is thus laid: she sacrificed her former

lover for her present one. Moreover, the Countess wrote, Monsieur de L. had already left Paris. *"Il est parti avec son amazone et ne plus reviendra de sa vie."* He already had a successor in the person of Savary.

Why did Mme. Metternich report all these secondary details to her most disagreeably surprised husband? For two reasons: first, to prove to Metternich that he was by no means the only one, and had no cause whatever to be conceited about his "grotto" adventure. This was the only satisfaction the oft-deceived wife claimed for herself. It was her commission, so to speak, for having so smoothly settled the affair. The other reason was a very practical one: she wanted to prevent Metternich from coming to Paris at once, since that would have been connected with some danger for him, and so she counseled him strongly against it. She did not utter a single word of reproach but, on the contrary, closed her letter with the sentence: *"Cher ami, revenez-nous bientôt . . . je vous embrasse, mon cher ami."* An aristocratic union! For only the day before, on February 6th, she had written him verbatim: *"Mais, que j'en ai passé des mauvaises nuits! Et que d'inquiétudes et d'angoisses j'en avais!"* But there she referred to Napoleon's wooing of Marie Louise. What a *grande dame!* And how well suited was her coolly controlled heart to the man who, in spite of everything, was and remained the man of her choice.

Metternich came to Paris, after all, not to settle a love intrigue, but to float an Austrian loan, in which undertaking he unfortunately had no success. In other respects, too, and in spite of the marriage of the Corsican Samson to the Austrian Delilah, he was unable to register any further political accomplishments on behalf of Austria, at least not at the first try. It was autumn, nevertheless, before he left Paris where, it is asserted, he walked about with the bracelet on his wrist which Queen Caroline had woven for him out of her own hair. Was it vanity that made him wear it? Or did he want again to mislead Marshal Junot who had long since ceased to be jealous? Or was it that he wanted to gloat inwardly over Napoleon whose own sister had once been his mistress?

When the great Norseman, Ibsen, was asked once by a curious admirer of his "Ghosts" if it had really been the carpenter Engstrand who had set fire to the "asylum," he answered after a few moments' reflection: "Well, I would not put it past him!" Metternich, too, while acting as Austria's negotiator at the Court of France, would have been capable of displaying Caroline's bracelet with the idea in mind that he wanted, at least inwardly, to defy his great antagonist Napoleon. Samson's locks, he may have thought to himself, are shorn by Delilah; but he, Metternich, who is no Samson, shears Delilah's hair.

"*Comte de Balance*"

I<small>F</small> it were Metternich's intention to restore Austria's greatly shrunken prestige by Napoleon's marriage to Marie Louise, his success during the couple's honeymoon was restricted to his own person. He was pampered and loved. Among the foreign diplomats he was the first man at Court and, for obvious reasons, was even in Napoleon's good books; for he had been the means of giving France a young Empress of age-old lineage, and the fact that she soon became an expectant mother raised the hopes for perpetuation of the new dynasty. Napoleon who, a year before at the outbreak of the war, was about to have him arrested and almost had him shot; who half a year before, was so outspoken in declining to have him assist in the drawing up of the peace treaty that Metternich was obliged to leave the conference room ignominiously—that same Napoleon now treated him most graciously and let no opportunity pass to flatter him with honeyed words. The master of the battle field was in those months nothing but a greatly enamoured husband who was blissfully happy and fortunately happened to have the leisure for it. He was quite ready to let those to whom he owed his happiness participate in it and was pleasantly aware that every attention he showed the seductive Austrian diplomat was at the same time an homage he paid to the charming young Austrian girl whom Metternich had procured for him. Napoleon felt, moreover, a certain natural sympathy for his dangerous antagonist. It was the irrational and hardly justifiable partiality of a genius for the very man who was to bring about his downfall. The logical explanation of this phenomenon is known probably only to God. It certainly is a fact that Napoleon had the same weakness, and for the same reason, for Talleyrand.

To be sure, pleasant words are one thing and success is quite another. This was a fact the Austrian statesman had eventually to admit to himself during those agreeable spring weeks in Paris which turned into equally agreeable summer months. If he had entertained any hopes of the unfortunate peace conditions being subsequently made easier because of the happy family relations now existing between the Houses of Habsburg and Bonaparte, he was forced reluctantly to admit to himself after six months of wily negotiations—in which, like every dictator, Napoleon was a past master—that they were in no way justified. All he finally brought home with him was a possible increase of the greatly reduced peace-time footing of the Austrian army—a first step, to be sure, in a rearmament program. Napoleon acquiesced probably because the step was to be taken at Austria's expense and not at France's. As for the planned loan, however, which Austria needed so very badly, Metternich returned to Vienna entirely empty-handed. Rebuffed! France, which meant Napoleon, although seemingly favoring the subject, never for a moment actually thought of lending money to Austria which had presented him with a wife. Such matters he magnanimously left to the French and Dutch bankers who, however, also refused to entertain the idea.

These were the reasons why Austria, half a year later, in February, 1811, announced the sad but well-prepared fact of her national bankruptcy, as the thing was bravely called in those unsophisticated days. In our day there would be a cold-blooded announcement of the currency's devaluation. At any rate, Austria had to suffer half a century from the consequences of the collapse, for which Metternich, too, was partly responsible. He, the Catholic, had refused to sanction a plan which provided for the use of the Hungarian church-lands to bolster up the crumbling State finances. But the main reason of the collapse lay in the precipitate signing of the marriage protocol, on February 7th, 1810, which was tantamount to an unconditional surrender of the Austrian position. Austria should have stipulated its financial conditions before, and not after the event. But the Austrian negotiator, Prince Schwarzenberg, lost his head. He was not equal to the task set him by Metternich and preferred to settle the matter in the manner of a cavalier.

This, unfortunately, is an experience which recurs in Austrian history. Fifty years later, Austria ceded the lagoon-bridge of Venice and the right-of-way of its Southern Railway, properties worth 80 million lire, without any indemnity whatever. It had simply been neglected to mention in the protocols these wonders of the technical science of those days. Again, in 1918, at the armistice negotiations with Italy, there was a failure to stipulate expressly whether the armistice was to be effective at the time of the dispatch of the Austrian telegram of acceptance, or only when it was received at Italian headquarters. The Italians maintained that hostilities were to cease only upon receipt of the Austrian reply, which they managed to delay a whole day. In the meantime, their motored columns advanced another few hundred kilometers, which cost Austria a quarter of a million soldiers who in the now occupied territory had to surrender their arms and submit to imprisonment because of a thoughtless mistake at Austrian headquarters. And what about March 11th, 1938, when Schuschnigg capitulated to Hitler without at least insisting —even if he submitted to everything else—upon amnesty for his own Government and a few thousands of his functionaries? Always the same mistake, the same precipitate haste, the same thoughtlessness; and always, too, the same consequences: lost credit, lost armies, lost country! Nothing, indeed, is more instructive than history; but nobody cares to be instructed.

To make up in a slight degree for the rebuffs he had suffered, Metternich, when he returned to Vienna in the autumn of 1810 after six months spent in Paris, was able to record a personal success. As a farewell gift he had been presented with a breast-piece of Napoleon and a few Sèvres vases valued at 8400 francs. It was not a great deal, in exchange for an Emperor's daughter, and certainly not more than a man of honor may accept on such an occasion. At any rate, he had some porcelain to show for the greatest and most successful coup of his still young career as a statesman. However, porcelain is fragile.

Austria, which had suddenly become France's mother-in-law, did not find herself in an enviable position when Metternich finally returned to Vienna. It was generally assumed there that the Chancellor's overthrow was at hand. This belief was not entirely unjustified, as he was soon to see.

He had remained in Paris a little too long and had not brought back enough. France had rejected the government-loan proposed by him; Vienna had refused to ratify the new trade-agreement he had with difficulty obtained in France; the prohibitively high war-indemnity had not been canceled, not even reduced; only the dates of payment had been slightly postponed. Added to all this was the growth of his own unpopularity. It is a strange fact that this Darling of the Gods had to suffer from it in Vienna all his life. In the present instance there was at least some justification for it. While in Paris, he had right under the nose of the Austrian Ambassador played a little too much at being himself the Ambassador. This had served to put out of joint not only Schwarzenberg's own nose, but also the noses of the whole Schwarzenberg coterie—in other words, by far the larger part of the Austrian nobility.

The Austrian patriots, on the other hand, had never ceased to feel as a deep disgrace the family union with the "arch-enemy," proposed and accomplished by Metternich. The Empress Maria Ludovika who no later than the spring of 1809 had presented for consecration at St. Stephen's Cathedral of Vienna the flags of the Austrian regiments and who still displayed a war-like spirit, found it difficult to be reconciled to the new order of things. She declared openly that she could not bear the sight of Metternich, and would not see him. The Archdukes—the nobly gifted Archduke Karl, unavailing victor of Aspern; and the nobly simple-minded Johann, dreamy hunter of chamois and helpless protector of the Tyrol—were of the same opinion as Her Majesty. Count Stadion, a true patriot, considered himself overthrown by Metternich, his successor in the Foreign Office. Count Wallis, the bankrupt Minister of Finances, saw himself abandoned by Metternich in his plans for financial reconstruction. Prince Liechtenstein, who in October of the previous year had conducted the unfortunate peace negotiations, could not forgive Metternich for considering him a jackass. Added to these were the envious ones, the offended, and those who had been passed over. With their enmity every minister has to count. Finally there was the social set of Vienna, which was always to be found on the side of mediocrity and of the outmoded, and was forever up in arms against any independent and autocratic talent. As a matter of fact, when Metternich came back from Paris, everyone was against him, with the exception of the Emperor himself. Metternich surveyed the situation and acknowledged the fact with a smile.

Firm in the knowledge of his Emperor's support, nothing would have been easier for Metternich at that moment than to slip off his gloves and show the hand of steel. And why did the Emperor uphold him? That he did it out of gratitude would be entirely too simple an explanation. In this instance, too, the reason possibly may be found in the basic character of the Habsburgs. The Austrian Emperor would permit neither public opinion nor that of the drawing-rooms to tell him when he had better dismiss one of his ministers. It was, on the contrary, a welcome opportunity to show people that one does what one has a mind to do. That is what Emperor Franz Joseph did for more than sixty years. Whenever a minister fell into disgrace with the people or in Parliament, the fact automatically prolonged his tenure of office. One of the most unpopular ministers under Franz Joseph, Count Taaffe, managed in that way to remain prime minister for thirteen years. Emperor Franz, who was Franz Joseph's great-uncle and model in many respects, proceeded along exactly the same lines. Joseph Redlich, the great Austrian historian, was justified in saying of Emperor

Franz that, although he died in 1836, he actually reigned in Austria until 1916, the year Franz Joseph died.

Whatever the state of affairs may have been, Metternich certainly did the cleverest thing he could have done under the circumstances. He simply acted as though he was not aware there was anyone against him in Vienna. He again went a good deal into society, as he had done when quite a young man; and he made it a special point to visit those homes and circles which were hostile to him. At the Russian Embassy, for instance, which he knew full well was the breeding place of most intrigues hatched against him, he came and went as if nothing had happened. He always honored with his presence the gatherings of nobility and patriots who would have liked nothing better than to oust him. He bowed low before the hostile Archdukes and the most ungracious Empress, of whom he may have thought to himself, he would ultimately get the better. And he remained in office.

At last, however, when the mischief-making would not end, and the flood of calumny which branded him as an arch-traitor, bought by France, washed its filth against the very steps of the Imperial throne, he surprisingly took the initiative. He had not watched Fouché in Paris for nothing. He had learned that one could get most people in one's power and mould them like wax if only one could get possession of their letters. As a matter of fact, in that connection there was not much the Paris police could have taught their Austrian colleagues of absolutist days, whose original teachers had been the Italians. Something of that must have remained in their blood, for when the Gestapo took possession of Vienna in 1938, the police there proved themselves extremely apt pupils. The only difference a hundred years ago at the time of Metternich, was that, if one had illegally got possession of someone else's secrets one did not make so much noise about it. So far as the "inviolability of letters" became a matter of police attention, a very sharp and conscientious distinction was made between what they called "chiffons" and "intercepts." The former were letters or notes thrown away after having been torn into little pieces. The fragments were gathered from waste-baskets or rubbish-boxes by treacherous employees in the pay of the secret police, and painstakingly pasted together again. "Intercepts" were detained letters which were carefully copied before they were forwarded again with but a slight delay. That was not a very difficult matter, for the postal authorities themselves attended to it in a specially equipped "black cabinet." It was all just as it is in Europe today.

In that manner Metternich had got possession of some rather strange and questionable, if not highly suspicious, correspondence. They were letters exchanged between the young Empress Maria Ludovika and her brother-in-law, the interesting Archduke Joseph, Palatine of Hungary, a younger brother of Emperor Franz. Joseph, who disapproved of his Imperial brother's Hungarian policy, was a member of the opposition, and so was the Empress, whose childless married life was not notable for its happiness. She was a beautiful woman of much temperament, who did not seem disinclined to kindle the spark of love in others, and then warm herself at the flames she had fanned to life. Among her great admirers was the sixty-year-old Goethe, in whose company she liked to be seen on the Karlsbad promenade. Her august presence so inspired the poet that he even composed a poem or two about her.

Just how far her relations with her brother-in-law Joseph
went is difficult to ascertain. It was asserted in Vienna that
they went as far as Pressburg where a rendezvous had been
arranged by letter. Politically they were of one mind, and
it would not have been surprising if, as the conspirators put
their heads together, not only their hands but their lips,
too, met. At any rate, there were a great many such allusions
in the letters, which Metternich, with hardly excusable un-
scrupulousness, submitted to his Emperor. His only excuse
may have been that he saw in his action a means for endur-
ingly securing his position with his most gracious Imperial
master, whose "bizarre whims" Maria Ludovika repeatedly
mentioned in her letters. Now that she was no longer permitted to go to Pressburg, it may have been a spirit of venge-
fulness that prompted the Emperor to keep the informer
in office; and the Court-party, although gnashing its teeth,
had to submit.

Whatever may be one's opinion of this act of rather far-
reaching self-defense which for the first time shows Metternich's moral indifference in official as well as private
matters, it certainly benefited the Foreign Minister and,
indirectly, Austria, too. Who knows what course history
would have taken if, influenced by Metternich's downfall,
the Francophile policy, of which he was accused, had been
abandoned. How little of "friendliness towards France"
there really was in it, was not suspected by anyone at that
time—not even by Metternich himself.

The fact remains that, at a time when Napoleon's star
was at its zenith and his son, the King of Rome and child
of the Habsburgs, lay in his cradle, Metternich could have
had no other wish than to be on good terms with France at

any cost. But even at that time he already included the other European Great Powers—Russia, England, and Prussia— in an ideological grouping which, as the so-called "pentarchy," was to safeguard European peace. This was his dream of a European equilibrium of which he talked so frequently and with so great a zeal that it began to attract attention—to the extent that Vienna society, never at a loss for a nickname, called him "Comte de Balance" behind his back.

The sobriquet fitted Metternich. But it was overlooked or unjustly forgotten that in this striving for a European equilibrium, which gradually became an *idée fixe* with Metternich, there was also a certain ethical idea; and in view of the lessons taught in recent days, the idea may be discerned more clearly today than was possible a hundred years ago. Metternich was the first Austrian and super-German statesman to understand what his country and Continent needed in order to have peace. Austria was at stake, to be sure; but Europe was drifting into a similar state. Gentz who was gifted with great foresight, called him the "Knight of Europe." Although Gentz may well be called a moral foot pad, nevertheless he was quite able to recognize the greatness of a new idea and on such occasions never failed to wave his dissolute hat in joyous salutation.

The Strangle Hold

For the time being, of course, a European equilibrium was out of the question. Napoleon's superiority decided everything. He sat enthroned in Paris in a flood of light which almost paled into insignificance the splendor of the "Sun-King," Louis XIV; and he dictated from there the fate of the continents. As he cast the lots, so they lay. The map of Europe was changed beyond recognition. Germany ceased to exist. It was replaced, for the present, by a broken ring of neutralized border states without a center and by the Austrian administrator of the defunct Empire. Those who reigned in these shadow states were petty princes, governors, or dummy rulers, unless some off shoot of the Napoleonic dynasty adorned the little throne. The Netherlands likewise had been wiped off the map and replaced forcibly by a Napoleonic puppet-state, the Kingdom of Holland. Belgium belonged entirely to France. Spain was a French protectorate, and so was Upper Italy, which was called the Cis-Alpine Republic. Prussia sulked embittered in a corner. Austria had been pushed back so far that it stood almost with one foot in Asia, and Metternich already at that time might have coined the malicious phrase later attributed to him: that Asia began at the Simmering Line (the eastern city-limit of Vienna). Russia and England alone, both protected by their geographical position, were, if not unconquerable, at least still unconquered. Therein lay the cause of the next war. Ostensibly, it was a war against Russia, but as a matter of fact it was a war against England.

Napoleon tried to settle England's fate in the same manner as England settled Germany's a century later: through a blockade; with the difference that it was a blockade reversed: *from* the Continent. It was called the Continental System. By cutting off all trade connections to and from the Continent the British Insular Kingdom was to be starved into submission and, like a hungry fortress, made ready for capitulation. For that purpose Napoleon needed the Spanish and Portuguese sea ports. That was a simple matter. He took them by establishing the Spanish protectorate. He also needed Italian harbors, and he secured them by controlling the North of Italy himself, while he let his own little sister Caroline, Metternich's former mistress and now Queen of Naples, exercise a strict control over the Southern part of Italy, over Naples, and also over Palermo. Caroline's husband, Murat, naturally had no objection; neither had Joseph in Spain, nor Louis Napoleon in Holland, nor the German subsidiary princes, nor the German Hansa cities, nor Austria in Venice, nor the Kingdom of Illyria on the Adriatic Sea.

Russia alone held aloof from this Napoleonic maritime encirclement. For a number of years, and at first by means of friendly diplomatic negotiations, Napoleon had tried to secure what wrestlers call a strangle hold, a grip which usually spells defeat for the other party. The Congress of Erfurt, 1808, when the great actor Talma played before a "pit of kings," was such a trial bout between the wrestlers Bonaparte and Alexander of Russia. On that occasion Talley-

rand, who furnished a cynical accompaniment to his master's political efforts, said to Alexander: "The French nation
is civilized, but its ruler is not; the Russian ruler is civilized,
but his people are not. What could be more fitting than an
alliance between the Russian ruler and the French nation?"
The civilized Alexander, however, was not particularly keen
on the proposition. Neither was the Grand-Duchess Anna,
for whose hand Napoleon confidentially asked Alexander
in Erfurt.

Instead of Anna, the Empress of France's name was now
Marie Louise. It was an indisputable fact, which those of a
fair mind should have put to Metternich's credit, that
through this matrimonial connection the threatened East-
West encirclement of the Habsburg Empire by France and
Russia was avoided, and Austria could at least breathe more
freely. It was also due to this conjugal union that the incipient Russo-French amity, Napoleon's political maneuver
with Alexander, was entirely wrecked. In the last analysis
the Russian campaign of 1812 had its initial cause in that
Paris marriage agreement of February, 1810. That agreement, although weakly engineered by Schwarzenberg, was
Metternich's original work. Consequently, if this war now
ended disastrously for Napoleon, it was also Metternich's
work and should be placed to his historical credit.

It is passing strange, though, that at first Metternich never
contemplated the possibility of France's failing in her risky
undertaking. He had been wiser than he himself had realized. Austria had entered the war virtually as Napoleon's
ally. The father-in-law marched along with Napoleon, while
his pretty daughter, made regent over-night for the duration
of her exalted husband's absence, remained in Paris. Even
if Metternich had been careful enough to restrict the Aus-

trian auxiliary forces under Schwarzenberg to a paltry 30,000 soldiers, he never doubted for a moment that he had thereby assured to himself a share in the spoils. In common with the rest of the world of those days, he counted upon a quick success for the French arms. His judgment seemed to be vindicated by events, for after a *"Blitzkreig"* of two months Napoleon, late in September, 1812, entered Moscow, the enemy's capital, ready and rather anxious immediately to dictate his peace terms. What both the victorious Emperor and Metternich left out of account were the possibilities that the negotiations might be protracted, and that snow might come sooner or fall heavier than usual. Does this weigh against Metternich? Not at all. A statesman cannot be expected to be a weather-prophet.

The question arises how, in the event of a French victory, Metternich's devilishly clever calculation to have Delilah conquer Samson could have come out right. The answer is that, to begin with, the calculation was not devilish at all but thoroughly human and that, furthermore, such calculations rarely turn out precisely as anticipated. Were it otherwise, history would be a matter of mathematics, and destiny a bureau of statistics. If Napoleon had been victorious in 1812, of which Metternich was, or seemed to be, firmly convinced in the summer of that year, Austria would have greatly benefited, and might have become the Great Power whose voice in Central European affairs would have been weighty, if not decisive. There would have been the chance, too, sooner or later, of entering into an English alliance against France. Time and straw make medlars ripe, was one of Metternich's cautious principles. A rather good principle, because a natural one. Even his lack of imagination, of which Metternich's adversaries were in the habit of

accusing him, worked out to his advantage. He always remained "master of the next step," because he lacked the
audacity to aim at mastery of the step beyond the next.
While attending to the settlement of history's documents as
they came to hand, he never lost track of his immovable
goal: the re-establishment of a condition of European equilibrium. Even if it had snowed a little less in the winter of
1812, he would have come nearer his goal.

While the pitiful remains of the Grand Army of France,
a weary, blood-stained, frost-bitten, and bedraggled mass
of starving misery, were crushed by the ice of the Beresina,
a sledge swiftly bore Napoleon to Paris through the wintry
quiet of Germany. There his Empress and his infant son—
how long would they still be his?—awaited him. A few
months, and he was again in the eastern part of Germany
at the head of a rejuvenated and enthusiastic army, determined to take up the fight once more and lead it to a victorious conclusion. Metternich urged him to consider a peace.
The Emperor did not heed the advice, failed even to reply
to it, and insisted upon Austria's fulfilling her duty as an ally.
Metternich observed it punctiliously. Prussia, too, observed it, to say nothing of Saxony which, although wavering, was still to be found on Napoleon's side at the Battle of
Leipsic. Tame princes and tamed Cabinets! But threaten-
ingly behind them rose the great multitude which pressed
forward relentlessly. What was the Austrian State-Chancellor's attitude towards that onward crush, to which history
was to give the beautiful name of the "Wars of German Independence," although it deserved only to be called a struggle for liberation from French domination? All his natural
instincts urged Metternich towards an attitude of repudia-

tion. He was no nationalist. Neither was he a friend of the people, and he hated crushes. He was loath to concede to the Germans a feeling of national self-consciousness. As for German unity, of which Baron von Stein, his Rhenish countryman of opposite views, dreamed so fervently and concerning which the German philosopher Fichte lectured so glowingly to the awakening youth, Metternich's views were almost identical with those of his master, Emperor Franz, who, in referring to this very same Fichte, made the distrustful remark: he had heard "that Herr Fichte was endeavoring to form some sort of a sect." Metternich repudiated all that so thoroughly that it was non-existent as far as he was concerned. National enthusiasm was to him identical with insurrection, revolution, and Jacobinism. The problem, as he viewed it, was not the German National State but the "historical State" which, in the name of Austria, ought to be re-established everywhere in Europe. That, however, was the concern of the Cabinets, whom the millions had to serve only when called upon, and then only in a soldier's uniform. Until such time the people should remain quiet and refrain from interfering in government affairs. Those who nevertheless insisted upon interfering were peremptorily arrested. This applied also to German go-betweens who, like Gruner or Boyen—the latter a member of the League of Virtue—made their meddlesome appearance in Austria. Metternich hated everything that smacked of German nationalism or rabid Teutonism.

Metternich was soon to have a welcome opportunity for an actual demonstration of his anti-nationalistic tendencies. The Austrian equivalent of the German League of Virtue, although it was not quite so virtuous, was the Alpine League. Then, as later, national feeling closely affiliated itself with the mountains. "On the mountains dwells our freedom"—or what is commonly considered freedom. Especially since 1809, and particularly in the Tyrol was the rallying cry heard. The Tyroleans, neighbors of the Swiss, had not without reason been the ones who in the "Year of Stress" revolted first and longest against the "Yoke of Foreign Tyranny." Their national indignation was so wholly Swiss in its thoroughness that it caused a good deal of consternation and embarrassment in Vienna, which henceforth lifted not a finger to come to the Tyroleans' assistance. Their leader, the black-bearded Andreas Hofer, was shot as a traitor at Mantua. His was a typically Austrian fate, recognizable as such by its high-minded futility.

Inflamed by the hot breath of history, the Tyrolean broth of liberty, which had been bubbling for quite a while, finally blew off the lid and boiled over. There were in 1813 several cooks who, ladles in hand, bent over it eagerly. One of them was the Director of the Habsburgs' Court and State Archives, a Baron Hormayr, intimate friend of the nationally inclined Caroline Pichler, who today would be a fanatical Nazi. Hormayr was the author of a large number of patriotically tinged biographies which he collected and published under the title: "Austrian Plutarch." There was also the Archduke Johann, younger brother of Emperor Franz, a romantic alpine climber, familiar and popular everywhere in the Province of Styria where to this day a majority of the inns are named in his honor. His oleograph may still be found, now and then, in a Styrian peasant-room. It presents to the beholder a serious, and even ill-humored, elongated provincial face which seems to look down into the valley from a high mountain. As a matter of fact, the usually quite amiable Archduke liked nothing better than to do that very thing. He lived in the mountains, for the mountains, and of the mountains. As a general pitted against Napoleon he does not seem to have covered himself with a great deal of glory, but as a hunter of chamois he was able to hold his own with anyone. His unassuming greatness seemed to be better suited to the alpenstock than to the marshal's baton. To wander, lost to the world, cloudward on lonely mountain paths was the exalted hunter's greatest delight. Of a child-like mind, he lived in his medieval ideas, despising the city, hating the Court, and thinking the worse of Metternich for associating too much with the "fine people." On the whole, and with the exception of the conspiracy of the Alpine League, which quickly blew over, he gave little further trouble to his Imperial brother—unless it be considered trouble that, a few years later, he married one Anna Plochl, the daughter of a rural post-master or, as Caroline Pichler would have expressed it, he elevated her to wifehood.

The matter of the Alpine League, however, was a real conspiracy and, as such, not the first one in which members of the Imperial family were implicated, and which Emperor Franz had to overcome. Two years before, Archduke Franz, the Empress' brother, had conceived a fantastic plan to build up on one of the Ionian Islands a "storm center" against Napoleon. Although he actually carried out his plan, there is no indication that Napoleon in St. Cloud or Fontainebleau felt greatly incommoded by the storm's blowing. Archduke Karl, the deeply aggrieved victor of Aspern, also had done some plotting; Archduke Joseph, the Palatine of Hungary and Empress Maria Ludovika's Pressburg cavalier, had done the same; and now Metternich had to halt Archduke Johann, the huntsman, in his nefarious scheming. He had much trouble with the archdukes.

The guileless Archduke, cleverly misled by English agents, had permitted himself to become implicated in a far-flung conspiracy, reaching as far as Venice and Bohemia and possibly even to the "storm center." Metternich was to have been assassinated by Russian officers, and a Kingdom of Illyria or Rhaetia founded under the leadership of Johann. England, planning a surprise sea attack on Venice, encouraged the founding of the new kingdom. The trouble was to have started in Tyrol, whereupon the Archduke who was already staying in Vienna for the purpose, was to "rush upon the scene" at Easter-time; at the same time, a connection was to be formed with the rising German movement for liberty in Silesia, by way of Bohemia. An English agent by the name of Danelon was for that purpose already en route to Prague in a mail-coach. In such affairs the presence of an English agent and that of a simple-hearted Austrian Archduke are inevitable, said Metternich, who knew how to be spiteful on occasions.

He had the Englishman's mail-coach attacked between Weisskirchen and Neutitschein by disguised robbers, who really were agents of his Gestapo. In addition to his luggage, the traveler lost all of his papers and documents. They plainly showed Hormayr's complicity and the Archduke's knowledge of the affair. The Archduke was immediately placed under surveillance, while Danelon was arrested, although, being an Englishman, he was subsequently released. Hormayr, who had the misfortune to be an Austrian, was taken to Munkacs, the political concentration-camp of those days, where the author of "The Austrian Plutarch" had ample time in cellar-vaults to reflect on the gratitude of the Imperial House. Metternich, by the way, later claimed to have saved the life of the man who was accused of high trea-

Lenoir Rhyne Colle
LIBRARY

son, by having kept him in prison for fully a year without trial. The unhappy Archduke, on the other hand, found that he was so closely watched in Vienna, that he was quite unable to leave the city and be in the Tyrol at Easter-time as had been planned. In the end there was nothing for him to do, but set out on the unpleasant errand of seeing Metternich. The latter received him very pleasantly, but the Archduke had to promise penitently that he would never do it again. During the remaining thirty years of his life Johann devoted himself almost exclusively to hunting chamois and to his Anna Plochl, the post-master's daughter. Once more only, in the revolutionary year of 1848, Johann, who in the meantime had become an old man, stepped again into the political foreground—though even on that occasion he was unable quite to disguise his Arcadian character.

Late in the summer of 1812, before Napoleon again joined his army, he once more gathered the European sovereigns around him in Dresden. As if they were servants to be left behind, he wanted to give them his last instructions before departing and graciously to receive the expressions of their submissiveness. The ceremonial observed on that occasion is so eloquent that the historian is able to restrict himself to playing the part of a reporter. The crowned heads assembled in a designated room in the Palace of Dresden, where Napoleon had established his headquarters. Whenever one of them entered the room the French Lord Steward of the Household announced his appearance: "The King of Württemberg!" he called into the room. "The King of Bavaria! The King of Saxony! The King of Prussia! The Emperor of Austria!" There ensued a pause of some little time. Only then, after he had solemnly tapped the floor three times with his white staff, he announced: "L'Empereur!" Quite simply: the Emperor! Napoleon entered the room at the double-quick and mingled, always hurried but affable, with the assembled potentates, whom he had kept waiting a little both because he was so very busy, but also to keep them from getting out of hand.

That was in August, 1812. On New Year's eve, however, of the very same year—the Russian campaign had been lost in the meantime—the Austrian Special Envoy in Paris, Count Bubna, acting upon instructions from Metternich, ventured to suggest to Napoleon with all due modesty that the time perhaps had come to conclude a reasonable peace with Russia, and that Austria would consider such a peace highly desirable. It is significant that Napoleon did not have the impertinent envoy dismissed, but said reservedly, bitingly, and contemptuously: "Well, let Austria bother about making peace. I have no objection!"

That was something, anyway, and a clever diplomat was able to make even more of it. Metternich immediately deduced from it a twofold further justification: first, the right to get in touch with Napoleon's foes, Russia and England, a step which Austria, nominally still France's ally, was not supposed to have taken; and second, the privilege of reminding the great Napoleon through his French Ambassador in Vienna, of the desirability, expediency, and even necessity of an early conclusion of peace, although at the same time chanting Napoleon's praises as a military genius without compare, and extolling his "victory" over Russia. In the meantime, Austria quietly but rapidly continued her program of military rearmament—as an ally of France, of course, and so as to assure Napoleon's victory in the event of renewed hostilities.

For the present, nothing happened; nothing in January, nothing in February; nothing in March except the suppression of the tempest-in-the-teapot revolution of the "Alpine League," the Austrian authorities' disproportionate ruthlessness having the twofold purpose of creating a good impression in Paris, and of camouflaging the rearmament activities. Then, in April, again nothing. In Eastern Germany things began to stir and throb everywhere. The snows melted, the roads became passable, and the waters hurled themselves valleywards. Russian hosts were already crossing the frontier. The Prussians under General York openly went over to the enemy. The King of Prussia condemned an action so contrary to treaty obligations, and threatened to have General York court-martialed and shot as a traitor. The King was a man of honor, but at the same time he was also a German patriot. So he proceeded to Breslau in April and there, timidly but openly and in a painful dilemma between his sworn duty and his sacred duty, deserted Napoleon. Prussia declared war upon France and allied herself with Russia. Austria rubbed her hands but remained neutral for the time being—and continued to arm.

It was highly interesting now to watch the slender wrestler Metternich cleverly dancing out of reach of his adversary's threatening hands while, with admirable foot work, looking for an opening. From time to time he stopped his dancing methods and, advancing half a step, planted himself squarely, legs apart, in front of his great adversary, whose gaze he met unflinchingly. But was he not justified in treating Napoleon in that manner? Had not the latter given him free play in his endeavors for a peace? The Corsican had certainly done so; but being a dictator, he had not meant the peace to cost him anything. Not an inch would he yield, he declared brusquely; not a single soul would he give up! And if they demanded that he renounce his claims upon Italy, and leave the Rhenish Confederation, they would, he thundered, have to come to Paris at the head of half a million soldiers and from the heights of Montmartre speak to him through the mouths of cannons. Prophetic words that made one shudder! Does it not seem as if Napoleon had intended to issue a warning to himself? But being a dictator, he refused to heed the warning.

Spring of 1813 had gradually changed into a sultry summer. The crops of hatred were ripening and would be gathered when autumn came. From month to month Metternich's attitude was one of increased firmness, in spite of Napoleon's temporary and partial military successes in Silesia. New peace conditions were suddenly added to those already formulated by Austria as the mediatory Power. Danzig would have to be ceded to Prussia—even then that was an issue!—and the Duchy of Warsaw, a Napoleonic blunder in which the beautiful Walewska had had a share, would have to disappear. Translated from diplomatic language into generally understandable words, that meant that Russia wanted Poland, and Germany the Baltic coast. Austria already spoke in their name, and in clanking armor. The peacetime-footing of her army had been raised to 180,000 men, a fact which clearly showed Metternich's next goal: armed intervention, for which his preparations had gone forward step by step. He was now where he wanted to be, and the shadowy contours of a coalition between Russia, Prussia, England, and Austria began to loom up on the political horizon. Emperor Franz had his troops drawn up in Bohemia and, at Metternich's suggestion, personally proceeded to Gitschin, which was located almost precisely half-way between the political and military fronts. At the same time, Metternich had a conference with Alexander of Russia at Reichenberg, singing the praises of his new ally, because he needed him. Constant secret connections also were maintained with Prussia, who had already started military operations of her own, and whose gallant warrior, Blücher, was operating in Silesia. In the face of all this, Metternich gave his word to the French Ambassador at the Court of Vienna that the Emperor of Austria would not, from Gitschin, get in touch either with the King of Prussia or with the Czar. Why should he? That was attended to most thoroughly by his minister at Reichenberg, so thoroughly that Napoleon, departing from his previous aloofness, suddenly made up his mind to request his presence in Dresden.

This clearly shows the devious road Metternich traveled between December, 1812, and June, 1813. It led from a military alliance with France to an armed intervention against France and represents a turn of 180 degrees. Napoleon realized his plight and knew now what Metternich had meant when, shortly after the Russian *débâcle,* he had let him know ambiguously that Emperor Franz could at any time raise fifty millions of Germany. That equivocal phrase had still further beguiled the deluded Emperor. He had assumed, as a matter of course, that these fifty millions would march with him, and now it suddenly appeared that Metternich might have had an entirely different interpretation in mind. Napoleon wanted, therefore, to talk to him.

Metternich accepted the invitation to Dresden and, having the Reichenberg agreements with the Czar in his pocket, respectfully put himself at the dictator's disposal. The memorable meeting took place at the Marcolini Palace, which today is a hospital, and most likely a military one. The wrestlers entered the ring. It was the greatest moment in Metternich's life and, at the same time, the deciding one in Napoleon's fate.

The portentous conversation was of Napoleonic dimensions. It continued eight hours without pause, from the forenoon into the evening. Metternich bravely faced the fire of Napoleon's arguments, permitting the genius of the battle field to spend all of his prodigious temperament without budging an inch from the position he had outlined. He demanded outright that the Emperor yield this time; that he evacuate Germany; that, well and good, he remain Europe's greatest man, but confine himself to his enlarged France; that he make peace and cease worrying his neighbors.

Napoleon had no mind to make any of these concessions. "You are no soldier, Count Metternich!" he exclaimed indignantly. "That accounts for your suggesting and expecting of me something that is contrary to my honor!" The phrase is sufficiently well known. When a dictator speaks of honor, he means power. Napoleon would have liked peace. Certainly! Why not? But without sacrificing anything, without relinquishing anything of what really was not his, without ceding anything, and without giving anything up. Why, after all, should he? Had he not always remained master of the field? Did he not owe all of his unheard-of successes to his iron inflexibility? Why should he not be successful now as he had always been? Why not, indeed? The pendulum was already swinging in the other direction, one that was to be fatal to Napoleon.

It was appreciated, however, by the fashionably clad Minister of His Majesty, the Emperor of Austria, who was not inclined to mince his words. "When the army of 20-year-olds, which you have once more been able to raise, will be used up, Sire, with what will you then wage war?" This was unheard-of language, and Napoleon answered accordingly: "And if victory should cost me a million soldiers . . . !" He said the words, he shouted them! To which Metternich, deadly calm, replied: "Let us fling open the windows, Sire, so that all Europe may hear these words!"

⌈Europe! It was Metternich's watchword, just as, in the last analysis, it was Napoleon's goal; with the only difference that Napoleon thought of a Europe under French hegemony, whereas Metternich considered a co-ordination of European Great Powers and of unilingual domains possible and desirable.⌉

"There is an abyss yawning between you and Europe," he said to Napoleon, "and it is up to you, and to you only, to bridge it." What he meant, of course, was: "I have no intention of yielding, either!"

It was then that the Man of Destiny lost patience. Determined to win the game at whatever cost, he played his last trump, the systematized fit of rage in which he had always indulged when everything was at stake and no other means seemed to avail. On such occasions he mobilized the force of his bad manners, because, as he knew from experience, that force never failed of its crushing effect upon well-bred people. In that way, in the beginning of his career, he had bullied his adversaries into accepting the peace terms of Campoformio, when he hurled the fine coffee-service to the floor at the decisive moment of the negotiations. The Austrian negotiator, Thugut, stood speechless, stared at the broken porcelain, and signed with a trembling hand. Now the ill-mannered great man tried the same maneuver once more, as if Metternich had been no more than a Thugut. He tore through the room, and in tearing past Metternich, hurled his Imperial hat at the Chancellor's feet. Then he rushed on until the wall stopped him, turned about, and rushed back again. As he passed his guest once more, the latter stood leaning nonchalantly against the console between the windows, still a cavalier to his finger-tips. The two-cornered hat Napoleon had flung to the floor still lay at his feet. Finally, there was nothing for the Corsican to do but to march back once more, pick up the hat himself, and throw it on a settee. It would have made too bad an impression had a servant seen it lying on the floor and deduced therefrom his master's defeat in the conversation.

It was a defeat, of that there could be no question; at first but a moral one, but for that very reason a decisive one. To grasp its importance one need only compare the scene which took place at that time at the Marcolini Palace in Dresden— a truly Shakespearean scene—with another scene enacted 125 years later, the consequences of which are still very much felt by a new generation of political spectators.

February, 1938, Berchtesgaden! Again, in a conversation of fateful and far-reaching importance, a dictator and an Austrian Minister, Hitler and Schuschnigg, are facing each other. While the dictator, also mobilizing his bad manners in the style of Napoleon, shouts down his visitor, the latter, endeavoring to keep at least some of his countenance, attempts to light a cigarette. The Führer interrupts him angrily, and forbids his visitor to smoke, justifying his action with the remark that smoke is not good for his health. And what does Schuschnigg do? He puts down his cigarette with polite surprise and continues to listen, with a half-averted bespectacled look and a well-bred immovable face, to all the ruffian still has to say to him. What would others have done in similar circumstances? Bismarck would have forged a weapon out of the churlish attitude of the other man, and likely stamped noisily out of the room; had Metternich been in Schuschnigg's place he would have kept his countenance, at least. He would have taken a few puffs from his cigarette, putting it out only at his leisure. Instead of turning aside the rude affront, the last Austrian Federal Chancellor puts up with it without uttering a word. Four weeks later the country in his charge has become a prey of the usurper.

Schuschnigg was a highly cultivated intellectual, but not a man of action. Metternich, too, was a man of intellect, but at the same time also a man of action, even at the time when he *failed* to do something by omitting to retrieve the hat Napoleon hurled to the floor. Had he picked it up, he would have been lost; for he could have handed it back to Napoleon only in a stooping attitude, like a lackey. As it was, Napoleon was lost, a fact of which Metternich informed him explicitly; almost his last words before leaving the Caesar's presence were: *"Sire, vous êtes perdu!"* At the conclusion of the interview Napoleon again had assumed the immobility of a bronze statue. He dismissed his visitor with that icy politeness which, in diplomatic intercourse as well as in love, marks the very end of an association.

Metternich walked through the silent ante-chamber. Silently the marshals, waiting in the evening twilight, gazed after him. One only, Berthier, saw him politely to his carriage. Before entering it, Metternich took leave of Berthier with the words: "His Majesty has told me all I need to know. His cause is lost."

The Austrian Chancellor dared to say it, and it came true. For now at last he had what he had aimed for all these months: the strangle hold! On August 11th, 1813, at the conclusion of the last armistice, Austria declared war upon France. She had three powerful allies: England, Russia, and Prussia, all of whom were already marching. With a sigh of relief Metternich was able to write to his father: "Europe may be saved!"

The words are significant for Metternich, the European, and for the Austrian conception of what was even then a chaotic condition of the world. He did not write: "We will humble France!" or "We must have Alsace-Lorraine!" or "Our 'Lebensraum' demands we have Paris!" He simply wrote on the eve of the Battle of Leipsic: "Europe may be saved!" He was never a greater man than when he penned this line and proved a vision encompassing infinitely more than events immediately surrounding him.

Minister of the Coalition

THROUGHOUT his life Metternich never suffered from any lack of self-assurance. It was not always pleasing to behold, and at times even made him look ridiculous. In his later years, for instance, he once said to the French statesman, Guizot, in a mood of complacency: "I have never been wrong!" That would be bad if it were true; what a dull man he must be who has never been wrong! Fortunately, however, it is not true. Metternich was repeatedly wrong, a fact proved very plainly by the history of his most dramatic years, between 1812 and 1815. He reckoned upon Napoleon's certain victory over Russia. He was wrong. He reckoned upon the possibility of an early conclusion of peace. Wrong again! He even reckoned upon the feasibility of maintaining the Napoleonic dynasty on the throne of France. Wrong once more.

It is surprising with what tenacity Metternich clung to this last mistake of his. Metternich, the man of order, and Napoleon, the "Son of the Revolution." And yet, Metternich continued to give him his support, and did so for a long time against the Bourbons, the hereditary ruling family. But that was just the point. They had been hereditary until the Revolution swept them away. Now, however, Napoleon had come to be the legitimate power, now *he* symbolized the existing order. Metternich had always been in favor of legitimacy and of order and, being the representative of Europe's most conservative Power, he had a decided aversion to any change of dynasty. This fact worked for a considerable time to the benefit of the Corsican usurper who was married to a woman of the Habsburg family. While, in the winter and spring of the year 1814, the allied armies fought their way ever closer to Paris, Metternich clung resolutely to his view that Emperor Franz' son-in-law and his wife should continue to reign in France. When things had finally reached the point where Napoleon had to be dethroned, it was Talleyrand, and not he, who was responsible for the accession of the Bourbons.

Were one to try to find apologies for Metternich's errors of judgment, two things might be said in his behalf: first, that his were only aberrations of the mode of attainment, and not of the goal which stood ever immovable and clear before his mental vision. That goal, of course, was the establishment of a permanent European order based upon principles of equilibrium—with the aid of Austria, needless to say. "Present and future are closely connected with Austria," was Gentz' way of expressing Metternich's thought. The second point in Metternich's favor is that if he did err, he became aware of his mistake in time. "As long as we cannot stop a development, we must at least try to guide it into proper channels," he said when before the gates of Paris he finally agreed to the return of Louis XVIII, who had grown lazy and fat in exile. There were plenty of instances in which Metternich, a conservative politician in a revolutionary era, fought against the tide of events. But if there was no other way out of it, he was willing to float with the tide and let it carry him to the conservative shore.

The diplomatic result of the great interview at the Marcolini Palace in Dresden was that Napoleon formally relieved Austria of her obligations as an ally. Emperor Franz
breathed an audible sigh of relief. He wanted to have a
clear conscience before attacking his son-in-law from behind. The clever Metternich saw to it that his Imperial conscience was relieved. No longer was Napoleon able to ac-
cuse him of treachery, as he had done at the beginning of
the Dresden interview. "How much did the English pay
you, Count Metternich, for betraying me?" he is said to
have asked the Austrian State-Chancellor. That is surely a
myth. But Napoleon probably entertained the thought in
some form; and the thought, the bitter suspicion, may have
had its share in influencing the tenor of the conversation
from its very first word. It is the tenor which counts in such
cases.

No sooner had Metternich escaped from the charge of
treachery than he had to put up with a similar accusation
from another quarter. The Allies, who became linked to
one another ever more strongly, charged him with having
wilfully extended until August 10th the armistice which it
had been agreed should terminate on July 20th. The North-
German camp especially raised a huge outcry, because according to the Reichenberg agreements Austria's declaration of war confidently had been expected on July 20th.
When it did not occur then, there were shouts of disappointed rage. "Perfidious Austria," hissed the Teutomani-
acs, whom Metternich could stomach as little as could his
great contemporary, Goethe.

Metternich let them shout and incriminate, as was, and
still is, their wont. He had more important things to attend
to, to make as sure of victory as possible. He had to make it

HOW TO DEFEAT NAPOLEON?

possible for the Austrian Supreme Commander, Prince Schwarzenberg, to draw up his troops circumspectly and deliberately in the Austrian tempo, which was quite different from the Napoleonic one. He also had to win new allies for the coalition so as to assure increasingly its military superiority.

At that time—it was the summer of 1813—the Rhenish Confederation still existed. Bavaria, among other States, was a member of that despotic creation of Napoleon. It was the largest of the Federal States to be taken into consideration. There was the fact, too, that Napoleon had known how to put its ruler under a personal obligation by raising—or lowering?—him to the status of a King: King of Bavaria by the grace of Napoleon.

Metternich proceeded to buy this venal King. It was not an easy bargain; Bavaria was dear. But Metternich was in a spending mood and prepared to pay any price. In compensation for the adjustment of the Salzburg frontier, he promised considerable indemnities on the left bank of the Rhine, plus Bavaria's full sovereignty despite any sort of reorganization within the German realm. Bavaria permitted herself to be persuaded. She left the Rhenish Confederation, bringing about its final collapse. The small border-States, Baden and Württemberg, could be all the more easily overcome under these circumstances. Their treatment was identical with that meted out to the Baltic States in 1939–40, condemned to impotence and compelled to keep silent. The methods of a diplomacy given to violence are always the same.

Bavaria, which in 1809 still fought on the side of Napoleon and made of the Tyrol the Finland of those days, had thus been won, and the way had been paved for the subsequent incorporation of the Tyrol in the Austrian Empire. Metternich had scored a great success which was supplemented by the concurrent advantage that the new friendship with Bavaria created a counter-weight against Prussia. Fifty years later, Bavaria's guaranteed German sovereignty turned out to be the greatest obstacle in the way of Bismarck when finally he enforced the unification of the German Empire—an event which Metternich wished to prevent at all cost and, as long as he lived, actually did prevent. All the same, it was not so much the unification he feared, as the unifying element. He always considered the Prussian military spirit a menace to all of Europe, and subsequent events proved the justification of his views.

After the Bavarian move on the European chess-board, still another pawn had to be maneuvred. This was Switzerland, whose co-operation in the planned military campaign was essential. Alexander of Russia desired as a matter of principle to respect that country's neutrality, although it had so far proved nothing but an "automaton in the hand of France." The Czar entertained liberal principles—abroad—a sense of vanity prompting him towards making ill-considered promises. Metternich, whose wishes lay in an entirely different direction, found himself confronted by the fascinating diplomatic task of duping both the autocratic Czar and democratic Switzerland. In this he succeeded.

At that time, Switzerland still lived in a transitional state of democracy. There was no universal belief as yet in the spirit of democracy in a country which formed the geographical center of a feudally organized Europe; nor was the country itself fully convinced of its own democracy. As a matter of fact, that is just as true today. In Switzerland, the oldest European democracy—and, strictly speaking, the only one—remnants of the oldest European aristocracy may still be found. When a Basle lady, conducting an Austrian visitor through her house in the Minster quarter, was asked how old the original part of the stoutly built edifice might be, her modest reply in drawling Swiss-German was: "Oh, a little older than the Habsburg dynasty." That would be about 700 years.

The Swiss democracy, resting upon the granite foundation of an age-old aristocracy, is influenced to no small degree by its geological formation, as is every form of State. Antique Greece, by virtue of its broken coast line, was condemned to remain a loose federation of small states; while Switzerland, through the inaccessible character of its Alpine landscape, is secure from any undue attempts at equalization. It is true that, as a beautiful line of poetry says, "freedom dwells on the mountain tops," but only for those who manage to get there; and those fortunate ones were in former centuries the aristocrats of Lucerne, Fribourg, and Berne.

They were the ones with whom the shrewd aristocrat Metternich allied himself against the northern plains, through which he was determined to march. He spun intrigues, played off one against the other; he was one man in Zurich and quite another again in Berne. Finally he attained his object: the passage of the Austrian troops was permitted, because—so it was stated—the majority of the Swiss population wished it. As is customary in such cases, no exact count was taken. But one day Schwarzenberg advanced upon France through the "Burgundian Gate" and threatened the flank of Napoleon's armies, tactics which are the alpha and omega of all strategic art. All in all, Metternich's action of those days did not differ greatly from Germany's in August, 1914, although there was no bloodshed. That, of course, makes quite a difference. Metternich, never ruthless, tried to be considerate whenever he snapped his fingers at international law.

On January 1st, 1814, the allied armies crossed the Rhine; Metternich, who took part in the campaign at headquarters, grew more and more to be "Minister of the Coalition," as he himself admitted, with a heavy sigh. A great satisfaction had recently come to him. After the Battle of Leipsic—the "Judgment of God," as the Allies called it—the Common Council of Vienna had made Metternich an Honorary Citizen of the City of Vienna. A festival cantata on the Ballhausplatz, under the windows of his Kaunitz Palace, was the high-light of the celebration glorifying his incomparable statesmanship. There were the usual "All Hail to Thee's" and all sorts of allegorical and symbolical scenes. When it is considered that, not so long before, the patriotic Viennese had accused him of having sold the Emperor's daughter to France, of having sold out Germany, and of having left Napoleon in the lurch, because he had sold himself to England; when it is further considered that his policies had been condemned almost universally by all circles of Vienna society, it is quite possible that the honors now bestowed, as vehement as they were sudden, was a rather bitter satisfaction to him. They were not able greatly to affect his attitude towards Vienna. He always disliked the city and never cared much for its opinion, which habitually lagged a step or two behind the facts.

Neither was there any lack of satisfaction for the Minister of the Coalition in the Allies' headquarters. One of the more

discreet ones lay in the fact that the beautiful Duchess of
Sagan conscientiously went through the advance upon Paris
in the entourage of the sovereigns. It is a moot question
whether she was a *cantinière* of love, or was actuated by
political curiosity. Altogether, however, the days and nights
which preceded Napoleon's dethronement were not easy
ones for Metternich. The Allies did not get along any too
well with one another, a fact which the military genius of
Napoleon knew how to turn to the utmost strategic advantage. Blücher, whose unorthodox way of expressing himself and coarse dryness considerably irritated the refined
Metternich, was forever for thrusting forward impetuously,
while Schwarzenberg was for holding back cautiously. Alexander had his mind set upon directing a battle, and re-
installing the Bourbons so that France would once and for
all be made dependent upon him. That was the very thing
Metternich was anxious to avoid, as he had all his life feared
nothing so much as a far-reaching entente between France
and Russia, whereby Austria's double-headed eagle would
be squeezed.

That was one of the reasons why he was for Napoleon and
against the Bourbons. If only Napoleon himself had not
made it so hard for him to be pro-Napoleonic. But there
was really no getting along with him any more. He was
like any dictator, after he has reached a certain point in his
development. He acted as though he had been stricken with
blindness and bereft of all reason. In Teplitz, before the
breach with Austria had occurred, all that was asked of him
was that he withdraw from the Rhenish Confederation and
from Italy. Napoleon said he would not be dishonored. In
Frankfort, that is, after the Battle of Leipsic, Metternich had
been responsible for the magnanimous offer of France's

natural boundaries, the Rhine and Pyrenees; but again Napoleon spoke of "dishonor" and insisted upon the Teplitz conditions. Then, forced back upon an interior line of defense, fighting for his life with his back against Paris, the Congress of Chatillon still would have made it possible for him to retain France within its "historical boundaries" of 1792. He declined because, unfortunately for him, in the meantime he had succeeded in gaining a few unimportant though spectacular victories at Brienne and La Rothières. He might not have been disinclined then to accept the Frankfort terms—Rhine and Pyrenees—but now, at Chatillon, Metternich was no longer willing to concede them. And so the fighting and the shedding of blood went on, Napoleon claiming victory after victory. If one reads the dispatches sent by Napoleon to Paris during those last weeks of the Empire, one would gain the impression that he proceeded from triumph to triumph. In a sense, this was true. He was not the only one in the history of wars who, in an impoverished country, virtually perished by his own victories.

In the meantime Marie Louise, whom Fate had so far overlooked, played in Paris the thankless part of a regent who as a matter of fact had no authority whatsoever. She received ten captured flags; they may have reminded her of the fact that no more than five years before, at St. Stephen's Cathedral in Vienna, she had witnessed with glowing cheeks a consecration of the colors, against the arch-enemy who was now her husband. She also wrote confidential letters to the cities threatened by the invasion, suggesting the forming of a national guard. In between she may have written touching letters to the ever closer approaching *"très cher Papa,"* whose embarrassed and apologetic replies were carefully suggested by Metternich. It was indeed a thankless task for so very young a woman, especially since her husband sulkily forbade her to make any effort in that direction. *"Je ne veux pas être protégé par ma femme."* At any rate, she tried to comfort him two weeks before the final collapse with the cheering sentence: *"Tout Paris est rempli de bonnes nouvelles,"* which surely was an exaggeration. At the same time she implored her *très cher Papa* to conclude a reasonable peace at last *"et de ne pas sacrifier l'Europe entière à l'avidité de l'Angleterre."* This phrase has a familiar ring. Like a person displaying symptoms of virility in the advanced stages of consumption, in the name of Napoleon, she indignantly rejected a renunciation of Antwerp: *"Rien ne l'amènera de céder l'Anvers!"* A few weeks before, Napoleon, in a message from the battle field, had urged her not to join a pilgrimage to St. Genevieve; a plea for mercy just then, he wrote, would make a disastrous impression in Paris. We see a new Napoleon, no longer the ever victorious hero.

Late in March, all of France knew that the end was in sight. Napoleon made a last attempt, as daring as it was desperate, to attack his enemy from the rear by making a flanking retreat towards the Marne before the steadily advancing armies of the Allies. But already he had given instructions as to where his wife and child were to go in the event that Paris had to be evacuated. He wanted to save his son "from the fate of Astyanax who fell into the hands of the Greek." He sought death in battle—without finding it.

Both strategically and politically, the net was drawn ever tighter round Napoleon. Baron de Vitrolles, acting in secret agreement with Talleyrand, managed to insinuate himself into the enemies' lines and get in touch with Count Artois.

He was received at headquarters by Castlereagh, Nesselrode, Hardenberg, and Metternich, who listened to what Talleyrand had to say to them. "Talleyrand," the valiant messenger said, "has in his heart always been for the Bourbons." "In his heart?" was the mocking reply. Perhaps it was Metternich who put the ironical question. Vitrolles corrected himself, while everyone laughed: "In his head, I meant to say."

Metternich finally conceded the point of the Bourbon succession. On April 11th, 1814, Metternich arrived in Paris, preceded by a few days by the Russian Czar who had put up at Talleyrand's house. There, we are told by a French diplomat who claims to have surprised him at it, Metternich's first concern was for his *coiffure* which had been neglected somewhat in the field and which he wished to restore to its usual perfection. Napoleon—pushed off the field, beaten, betrayed, and sold—staggered, fell, and was overthrown. Metternich, enthroned before a looking-glass in a hair-dresser's wrapper, had his locks crimped. History, indeed, provides many a contrast. As a matter of fact, it consists of nothing else.

It must have been in those April days of 1814 that old Blücher, who had an illiterate way of expressing himself but also the keen judgment of the Berlin corner-prophet, shook his head and growled under his bristling white moustache the words Metternich smilingly handed down to posterity. They were both standing in the castle-courtyard of St. Cloud, the incautious victor and the cautious one, gazing at each other still partly stunned by the magnitude of their victory. The old Marshal-"up-and-at-'em" said: "Must 'a' been a damn' fool, havin' all this, and then cut and run for Moscow!"

After all that had gone before, it was a lenient peace which Metternich dictated. If one compares it with the Treaty of Versailles, of 1918, one is forced to admire not only the moderation but also the far-sightedness of the Austrian statesman. He laid no claim to Alsace-Lorraine, although he could have pocketed it without trouble. He refused to take advantage of France's momentary helplessness, which would have made it easy for him to plunge it into permanent bondage. He was no Shylock insisting upon his pound of flesh. He left it to the subdued country to form a new government, without any intervening period of lawlessness. He was not a Clemenceau—not a genius of hatred; not only because he never was a genius, nor a man of great passions, but also because he was wise enough to know that hatred could never create a permanent solution and because he desired above all the pacification of Europe.

In one respect only, did he proceed without mercy, and almost inhumanly. He insisted upon destroying Napoleon's marriage. He may have felt it his duty, because it had been he who brought it about. He had married Samson to Delilah. Now he was determined to tear asunder what he had been instrumental in creating. Sensitive historians—there were some in the last century—spoke of "devilry." "Politics," however, would have been better. It was a political necessity to separate the daughter of the Habsburgs from the dethroned dictator, thus placing him outside the pale of the law. To permit him to retain his family—his wife and a growing successor—to be united and keep an Emperor's Court in exile, virtually would have meant the establishment of a French counter-government and a storm-center of future developments. Merely to banish to Elba the man who, after all, remained the idol of his soldiers, though not of all of his marshals, was a half-measure anyway, for which a heavy penalty was to be paid. But the leading statesmen of that era, Metternich included, were faced by an entirely novel situation, and they were not able to cope with it at the first try. What to do with overthrown dictators was a chapter that still had to be learned. . . .

Metternich should not be criticized for his attitude and procedure of those days, no matter how heartless they may seem. It was not for him as a statesman to prove on that occasion that he had a heart. It would have been Marie Louise's moral obligation to stand by her husband and by the father of her child in the most difficult hour of his life. She might easily have done so, and there was no one who could have opposed her. But she did not do it. She declaimed a little—*"mon devoir est d'être auprès de l'Empereur dans un moment, ou il doit être si malheureux"*—but she remained in Blois, whither she had gone from Paris in the early days of April, in great haste, but nevertheless accompanied by 48 hats, 85 pairs of shoes, and 30 pairs of boots. Why did she stay in Blois, idling away her time, while the dethroned Caesar, after signing the deed of abdication, waited for her at nearby Fontainebleau? It was because of her impaired health—in a letter to her *très cher Papa* she even claimed that she was coughing blood—and because those about her wished it. Those about her were the Duchess of Montebello, who was in league with the Allies, and the two Kings, Jérôme and Joseph Bonaparte, who clung to her skirts in the hope of obtaining better terms of abdication for themselves. Napoleon, who all his life had been convinced of the baseness of human nature, got a real taste of it now. Marmont's treachery had put an end to military proceedings, Talleyrand went over to the political camp of the

Bourbons, and the Guard refused to march upon Paris. Now, even his wife forsook him; not all at once, but step by step, wavering for some time, as a vacillating woman who finally deserts her husband will do. Not long before, in March, she had written him a beautiful letter when he had been in the field, submitting most meekly to all his wishes; she reported about the disturbed sleep of the King of Rome who had wept in his sleep because he had dreamt of his father; and she closed, after having alluded to the all-important matter of the weather, with words that were more charming than they were regal: *"Le temps est assez doux, pour que je puisse monter à cheval. Cela m'a fait grand bien, mais ce qui me ferais plus de bien que tout cela, ce serait de te revoir et de ne plus être tourmentée. Ta fidèle amie, Louise."* But now, in April, when the man whom she pretended to love so dearly was longingly waiting for her at Fontainebleau, she permitted Shuvalov, the Czar's adjutant, to persuade her to repair to Orléans, which is a little farther away from Fontainebleau. From Orléans to Rambouillet, where Papa was, is but a step. Was it not at Blois where François Grand cut into a window-pane with a diamond: *"Souvent femme varie, bien fol qui s'y fie"?*

Again it was Metternich who was the determining factor in this last and most un-Imperial decision of the Empress. He arrived in Paris on April 11th, and hardly did he have his hair attended to when he dispatched a prepared letter to Marie Louise. In it he offered her Parma, Piacenza, and Guastalla for her maintenance, advising her at the same time in the name of her *cher Papa* to return to Austria as soon as possible and without proceeding to Fontainebleau, although the latter name was not mentioned.

Marie Louise had the choice between Piacenza and Fontainebleau, and her decision was no surprise. Fontainebleau meant Elba, the sharing of the banished man's fate on the little Italian island. This she considered below her Imperial dignity. No sooner had she heard of it than she wrote to Emperor Franz, on April 8th, demanding treatment to which her birth entitled her. She also wrote in the name of her son *"qui est innocent de toutes les fautes de son père."* There was treachery already in these words; they foreshadowed Delilah's conquest of Samson, and it is not at all unlikely that Metternich's letter of April 11th was partly inspired by them, and thus little more than a reply. If such was the case, it would go a long way towards exonerating Metternich, and the diabolical cleverness with which he managed to prevent any further meeting of Marie Louise with Napoleon by seemingly leaving it to her choice, would not be so blameworthy, after all. Her own character failed Marie Louise at a moment when, humanly speaking, it should never have failed her, no matter what "knights without fear and reproach," of whom there has never been any dearth until the most recent past, may have to say in her favor.

While she cannot be exculpated, Marie Louise may be granted a mitigating circumstance in the fact that she was married without having been wooed. She had then been but the object of someone else's decision, and it was the same now. She was taken away from her husband as she had been taken to him: without being asked. This was not an unusual procedure, especially not in Austria. But it reveals Marie Louise's character: fatalistically declining to make her own decisions, she meekly permitted Fate to rule her destiny. It also reveals a submission to Habsburg traditions which provide that only one will is authoritative, that of the Head of the House; in this instance, Emperor Franz. She left her husband's written appeal unanswered and, instead of writing or setting out on her way, rested her elbows on her knees and allowed her tears to flow freely; the Emperor's daughter in her had definitely conquered the woman.

When everything was arranged and Napoleon, at once touching and admirable in his magnificent and theoretically unsubdued creative power, already had begun to establish his miniature Empire on the island of Elba, Prince Metternich returned to Vienna to attend there to the necessary preparations for the Congress of Vienna. He had become a Prince over night. It was his Emperor's gift and reward after the Battle of Leipsic. Just as Lord Byron was able to say of himself that he woke up one morning and found himself famous, Count Metternich woke up to find himself a Prince. His well-trained valet, a servant ready for any emergency, a gentleman's gentleman of perfect manners, and with a sense of humor, addressed him in the following inimitable manner: "Will His Highness wear the same suit today which His Excellency wore yesterday?" A more tactful way of putting the question could hardly be imagined.

The Victory Feast

METTERNICH'S unparalleled accomplishments in the two years between Napoleon's Russian campaign and the Congress of Vienna may have surprised even himself. For not only had he, in the course of a few months, changed his political attitude to such an extent that, in July, 1814, he did the very thing that had caused him to have Hormayr arrested in the autumn of 1813; but as a result of the gigantic wrestling match he had engaged in, he had also achieved considerably more than he had set out to accomplish. One morning, his hair neatly crimped, he stood before his dressing-glass and found himself the conqueror of Napoleon. He had done even more than conquer him; he had actually deposed him—a fact that had not entered into his calculations. Or had it, after all, although only in what later scientists called his subconscious mind? It is a fact, at any rate, that his conscious mind had uttered assurances to the contrary so loudly and frequently that he himself had come to believe them. Like Pilate, he washed his hands in complete innocence and, in the bargain, was able to enjoy with a perfectly clear conscience the unlooked-for fruits of his double-dealings. A delightful soufflé, indeed!

The name of the political soufflé that followed upon the carnage was the Congress of Vienna. The Allies, as they were closing in on Paris, had decided on it at the last moment; they assumed correctly that they would not be able to come to an easy understanding concerning the division of the spoils and therefore considered it advisable to put off for a few months the expected non-agreement. September witnessed a happy reunion in Vienna.

Things happened as they do at every Congress: in the beginning no one was quite ready, and in the end nothing was completed. Meanwhile, the days were spent in bickering and the nights in dancing.

The opening of the historical bout was set for October 1st. A week before, Talleyrand, France's representative, arrived in Vienna. From that moment, Metternich, who in his clever way was already presiding over the Congress without actually being its president, had an opponent who was a match for him. Talleyrand was eighteen years older than Metternich, who had learned a great deal from him in his Paris days. Being a grateful pupil, he had ample opportunity now for proving to the Frenchman his acquired mastery.

While these two men had much in common, they were yet totally different. Talleyrand was wholly a Frenchman— the "Frenchest Frenchman," Prince de Ligne had called him—while Metternich was considerably more of a German than he knew or was ready to admit. What was typically German in him was his need of a metaphysically founded ideology. Every nation is apt to do things that are stupid, bad, or incomprehensible; but the Germans are the only ones who, in such an event, feel compelled conscientiously and ideologically to reinforce the foundations of what has happened or what they have perpetrated.

If that be philosophy, it was the German element in Metternich's character that made him the philosopher he always

was, both as a statesman and even as a lover, while Talleyrand had nothing at all of the philosopher in his make-up.
Talleyrand was a keen thinker, a much keener one than
even Metternich, because he excluded everything that was
unclear; but he would never have said of himself as Metternich did: "I was born a thinker." On the other hand, the
worldly Metternich was fundamentally much more religious
than the former cowled Bishop of Autun. Talleyrand believed in nothing, not even in the devil; there were times
when Metternich was ready to ally himself with the devil,
so as to be able to praise God all the more fervently afterwards. He was never cynical; Talleyrand always was. Talleyrand had no conscience; Metternich sometimes disregarded
his. He was also fond of speaking of his heart, an organ
Talleyrand never mentioned. Being diplomats of the classical school, they were both consummate liars; but if it is
permissible to say so, Metternich was the more honest liar
of the two, while Talleyrand was the more determined.
Metternich was apt, in the end, to believe his own lies, a
fact maliciously emphasized by Grillparzer in his characterization of the man. Talleyrand was much too shrewd to be
taken in by a man like Talleyrand. When in society, Talleyrand was the wittier conversationalist, while Metternich was
the more amiable of the two.

When they were eighty, both men were still pampered by
women. They had one common characteristic: their active
fondness of the other sex which manifested itself in both
cases over a stretch of fully fifty years.

Being so strongly attached to women, they never had a
great deal of time for men, unless their official activities
brought them in contact with them. There had been ample

opportunity in Paris for Talleyrand and Metternich to meet, but no close association had resulted. That their connection was more than a superficial one, however, is proved by the fact that Metternich was instrumental in getting for Talleyrand from the Vienna Court the sum of 100,000 francs, a little gift discreetly handed over to the French statesman in consideration of his support of the Austrian policy. Talleyrand was not small-minded in money matters, and Metternich was certainly liberal in this respect. But even on this point he had his principles. Serious historians assert that at the termination of the Wars of Independence, when Napoleon was defeated, the Senate of the City of Frankfort made Metternich a grant of 10,000 ducats. But when, near the end of his life and to relieve the needs of his exile, Czar Nicholas placed at his disposal the sum of 100,000 rubles, he accepted the present only as a loan, which he later dutifully repaid. It was his principle to accept gifts of money only from friendly Powers, and he could never make up his mind to count Russia among them. He was an ideologist even in that respect!

As diplomats—in their very own domain, that is—the two men were a match for each other, though the younger of the two, Metternich, was but Talleyrand's most gifted pupil. Metternich's biographer, Grunwald, said of them that, while Metternich was more the tactician, Talleyrand was the better strategist. That may be so; but as the tactician and the strategist are active rather rarely at the same headquarters, they saw little of each other except at conferences. There could hardly be any talk of a personal, confidential, let alone friendly intercourse between them. The fact that they were rivals almost all the time made that quite unlikely.

There was the added matter of success; if it occurs within the same sphere of activity, it is apt to estrange men rather than to unite them.

Talleyrand arrived in Vienna on September 23rd and immediately began to be dissatisfied. This he did no doubt to fortify his position, realizing that, after all, he was the representative of a defeated country. The very first meeting furnished him with a pretext. The representatives of the victorious Powers—Austria, Russia, Prussia, and England—had been in Vienna for some time. There were, before the official opening of the Congress, a few informal meetings to which it was not deemed advisable to invite Talleyrand. The Frenchman's resentment of the slight finally forced Metternich to ask him to join one of these conferences. When Talleyrand turned up, the other delegates were already in session. Knowing that the conference would have been held even if he had not been asked to attend, Talleyrand was justified in considering himself called in rather than invited. This view was further substantiated by the fact that, although he had turned up punctually, the others were already busily deliberating round the conference table under the chairmanship of Lord Castlereagh, the representative of England.

Talleyrand seated himself in an empty arm chair next to that of the presiding delegate. While the chair may have been reserved for him, no one had invited him to occupy it. Lifting his lorgnette to his eyes he scanned the circle of those present and immediately opened diplomatic hostilities by inquiring with polite surprise why his delegation—he had brought two associates with him to Vienna—had not also been invited. It was pointed out to him with equal politeness that only the heads of the various delegations

had been invited. But Talleyrand—here we follow Duff-
Cooper's description in his brilliant biography of Talleyrand—continued to be surprised: if that were a fact, how
was it that Spain was represented by Monsieur Labrador
who, as far as was known, was not the head of the Spanish
delegation? Because the head of that delegation had not as
yet arrived in Vienna. And Prussia, persisted Talleyrand,
still fingering his long-handled eye-glass: what was the reason of that country being represented by two delegates,
Humboldt and Hardenberg? Because of the ailment of one
of them, he was told in a subdued voice. The answer might
as well have been shouted, for Humboldt was stone deaf.
"Well," replied Talleyrand with charming suavity, "we all
have our little ailments." Having managed to drive the
others into a corner, there was nothing left but to concede
that from then on the three French delegates would be
invited: Monsieur Dalberg, Monsieur du Pin, and he.

Thus he succeeded in creating for himself a position
which he immediately proceeded to reinforce. A protocol
was read concerning what had happened, and had been accomplished since Chaumont. In the statement the word
"Allies" occurred. Talleyrand interrupted: "If there are
still Allies, this is no place for me." It was pointed out to
him apologetically, that the expression had been chosen
merely for its brevity. "Regrettable," remarked Talleyrand;
"brevity should never be purchased at the price of ac-
curacy." He was right; and so "Allies" had to be stricken
from the protocol. On the other hand, Talleyrand immediately extended his front by taking into his camp the dissatisfied Portuguese Ambassador who had complained in
a letter about not having been invited to the sessions.
Adroitly, Talleyrand not only espoused the man's case but

in a trice had made it the basis of a generalization. With him as the spokesman, France became the advocate not only of Portugal, but of all the small States. Was there not something like a morality of international law? Talleyrand was ready to uphold it, though it was by all means the only morality he had ever upheld. He was also quickly prepared to drape the cloak of Christian charity round the frail shoulders of that decrepit morality. France, so her shrewd representative asserted with his tongue in his cheek, was the only Power at the Congress which had no aspirations of territorial gains. Its natural altruism prompted it to be satisfied with the boundaries conceded to it; which in turn prompted Talleyrand to extend his own boundaries all the more immodestly. It was a masterpiece of diplomacy comparable only to the Napoleonic campaigns. Even Metternich's subtle tenacity was not able to change the fact. True, he had won the war against France, but at the green table he was forced to retreat step by step.

On one occasion, after the Congress had been in session three months, and its participants had rushed feverishly from one entertainment to the other, the existing differences of opinion came near causing a war. Russia wanted to "liberate" Poland, and Prussia wanted to have Saxony, and Austria did not desire either of these two things to occur. That meant war against Austria! On Elba, Napoleon was beginning to rub his hands gleefully; he could already see his day dawning. At the last moment, however, an alliance was effected between England, France, and Austria which succeeded in driving the opposing forces into a corner. It was an occasion when Metternich was victorious not against, but on the side of, Talleyrand. Nevertheless, it was a fact that Talleyrand's victory was the greater. For France already had become the determining Great Power of the Congress.

On another occasion, the Austrian Chancellor was even more embarrassingly cornered by his old rival for the diplomatic leadership of Europe. There would be justification to speak even of a diplomatic defeat of Metternich. But it was a smiling defeat which had to do with former victories on more discreet battle fields. The case concerned Naples; to be exact it concerned Caroline of Naples, for Murat, her war-busied husband, gave Metternich but little concern. As a matter of fact, he rather disliked the man, a fate not infrequently shared by cuckolded husbands.

Seven years before, in Paris, and even as late as four years before, Metternich had been *aux mieux* with Caroline. He still cherished fond memories of the tousled little Cromwell-head; and the fact that in the meantime she had adorned it with a crownlet, the Crown of Naples, rather flattered his not inconsiderable vanity.

It was true, though, that the little head was not easily managed. It was full of ambitions and lusted after power. There was significance in the fact that Caroline was the sister of Napoleon, who once had said of himself: "I can never see a throne without being tempted to sit on it." The little sister greatly desired to remain Queen of Naples. That was not easily accomplished now that Napoleon had been overthrown and the Bourbons had returned to France. Naples, too, formerly had been a Bourbon domain, and they wished to return there also. Talleyrand was in favor of their claim which, from the standpoint of a Frenchman, was entirely logical.

Caroline, however, was not ready to give up without a struggle. A woman of her type never permits a man to share the privacy of her bedroom without feeling that it will have to benefit her some day, somehow. The moment had now arrived. Metternich, himself, had brought it about. Hardly had he arrived on French soil, on January 11th, 1814, when he wrote a letter to Caroline endeavoring to assure himself of her political allegiance by discreetly reminding her of their old liaison. At that time he had proposed an alliance between Naples and Austria. Caroline had agreed to it and, due to her influence, her royal husband had not hesitated to join the camp of the Allies. Naturally, he expected to get his reward now for having betrayed Napoleon: the Congress of Vienna was to impart permanence and steadiness to his shaky crown. Metternich was for it, Talleyrand against. "Who is that—Murat? I don't know such a man!" the latter said when, at one of the Congressional sessions the name of the then King of Naples was mentioned tentatively.

Clio, the Muse of history, must regret not having been asked to that session. Its central point of interest was an *affaire de coeur* which, with the exception of Metternich, must have profoundly delighted all those in attendance. If Talleyrand attacked Murat, what was the Austrian State-Minister to say in reply? What could he say? That Caroline and he had been rather more than friends was no argument to be discussed publicly at a session of the Congress. It was a compelling argument, nevertheless, although it was so only for Metternich personally, and so he was quite unable to bring it forward. There are situations in which even the most eloquent ladies' man must be silent, and this was one of them. Whenever the discussion turned to her person, the lips Caroline had kissed so often were sealed. He had to confine himself to speaking about her husband, the general of cavalry, against whom Talleyrand, probably highly amused at Metternich's discomfiture, led the violent charge.

In the end there was nothing for Metternich to do but yield gracefully in that point, too. It was unanimously decided to drop Murat, and it was probably at the suggestion of Talleyrand that the execution was entrusted to Metternich, who was only to await the opportune moment. That moment would come when Murat was guilty of his first piece of stupidity. It was not long in coming: when, during the reign of The Hundred Days, he placed himself once more at the side of Napoleon, he was definitely done for. Caroline had to thank Metternich for finding sanctuary in the Austrian hereditary lands, where she died in the year 1839.

Much has been said about the Congress of Vienna, and by many able writers. Beginning with De La Garde, the dissolute Homer of this amusing Iliad, the glamorous event has been the subject of innumerable historians, diarists, and fair writers of letters who liked to mirror themselves and their impressions in their little ink-wells. A number of more or less successful comedies, too, have been written on the subject, the present writer being among those who must plead guilty to that indictment. The social aspect of the Congress has been most prettily characterized by the clever Rahel Varnhagen who, in untranslatable Berlin dialect, said: "They amused themselves." Mention must also be made of the hackneyed words of the old Prince de Ligne: "The Congress dances, but it does not march!" The equivocal element which forms part of all social activities is wittily expressed in such ambiguous sayings.

The Congress was pre-eminently a social affair, and in that respect Vienna was its most appropriate scene. "You are Europe, no longer a city!" is the way Gentz apostrophizes the pleasure-loving modern Babylon on the banks of the Danube. Gentz represents Metternich's other side, perhaps even his better side. He was reaction's publicist leader of the dance, while Metternich was the time-beating conductor of a reactionary movement which then had its inception and was soon to sweep the whole of Europe.

For the time being, however, the Congress was a Victory Feast and nothing else. At one time a new sovereign arrived in Vienna almost every day, putting up at the Palace of the Emperor of Austria, as if the "Emperor of Austria" was a hotel. As a matter of fact, it was. Two emperors, two empresses, four kings, and half a dozen archdukes were living at the "Burg" together with their entire retinues. Three hundred carriages were kept in readiness for their use day and night. The Imperial horses' manes were festively adorned with colored ribbons, and the spokes of the carriages' wheels were gilt. Ordinarily, only the immediate members of the Court were permitted to ride in these carriages. This was symptomatic of everything else: balls, masques, receptions, equestrian displays, military reviews —the largest of which occurred on October 18th, in commemoration of the Battle of Leipsic—thanksgiving functions, sleighing-parties, and tournaments. If one day an equestrian tournament took place at the Court Riding-School, it was followed the next day by a heron-hawking at Laxenburg, one of the Imperial country-estates in the suburbs of Vienna. There was, of course, the usual round of concerts and theatrical events. There were again performances at the Opera of Beethoven's "Fidelio" which after a lapse of ten years had at last become successful even in Vienna. The attraction at a popular playhouse was "The Burghers of Vienna." All these burghers were permitted to do, by the way, was to look on and gape at the passing coaches. They loved to line the streets and watch the parade. They did the same in the spring of 1938, and not unwillingly either. That some spectacle or other may be watched has always been of greater importance to the Viennese than the significance of the spectacle itself. It is an inordinately curious city; ready to sell its soul for the privilege of being able to say: "I was there!"

The "good" Emperor Franz, being a liberal host, was determined to do everything in grand style. A caricature from those days is eloquent of the fact. In it we see the six "Kings on Vacation"—another of Prince de Ligne's *mots*—united in an amusing picture which bore the following sarcastic legend: "The Emperor of Russia—loves for all; the King of Prussia—thinks for all; the King of Denmark—speaks for all; the King of Bavaria—drinks for all; the King of Württemberg—eats for all; and the Emperor of Austria—pays for all." Of course, it only appeared as if he did. As a matter of fact, an additional 50% of taxes were levied, thus making the well-known general public bear the burden of the expense. "There they go for our fifty per-cent," the Viennese used to grumble on the occasion of the great sleighing parties, as they gazed with anything but a benevolent mien after His Majesty's exalted guests in their costly furs.

The high spirits of the guests left nothing to be desired. A royal good time was had at the sleighing-parties, tournaments, and masked fêtes, and there was laughter even at the Emperor's table. The Empress of Austria, who was deaf in her right ear, sat on the left of the King of Prussia, whose left ear was similarly afflicted. It was a treat to watch them, as neither could understand what the other was saying. The Czar of Russia, who sat next to Emperor Franz, noticed that a giant peacock which had been handed around as a show-dish was carried away and, instead of finding its way back into the kitchens, was taken to the servants' quarters. "Did you see that?" the Czar said teasingly to his Imperial brother. Emperor Franz, without moving a muscle of his face, as is the way of some comedians, said quite drily: "Indeed, I did —and that gives you a slight idea of what is being stolen in your Russia!"

Metternich seemingly was in all places at once, a veritable *maître de plaisir*. He was now called "Ministre Papillon" behind his back. He flitted from one party to the other, from one session to the other, from one fête to the other. Every Monday he gave a reception at his beautiful home on the Rennweg which, until 1938, was the seat of the Italian Legation, but which in those days was still on the outskirts of the city, surrounded by an attractive private park with great trees and winding paths. The most magnificent of these receptions took place on the anniversary of the Battle of Leipsic; Princess Metternich presided as a perfect hostess, while Metternich himself received his guests with a coquettish grace. A sort of pantomime was produced which—what a joke!—mythologically represented the triumph of concord over discord. The ladies were all dressed in blue, supposedly in homage to the Bourbons, and wore olive branches in their hair. So great was the crush that the Danish Countess Bernsdorff was forced to wait two hours before she was able to alight from her coach. Needless to say, all the crowned heads were present. Each one of them already had his coterie, his following, and his favorite, whom he elevated above all other ladies. Society soon found nicknames for the prominent ladies, so that they could differentiate between them like connoisseurs do among various kinds of wine. One of them was called *"beauté céleste,"* another one was known as the *"beauté du diable,"* and a third one was simply the *"beauté* who gave you delicious chills."

Czar Alexander, one of his epoch's most sedulous and at the same time most harmless admirers of the fair sex, liked best to have his tea at Princess Bagration's, the *"bèl ange nu"* whose acquaintance we made in Dresden. She had now a marked tendency towards plumpness, but the more material she needed for her dresses, the less she actually used, thus making the display of her charms an international exhibition. As far as Metternich was concerned, she had been his mistress and remained a discarded one. It is not surprising, then, that during the Congress the relations between the Czar and Metternich grew steadily worse, from one of Alexander's tea-visits at the Bagration's to the other. If she had become the Czar's mistress, it probably would have come to a war between Russia and Austria; but as it was, there were only some diplomatic fireworks. In spite of the liberality of the Bagration's displays she could not get any further, after all.

Princess Bagration lived at Prince Palm's palace, adjacent to the Imperial Palace; and in another wing of the same house—which may be seen to this day—lived, *maigre et ardente,* the Duchess of Sagan, Metternich's intermittent love, and *vivandière* of the heart from French headquarters-days. What a situation, to have both these queen-bees living in the same society bee-house, where visitors went flying in and out day and night! While the Austrian State-Chancellor stole up to his beloved over the well-worn stairs of the old palace, the Autocrat of all the Russias may have been seen to steal down another stairway, or perhaps even the same one, on his way from his love. There were others, too, by the way, who did some "stealing." Foremost among them was the young Prince Windisch-Grätz, who went to see the woman who "loves as one dines." Metternich was made to feel once more that he was, after all, but a guest. His life, blest with an abundant harvest, had now reached its midsummer days. There were at times sultry skies, followed by thunderstorms. La Sagan, supposed to be the woman for his lighter moods, did not always make things easy for him, a fact of which his contemporaries took notice with a good deal of malicious satisfaction. Why should one man have everything? That was Princess Sagan's way of thinking, too.

A story was circulated that one of Metternich's visits with the beautiful Duchess, lasting throughout the night, cost Austria a considerable part of Bavaria. Bavaria was to have ceded it and be indemnified with a large slice of Italy. All arrangements had been made, and on the following morning the treaty was to have been signed in solemn session. Everyone was present on November 11th, 1814, waiting for the Austrian plenipotentiary, who failed to arrive because he had overslept. Bavaria thought better of the matter and withdrew at the very last moment.

This is a legend of North-German origin. If Metternich overslept on that November morning, it may safely be assumed that he knew what he was doing. Certainly he would have been pleased to receive an added piece of Bavaria, beyond Salzburg, but he begrudged Bavaria the portion of Italy it was to receive in return. His visit at the Duchess of Sagan's and its unfavorable consequences were nothing but pretense, designed to make the Viennese smile. The facts of the matter were quite different. He preferred to forget his appointment because he happened to remember in time that it was more opportune to forget. Even when he was absent minded, there was a purpose behind it. In that respect, too, he resembled his master Talleyrand who, when he died, caused one of his contemporaries to remark: "I wonder what his motive was!"

The beautiful Duchess of Sagan had an equally beautiful sister, the Countess of Périgord, and as it happened Talleyrand's mistress. Here, too, the authors of comedies may have found a mine of material involving the two champion politicians and the noble sisters, each one of whom jealously maintained her place on the map. The two sisters, living in the same house, intrigued and stirred up trouble. Vienna used to call them *"les deux Sybilles."* It was a mythological era, and whenever old Prince de Ligne composed a poem about the Congress, all Olympus had to turn out. His world of fancies lay between Venus, Mars, and Cupid.

The old gentleman himself was by no means insensible to feminine charms. It was at a mid-winter rendezvous on the "Bastion" that the octogenarian caught the cold to which he succumbed in the third month of the Congress. When he was on his death-bed he is said to have given vent to one of those witty phrases which authors of comedies like to put in the mouths of their characters before their exit: "A Marshal's funeral is about the only thing the Vienna Congress has not yet been able to enjoy." After many a display of mental fireworks, now he even provided that macabre spectacle for the Viennese. His narrow-fronted house on the "Mölkerbastei" was empty all of a sudden. He had occupied the upper story, to which the Viennese referred to as the "parrot's perch." It had been rose-colored like the mood of its master; like the silver-lace-covered liveries of his servants; and like his style of writing: a varnished nothing, wittily wound about with rose-colored ribbons. Metternich owed much to the man's undeniable charm of manner, which charm was augmented by a gracious heart and mind. It would be interesting to know if the State-Chancellor attended the old man's funeral. However, it was rather a long way to the "Kahlenberg" where, under waving tree-tops, the body of Prince de Ligne was laid to rest. The mountain-grave may still be seen there, and there is none in Vienna that is higher.

The Congress of Vienna was the high-water mark in the history of Metternich's life as well as in the history of Vienna. It was the occasion for Vienna's growth from an "Imperial City" into a metropolis, which it remained for more than a century. This ought not to lead one to the conclusion, however, that because of the service he had rendered to the city in bringing the Congress to Vienna, Metternich was particularly popular there, then or later. On the contrary, he was extremely unpopular, and even hated.

This remarkable lack of popularity, which seems to have been the share of this favorite of fortune throughout his life, is a puzzle only partly solved by Vienna's traditional ingratitude. There must have been other reasons, too; reasons which had to do with his personality and his fate. Perhaps it was because of his many affairs of the heart. As in the case of Count Leicester in Schiller's "Mary Stuart," he had bribed judges on every women's council. This fact may have alienated the sympathies of the associate judges in the council. The world treated him as some cuckolded husbands would have done: ready to acquiesce, but never forgetting.

To a reviewer of Metternich's social and historical position in the Vienna of Congress days it must seem that, with the exception of the Emperor himself, he had everyone

against him: the Empress; the Archdukes; the high aristocracy—"Starhemberg & Co." the Viennese called them jocularly—the "patriots"; the ministers, who were no longer
patriotic; and the ultra-Germans, who could never be patriotic. They all felt, and not without some justification, as
though he had duped and cheated them. True, he did not
want a powerful and united German Reich, but a powerless and disunited one; therefore he placed obstacles in the
way of a unification instead of removing them. While this
is undoubtedly true, one might think that the dyed-in-the-
wool Austrians, the Prussian-haters, and the Habsburg adherents should have been grateful to him. They were, on the
contrary, his worst and most relentless enemies. The Wal-
lises, the Schwarzenbergs, and the Choteks, all of them members of the highest aristocracy—to say nothing of Stadion,
to whose political position he had succeeded—all had something against him. This animosity extended even far into
the middle and lower classes. One half of the Viennese found
fault with him because he had married Marie Louise to
Napoleon, while the other half blamed him for having
betrayed Napoleon too late. Among both halves, moreover,
and among the so-called "Vienna patriots," whose sentiments
were not always wholly uninfluenced by financial considerations, there were even those who found fault with him for
having deserted Napoleon.

Nor would the ambassadors and foreign dignitaries allow
him one good quality. One thought he did too much, the
other that he did not do enough. "A good diplomat," he
was called, "but a bad minister." "He shows enterprise only
when he is alone with a woman," said another of him. That
was also the opinion of the old Countesses, in whose good
graces his father had admonished him to remain twenty

years before. They never grew tired now of decrying at their tea-parties the all-too-attractive Chancellor. "The poor Princess!" they would say of his wife. "But she is good enough to receive his guests on a Monday, the poor Lori!" Their Excellencies' opinions were no different. "He will keep two ambassadors waiting in his ante-chamber, while arranging *tableaux vivants* with his daughter," Humboldt, the German chargé d'affaires might have been heard to grumble. There was some truth in that. It was Metternich's daughter, Marie, then a half-grown girl, who was the best loved of his children. (Even here he was a ladies' man!) And then there was the Church, represented by the Papal Secretary, Monsignore Evangelisti. He considered Metternich a downright lost soul, "abandoned to the mysteries of Isis, of Ceres, and to free-masonry."

The assembled majesties, too, were not favorably disposed towards him. The King of Denmark complained about Metternich's remaining seated, while speaking to him. The King of Prussia, whom the Viennese called "King Infinitive" because he considered it his kingly prerogative not to conjugate his verbs, was often heard to speak disparagingly of him. He had no confidence in Metternich, thought that he was trying to cheat, had a number of violent altercations with him, and at one time refused to see him for several weeks.

Worst of all, however, was Czar Alexander, whom the Bagration woman set against Metternich whenever the Russian ruler came to have tea with her. On one occasion he shouted at Metternich: "You are the only man in Austria who dares talk to me in this manner!" Another time, during a conversation, he threw his sword on the table and challenged Metternich to a duel. For weeks afterwards he passed him at social gatherings without a word or even a nod. In the end they made up again, and Metternich was able to attain all his objectives. He reconciled Prussia by ceding to it a piece of Saxony and Poland, while he handed the rest of the latter country to the Czar who, disregarding his oft-professed liberalism, had no compunction about swallowing it.

Altogether it became more and more apparent, as the Congress drew to its close, that a statesman, having attained to a certain prominence, is able to achieve more through his unpopularity than through the greatest popularity. All had heaped calumny upon him, many had tried to vanquish him, and some, like Talleyrand, had actually vanquished him in some secondary skirmishes. But when the inventory was finally taken it showed that of all the States represented at the Congress, Austria had fared best. She got Lombardy and Venetia, a piece of Illyria, a large part of Galicia, and the charming Salzburg, whose international summer visitors little thought, a hundred years later, as they attended some Reinhardt production, that they owed to the maligned Metternich this most Austrian piece of Austria.

The Congress of Vienna does not enjoy a good repute among professors of history. It has, in their opinion, the unpardonable fault of having been entertaining. True, it would be difficult to acquit it of that charge; but the question arises whether it is actually only boredom which is of political consequence, a view held by German scholars for over a century. These pedants are in the habit of asserting in their pompous manner that there is always too much talking in Vienna and not enough action; to which a Vienna journalist in Berlin once had a rather neat reply. When in his presence his Berlin fellow-journalists implacably held to this opinion, he interrupted them with the modest rejoinder: "There is plenty of work being done in Vienna. Only the *talk* about the work is better organized in Berlin." The same may be said of the Congress of Vienna when comparing it with the Congress of Berlin, in 1878, the other and better organized great event of a similar kind. It is all the more true if a comparison is made with the great session of Versailles, a century later. After twenty-one years, in 1940, there is not much left of Versailles!

The Congress of Vienna created a European order which was able to hold its own until the beginning of the 20th century. The alliance between Austria, Russia, and Prussia guaranteed the permanence of that order; and only when it collapsed did Bismarck, who had unshakably held fast to it, feel justified in sounding a warning of approaching chaos. Between the downfall of Bismarck and the Congress of Vienna lies a span of seventy-five years. If these eight decades assumed the character of an Age of Peace for the peoples of Europe, it is due in no small degree to the pleasure-loving Congress of Vienna and to him who called it into being, without renouncing the pleasures of life in doing so. "Ere he sings and ere he ceases—Must the poet live!" said Goethe. But why only the poet? Why not also the statesman? They are surely not the worst who appreciate existence by enjoying life.

"Oh Monde!"

WHILE the Congress of Vienna evolved, revolved, and dissolved, Marie Louise's fate, comparatively insignificant, had long since reached the point towards which Metternich's clever hand steered it with cold placidity. The times did not permit of any new love affair. His experiences with the Duchess of Sagan were hardly exciting any more. So, in the absence of a new romance, he contented himself from sheer necessity with adding another thrilling chapter to the unfinished novel of the dethroned young Empress. It was at best a sad business, this spare-time work, and not entirely worthy of a statesman of his rank. But he had little choice in the matter. Napoleon had to be removed once and for all. To accomplish that, he had to cease being the Emperor of Austria's son-in-law.

Marie Louise was obliged to wait three days for her Papa in Rambouillet. Then she was the recipient of a fatherly embrace, and of a suggestion that she return to Austria as soon as possible. First of all, she should recruit her strength and then make her own choice as to the opportune moment to see her husband again. There was seemingly no objection to her visiting him, from either Emperor Franz or Metternich. This is documented by a confidential letter, drawn up by Metternich and sent by Emperor Franz to Napoleon.

In the meantime, his wife, turning her back upon historical developments and traveling by way of Switzerland, Tyrol, and Salzburg, journeyed back to Vienna, her little son on her knees. On her way through the Austrian hereditary lands she was everywhere received with jubilant acclaim; wherever she stopped, flowers were thrown into her coach. How could it have been otherwise? Was she not an Emperor's daughter, the child of their beloved monarch? Emperor Franz' popularity was as inexplicable as was Metternich's unpopularity. But, anyway, here was a pretty young woman and mother. She was hardly twenty-three years old, and at her side was a darling little bit of a man who answered to the name of King of Rome, and who put his curly head out of the window whenever she showed herself to the people. How could they have failed to be delighted, the good, faithful Austrian people? It did not matter a straw to them that this woman was the wife of their archenemy; they saw only a dethroned Empress and a young mother deprived of her natural support. And so they rejoiced, and threw flowers.

In Vienna, at Schönbrunn Palace, the physical recuperation of the sorely tried woman still left much to be desired; therefore His Majesty's private physician ordered her to journey to a Swiss watering-place. He considered Aix-les-Bains the right place: the air was mild, and so were the baths. Besides, it was not too far from Parma, nor from Elba, where Napoleon, as great in small surroundings as he had been in vast ones, was occupied in expertly developing his miniature State. Without hesitating a moment, Marie Louise agreed and gaily made her preparations for the journey. It was probably due to Metternich's instigation that she was not permitted, though, to take her boy with her. She was a little put out about this, but only at first. She was more woman than mother.

Whenever an empress traveled, no matter if she were but a dethroned empress, she needed a royal courier. Prince Esterházy was appointed in that capacity, and there could certainly be no objection to him. He was a cavalier, an old dignified, and highly chivalrous Magyar. Suddenly, however, when Marie Louise had already started, the appointment was canceled, and another man was surprisingly put in Esterházy's place. Metternich's fine hand became visible. The new courier was a Count Neipperg, a man recommended by Prince Schwarzenberg in Paris, and whose general reputation was not too good. Women, on the other hand, considered it quite excellent.

Neipperg was forty-two years old, a general, and was in the service of Austria as divisional commander in Parma. He had lately been Ambassador to Naples, where he had been able to render valuable services to the cause of the Allies. Four years before, in Paris, he had been informally presented to the Empress.

Now at Carrouge, which is in the immediate neighborhood of Aix, he rode to meet her. He was clad in the fur-trimmed uniform of a Hungarian hussar, and wore on his tunic the Maria Theresa Cross, the highest Austrian military decoration. A black bandage covered one of his eyes which he had lost by a sword cut in the War of 1813. Although the wound did him honor, the bandage gave him a suspicious and sinister look. The one-eyed cavalier, no matter how well he sat his horse, was rather repulsive to her at the first glance.

Well, Napoleon, too, had been highly unsympathetic to her when she was a young girl. Why, it is said that she had actually hated him and in her nursery shot at his picture with her little cross-bow. Yet she became his wife. That should not be held against her. If there existed statistics concerning the beginnings of loves, it would be shown that from the women's side, the attachments beginning with dislike, outnumber those arising from sympathy. Love at first sight, if there is such a thing, presupposes a fully developed personality, which Marie Louise was not to the end of her days. She was an average little woman, not better and not worse than millions of others.

Now the courier-general took charge of the little traveling procession which proceeded at a smart trot towards Aix-les-Bains. There the mild cure prescribed by the Vienna Court physician was to begin. The young woman had a somewhat delicate chest—the Vienna disease, unfortunately —and its cure in those days consisted of whey, and tepid baths. Marie Louise dutifully gulped her whey-pap every day and as dutifully bathed at the prescribed hours in the supposedly miraculous waters. In the evenings she would dance a little, and on such occasions the sinister-looking Count Neipperg turned out to be a splendid and graceful dancer. Also there were evenings when, to make the time pass, there was some music; and it appeared that Count Neipperg had a magnificent singing voice, which he knew how to use to good advantage. Rolling his one eye, the cavalry general sang so dramatically, that the walls resounded.

Marie Louise felt better in Aix-les-Bains from day to day, and her health improved visibly. The splendid surroundings attracted and urged her to make excursions into the mountains, which she had been unable to do for a long time. At first, these excursions were short; then they grew longer

and were undertaken either on horseback or on foot. Count
Neipperg was her constant companion, which was his duty
as well as almost his right. He proved himself a highly skilled
horseman on mountain paths, and a mountain climber of
great endurance. He knew every way and by-path as far as
the snow line, and was never at a loss for information or
advice. Even in the shelter huts, when he was alone with
the young woman, he knew how to behave properly, if the
travel chronicler, Meneval, is to be believed.

But hadn't Marie Louise intended to proceed to Elba
and visit Napoleon as soon as her health improved a little?
She was feeling considerably better now; why, she was even
feeling quite well again, and yet she delayed her proposed
visit. It seems that the longer she stayed the better she liked
Aix-les-Bains. "*Elle s'amuse,*" confidential reports to Vienna
stated. She danced at the public subscription balls, which was
not at all Imperial; but it made her downright popular.
She put on the new clothes she had brought along to be
prepared in case of need; she blossomed, she laughed, and
she sang little snatches of song all day. What had become
of the mild cure prescribed by the Imperial physician in
Vienna? Eating her whey as if it had been ice-cream, and
eating ice-cream as if it had been the prescribed whey, she
enjoyed her young life without thought or care. The young
Empress acted as if she had never been dethroned and her
husband had not, quite recently, been banished to Elba. It
was the very fact of her behavior, however, that caused bad
blood among the French, who have little use for want of
tact on the part of a woman in Marie Louise's position. The
French Government, using Talleyrand as their mouthpiece,
expressed the wish that the Austrian authorities cause Marie
Louise's visit to be terminated as soon as possible. Emperor

Franz sent a letter, composed by Metternich, to Aix-les-Bains, in which the gay and pleasure-loving little lady was commanded to leave the watering-place at once. At the same time her entourage was also recalled—with the exception of Count Neipperg.

Marie Louise ordered her trunks packed. A few days previous, however, on August 10th, before she could have known of Talleyrand's protest, she had already canceled her visit to Elba. She stated as her reason that unfortunately she had to return to Vienna hurriedly; but she would surely come soon, many kisses! It was her last letter.

Those who had been in attendance upon Marie Louise were already scattered—Metternich's work again. One of them was ill, another, Monsieur Meneval, was detained in Paris. The ex-Empress remained alone with Neipperg and, finding Alpine tours more and more to her taste, roamed the Bernese Oberland with him for some time. Much later, after having lived with him, she married him, though he had been married before to the wife of another man whom he had seduced, and who had presented him with five children. Nevertheless, Neipperg had been appointed Honorary Attendant to the Empress and, after some time, he was elevated to the rank of Prince Montenuovo (Neipperg—Neuberg—New Mountain—Montenuovo), "for services rendered."

This court-intrigue portrayed Metternich in the far from sympathetic rôle of an almost pandering State-Minister in the style of the 18th century; but the touching figure was the deceived husband, Napoleon. From the moment when, in Fontainebleau on April 8th, 1814, he swallowed poison because Marie Louise had failed to come to him, he never ceased to woo her and to wait for her. On his exile-bound journey to Elba he proposed to her a rendezvous in Brière, which she disdained to keep. No sooner had he arrived on the island of Elba than he wrote to her, proposing without rancor and in the tenderest expressions that she join him at least for a visit. She would reside in Parma, while he remained on Elba; but at any rate they would be able to see each other from time to time. He was sure she would not fail him this time; he confidently expected her visit during the summer weeks and gave orders adequately to remodel the country seat he had equipped for himself above Porto Ferraio. The coolest rooms were to be decorated first and kept in readiness for the Empress. He also arranged for a display of fireworks upon her arrival, to entertain her.

Marie Louise chose an idle pretext for her failure to go to Napoleon who patiently continued to write her, although he received no further replies. When, after his escape from Elba, he started upon his unparalleled triumphal march on Paris, he actually addressed no less than seven letters to her between March 8th and April 4th, 1815, during which time events of world-importance followed one another with lightning rapidity. From Lyon, before he entered Paris, he commanded, nay, he begged her: *"Sois à Strassbourg de 15 au 20 avril!"* It was the S.O.S. call of a dying heart, destined like all other calls to remain unanswered by the beloved wife who already received a monthly allowance of 1200 francs from her Papa and had no intention of jeopardizing it. But the great man's heart did not die; it was immortal!

The Empress, to be sure, might have behaved in a manner more becoming her station as an historical figure. But, as Masson cleverly said at the conclusion of his book on Marie Louise: "History begins when one is dead, and Marie

Louise wanted to live." So she continued to live in Parma with her Honorary Attendant and, as the years passed by—so Masson tells us—there was nothing to remind her of Napoleon at Parma except perhaps the violets, his favorite flower in the days of his glory, the flower of the Empire.

Two hearts—great and small! The great one never ceased to beat for her, and it seems that we can still feel its palpitation if we consult the records of Napoleon's attitude towards her when, on St. Helena, an ocean separated them. During six long years not a day passed without his mentioning her name in conversation. Repeatedly he attempted to get in touch with her. His unshakable love found a thousand excuses for her, who was unworthy of one. He never condemned her; he never even judged her. Her disloyalty? Why, he simply ignored it. Forced to choose between the alternatives of contempt and blindness, he deliberately chose blindness. When he died, he left to her his laces and his heart. *"Je lègue à l'Imperatrice mes dentelles."* How much tenderness there is in this simple sentence! As for his heart, he never ceased to consider it her personal property. He directed in his will that it be preserved in alcohol and sent to her as a final proof *"que je l'ai tendrement aimé et que je n'ai cessé de l'aimer!"*

Human greatness! Measured by Napoleon, Metternich did not possess much of it. But there were times when it dawned upon him how much he was lacking in it; they were the times, during later years, when he spoke of Napoleon; and he spoke of him increasingly as he grew older. It was strange, indeed: since he had conquered Napoleon he could not keep from talking about him. He had used the Emperor ill and yet—or was it because of it?—remained his debtor throughout his life.

To be sure, Napoleon was not yet entirely vanquished, a fact which was soon to become apparent. While the Congress of Vienna continued to dawdle along endlessly—a diplomatic minuet, a be-ribboned barter of the peoples, a mart of love, and a waltz-dream of politics—the incredible news was circulated in Vienna one morning, that Napoleon had escaped from Elba, and had gone ashore at Cannes. It is said that Metternich, awakened by his valet, got the message at 7 o'clock; losing no time, he was at the Emperor's apartments at 8. De La Garde even asserts that the bomb burst at a ball and tore a Vienna waltz right in two. The King of Prussia, accompanied by the Czar, was seen to leave the party at once: Metternich, on the arm of the Duke of Wellington, followed them presently. The ball was over.

That was about the gist of it, even if it did not happen in exactly that manner. After deducting the decorations of history, two facts remain. First, during the latter half of the Congress of Vienna it had already become apparent that in the long run Elba would not do as an exile; it was too near the coast and especially too near the estates of Parma and Piacenza, the future residence of Empress Marie Louise. Another place of exile long had been contemplated in the intimate circle of the leading statesmen, and the name of St. Helena already had been mentioned. Napoleon did not worsen his fate by the theatrical coup of The Hundred Days, although thoughtful historians are inclined to find fault with his conduct. He merely stole a march upon Fate and, hero that he was, bravely faced it. It is more than likely that he would have been sent to St. Helena anyway.

The other fact is, that no sooner had Metternich received the news of the Emperor's escape than he managed to establish a defensive front and revive the Coalition. Napoleon was declared an outlaw, which would hardly have been possible had Marie Louise still been his wife, and war against him declared at once. The "Hundred Days" rushed by as if on eagles' wings. In their mighty rush and roar dwells an echo of the eternal world-melody which encompasses all of life and all human history. Only Shakespeare or Beethoven could have given forth with equal magnificence the glories of this heroic song.

In contrast to an heroic song stands human infamy, the wretchedness of small minds, and the depravity of public opinion, whose utter corruptibility becomes plainly visible on such occasions. After Napoleon had set foot on French soil with the epigrammatic words: "The Congress is dissolved!" he started upon a triumphal march through France, the like of which the world has never experienced before or since. The battalions, the regiments, the divisions of the Bourbons went over to him, and while he rode at their head the train of his followers grew into a mighty host. The words of his manifesto seemed actually to become true: the Imperial eagle flew from church-steeple to church-steeple until it alighted on the Cathedral of Notre Dame.

It is interesting to contemplate the reflections of this triumphal procession, this onward march into eternity, in the ink-wells of contemporary journalism. Alas, that journalism must always be contemporary! "The monster has escaped from Elba!" announced the Bourbon press; "The tiger has gone ashore at Cannes!"; "The demon has arrived in Grenobles!"; "The tyrant marches upon Lyon!"; "The usurper threatens Orleans!"; "Napoleon arrives in Orleans!"; "The Emperor in Paris!"

Within three weeks the entire Bourbon press was Napoleonic again. Today it would take but twenty-four hours to perform the miracle. The means of communication have multiplied enormously, and there are no longer any distances or limits—not even to people's want of principles, as we know from all-too-recent experience.

Between the landing at Cannes and Waterloo, where the fate of Europe was decided for another century—in this breathless space of history, Metternich scarcely had the leisure to form a clear picture of what he had achieved, or failed to achieve, at the Congress of Vienna. Not only journalists but historians, too, are at times "bewildered by the parties' grace or hatred"; so it comes about that even competent historians are not quite clear on the subject, although one point seems to be firmly established: he made Austria great again; greater than she had ever been. But, the North-German historians immediately add modifyingly, "at the expense of Germany." They reproach Metternich for having forgotten at the Congressional house-cleaning to set the German house in order.

True, when in the winter of 1814 the Imperial German Crown was offered to Emperor Franz for the second time, he declined it. In the draft of a confidential message addressed to Generalissimo Prince Schwarzenberg he replaced the word "fatherland" with "My peoples" and "My State." By the use of the possessive pronoun and the capital "M" he raised them to the status of a family possession. There is no avoiding the fact that, to Metternich, Nationalism meant Jacobinism. For this, German nationalist circles attacked him bitterly for fully a century, until it was shown mordantly, quite recently, that Nationalism actually *is* Jacobinism.

This point is the most interesting one in every biography of Metternich; and it is, at the same time, the one in which discernment or the lack of it most clearly manifests itself. This may be ascertained especially in works written since the flare-up of National-Socialism in Germany. In this connection it is highly instructive to note that critics with inclinations towards the Right have a tendency to forgive Metternich his reactionary views, while they attack him for his internationalism. Thus Metternich has gained nothing except a change of the front from which he is attacked: for a century the attacks came from the Left, while today adverse criticism comes mostly from the Right. Especially those in the Austrian nationalist camp are keen on branding him an "Austrian traitor" who, because of an inherent want of principle and a typically Austrian epicureanism, missed the opportune moment for making Austria the leading German power in Central Europe—which is to say that he should have laid the foundation of a German Central Europe, perhaps even a German Europe.

When and how could he have made this Niebelung dream come true? Some say in reply: at the Congress of Vienna, on the morning which followed the night he so unpardonably spent with the Duchess of Sagan. If he had not overslept, South Bavaria would have fallen to Austria. Then Austria, protected in the north, would have been able to re-create the Greater Germany under its aegis. By permitting this unique opportunity to slip out of his grasp Metternich condemned himself to historical insignificance. In that night spent with the *"maudite femme,"* as Gentz called her, he relinquished once and for all any claim to heroic greatness in favor of his love of pleasure. From that day, he wasted the rest of his life, more than forty years, in following a sad and dull governmental routine which was never able to satisfy him.

This concept has much in common with that of Walter Tritsch, one of the more recent Austrian writers, and one who is obviously inspired by National-Socialist ideologies. He makes this view the starting-point of his nationalistically colored Metternich biography, published in 1934. Tritsch is of the opinion that the career of Metternich, who abjured German nationalism, was virtually closed when he was forty-two years old; the rest safely may be passed over. That was Clemens Metternich's age when Lawrence painted his portrait. It shows him sitting in the conference chair at the Congress of Vienna, his legs crossed, leaning back slightly, and in a pleasantly relaxed attitude. It must be admitted that in this painting he looks less like a grim and formidable German warrior than a French or English statesman of his period, somewhere between Pitt and Talleyrand. As a matter of fact, he looks typically European.

It is this very fact which Tritsch and those of his ilk forget, or rather try to make us forget: Metternich was a European in the first place, an Austrian in the second, and a German only in the third. It was a balanced and happy group of nations in Europe that he visualized always.

Even now, when after Napoleon's spectacular attempt the tragedy unfolded stormily to the thundering of cannons, Metternich never lost sight of his goal. Standing on the deck of the "Northumberland," the English man-of-war that carried him to St. Helena, Napoleon uttered the words *"Oh monde!"* as he saw the coast line of France sink below the horizon. It was not only France but Europe which faded from his vision. But to Metternich, who had conquered him, Europe was only then beginning its ascent; and that was even more important to him than his victory over Napoleon.

BOOK THREE

The Dictator of Europe

Metternich in Profile

Success rarely improves a man. Reverses, on the contrary, enoble and steel human character, provided that a man is great enough to live down his misfortune. For misfortune in itself is no cause for admiration. The capacity for growth and development, of ability to meet and master crushing opposition is the important quality we must seek.

Did Metternich's character possess these decisive faculties to grow and evolve? He was a man of the old order which rejected development, because it believed in the static. That was Metternich's primary belief. There are existing facts, but no progress. There are only the eternal laws to which everything must revert in the end. It is logical, therefore, that looking back on his life, Metternich should deny a gradual growth of his own nature and character, considering them an inborn and immutable part of his being. "I was the same at seventeen as I am today" (at 46), he wrote to Princess Lieven. Fortunately, however, commentaries of this kind are hardly to be taken more seriously than a patient's diagnosis of his own case before the physician has examined him. A percussion of Metternich's personality and an auscultation of his historical heart-beat would reveal facts which contradict his self-asserted immutability in the course of a life of more than eighty years.

To practise character analysis is a rather abstract pleasure. That is why poets have found another method for grasping the essential nature of a human being: they synthesize a character without analysing it. Painters, in their way, do the same thing. A portrait amounts to nothing unless it be a character study, the reflection of a personality. A deep knowledge and understanding of the portrayed person is the background upon which it is painted. This being so, let us see what the painters have to say.

As far as the Metternich of the first half of his life is concerned, there are two portraits. One was painted by Gérard in the early days of the young diplomat's life in Paris, while the other is by Lawrence and dates back to the time of the Congress of Vienna. Both are excellent examples of portraiture, painted within seven or eight years of each other. A comparison of the two clearly shows the development of the personality.

Out of Gérard's rosy full-face portrait a young courtier, elegantly dressed, gazes at the beholder. Clemens Metternich was thirty-five years old when this portrait was painted in Paris, and in it he looks even younger. One is almost tempted to speak of a handsome boy's head, were it not for the knowing expression round the mouth, and the discreet smile. The smile indicates not only a secret ridicule of the courtier he pretends to be, but also a certain impertinence which, though cleverly held in leash, practically renders the courtier null and void. The mouth is already in evidence, the ingeniously eloquent Metternich mouth; there are indications, too, of the somewhat protruding and cynically pendulous lower lip, while the nose is not yet a prominent feature in the slightly too round and full voluptuary's face. It is still an ordinary nose. And that may also apply to the whole person: a festively adorned *Ambassadeur* with all appurtenances; the beautiful star of an order on his chest and a grand-cordon swathing his neck which seems protected and secured, as by rampart and moat, by a triply folded starched cravat and a steeply mounting coat-collar. A not altogether pleasant self-assertion and an undisguised self-complacency hover round the enterprising young Ambassador's head, with its artistically disarranged coiffure.

In the portrait painted by Lawrence seven years later in the crush of the Congress, the self-assertion is visibly replaced by the entirely natural superiority of a man so firmly entrenched that he can afford to smile at his own superiority. Lawrence painted Metternich in a sitting position, yet the canvas vividly and cleverly shows the entire figure from the tips of his toes to the still carefully arranged profusion of locks. We see the hand, the fine knee, the handsomely formed legs in their white silk stockings, the heavily gold-embroidered full-dress coat, and the broad sash adorned with the order of the Golden Fleece, which had been bestowed upon Metternich in 1809 on the occasion of Marie Louise's marriage. More important, though, than all these externals which their owner himself, gracefully reclining in his armchair, seems to belittle by the mocking expression of his face, is the unique and unmistakable air of a matured personality at the zenith of life. Gérard's breast-piece is the portrait of a man who does not differ essentially from dozens of fortunate young men of the same age and period; what Lawrence painted is Clemens Metternich and no one else. No matter if Pitt, or perhaps even Beau Brummell, the great king of fashion, had taught him to cross his legs so nonchalantly and unconstrainedly and to let his beautifully shaped hand dangle so artlessly over the arm of the chair;

no matter if the highly arched Mephistophelian brow and the still more Mephistophelian smile on the disillusioned lips were copied from Prince de Ligne; it all had become genuinely Metternich, in that Lawrence portrait. And there is one added detail that encompasses everything: the pose of the profile which causes the finely chiseled and decidedly prominent nose in the more thinly modeled face to dominate an almost theatrical animation of the features. It is Metternich's first portrait showing us that side, and the first one, also, which by emphasizing his profile, plastically presents his personality. A man's profile perhaps indicates what Fate's intention towards him has been, while a full-face view often shows what Life has made of him. The "Congress Portrait," at least, seems to bear out this contention. We behold the temporal and the super-temporal Metternich; we behold him in the last glow of youth and yet already *sub specie aeternitatis*. We behold the statesman, aristocrat, and *viveur*. Do we also behold a great man? An important man, at any rate! That he had the courage to place so little emphasis upon his own importance may detract from his value in the eyes of North-German observers, who are so apt to confound grimness with greatness and who must tremble before they can admire.

Let us not be confused by outward appearances. This slender prince with the ironic smile and the Golden Fleece who wears smoothly fitting white silk stockings in preference to knightly armor and disdains to strike a Napoleonic attitude by heroically crossing his arms over his chest; this amiable Congressional Chancellor whose insouciance caused a whole country to have a small opinion of his importance; this man, in the years following upon the Congress, actually

possessed and wielded a power scarcely second to Napoleon's. If we picture to ourselves the map of the Europe of
those days, we see not only a mightily grown Austria, but an
Austria also reinforced by old and new "hereditary" lands
and ruling over Italy and Germany. In January, 1815, Emperor Franz for the second time refused the German Imperial Crown. Nevertheless, Austria maintained her presiding seat in the German League, and whatever she desired
and ordered—although it was not always reasonable and correct—was done, and continued to be done in the German
Federal Lands, for the ensuing fifty years. Relations with
Italy were about the same. Far into the South, even as far as
Ravenna, there was an Austrian garrison in every town of
any considerable size. Not only Lombardy and Venetia belonged to Austria—Emperor Franz Joseph was permitted to
call himself King of Lombardy to the end of his days—but
Tuscany, Modena, Parma, and Piacenza were either wholly
or partly Austrian. The same was true of Naples and Sicily,
or soon would become true through marriage. Austrian
troops of occupation were to be found in France; and as far
as the Black Sea and Turkey, there was felt the powerful
influence of the Metternich-created Danube Convention
which made the Danube and not the Rhine the great artery
of Europe. Even in Spain, for two whole decades things
moved along a course either prescribed or desired by Austria. Until Greece declared its independence in 1827, nothing was done by either England or Russia to offend the
Habsburgs. From the Thames to the Neva the principles of
the "Holy Alliance" assured to Metternich the exertion of
his power as an inviolable right. "Might by Right" was the
heraldic motto he chose when he was made a Prince. In addition Emperor Franz conceded to him the unique preroga-

tive of including the Imperial escutcheon, that of Austria, in his own. He was the country's virtual regent to the same extent that Mussolini, a century after him, was the leader of Italy. Actuated by his unflinching desire to maintain the existing dynasty, Metternich was at the same time dictator of Europe.

This dictatorship actually was exerted by Metternich for several decades. It was a dictatorship in velvet gloves, in contrast to what dictatorships were to be a century later. History persisted long in surrounding it with the halo of a "Holy Alliance." This was due rather to the liberal tendencies of 19th-century historians than to the reported mystical inclinations of Czar Alexander, who is said to have been the inventor of this Christian Brotherhood. Madame Juliane von Krüdener, a partly German Baltic baroness and one of the Czar's romantic-political tea-table friends, was credited with having converted the Russian autocrat to the idea, thereby also indirectly convincing Metternich that the Rock of the Church was the most secure foundation of an already existing grouping of the Powers. There are a few grains of truth in that, though most of it is purely fictitious. In the summer of 1815, shortly after the resumption of the war against Napoleon, Czar Alexander was seen to be reading a recent publication whose unmistakably German author was one Baeder. The professorial title read: Concerning the need of a New and Closer Relationship Between Religion and Politics as a Consequence of the French Revolution. Metternich, too, had read it; he was a great reader and always amenable to intellectual suggestions—and also he knew who Madame Krüdener was. He refused, however, to take her obscure cacklings more seriously than they deserved, and as the years went on turned more and more pointedly from her—even against her. When she induced Swiss peasants to emigrate to Odessa in 1817 and published a "Newspaper for the Poor," he actually declared her to be a "Jacobine," to him a synonym for: "A danger to the State." He had a fundamental distaste for every kind of popular movement and decidedly no use for the religious communism preached by the visionary baroness. In his capacity of regent, quiet and order were all he demanded; and to safeguard them he felt sufficiently well protected by his carefully planned and developed "pentarchy," the League of Five Powers, including France—though, for the time being, that country was still held in check by an army of occupation. This army, commanded by Wellington, was garrisoned in the North of France and in the eastern part of Central France, until the Congress of Aachen. The first line of the Vauban belt of fortresses at the Swiss and Baden frontiers—the Maginot Line of those days—had to be razed. Altogether, however, Metternich was a rather magnanimous victor, doing his best to check the imperialistic tendencies of various Powers, especially of Germany. Alsace-Lorraine remained a part of France, no matter how much the King of Bavaria yearned for them. The war indemnity to be paid by the French was reduced to 700 million francs, a very small amount. The Peace of Paris was no *Pax Romana*, nor was it a Peace of Warsaw. It was a durable peace which lasted for more than half a century.

French culture, intellectual life, and art remained wholly unaffected. Metternich insisted, however, that some of the art treasures which Napoleon had stolen from the Italians be returned. If in the Venice of today the Bronze Horses again adorn the Church of St. Mark and the Winged Lion, the Piazetta, the City of the Lagoons is indebted to Metternich. To be sure, Venice again had become an Austrian province, so that Metternich's artistic feelings were not without a patriotic admixture calculated to further tourist traffic in the Italian Provinces of the Habsburg Empire.

All that was brain-work and, it must be admitted, the work of a good brain. In the meantime, however, what had become of the organ that Metternich somewhat exaggeratedly called his heart, the disposal of which he considered at all times his most personal privilege? This highly active heart lately had been rather inactive; politics, that exacting lady, effectively blocked any new sentiments, though the old ones were painfully shopworn. What still tied him to the Duchess of Sagan was but a love without love and, what was even worse, a love without respect. This woman who "always wanted what she did not do, and always did what she did not want" and who "loved as one dines"—that is, because one happens to have an appetite and has been invited —as late as the march upon Paris, had reminded him from time to time of the beautiful Berlin days of his youth. The fact, though, that no sooner had he arrived in Paris than he devoted himself with a restored faithfulness to Madame Junot does not speak well for the durability of a tie which snapped as soon as another attraction was within reach. Then, during the Congress of Vienna, the Sagan appeared again at his elbow; she took quarters at the house occupied also by Mme. Bagration; there was no sympathy between these two ladies.

But the Duchess of Sagan was not Metternich's only attraction in Congressional Vienna, nor did the Duchess live and love for him alone. She was at that time a woman in her late thirties, still beautiful but with a faint tendency towards the witch-like. This tendency became more marked as the years passed on. On one of her pictures her sharp slit of a mouth and her staring gaze under a somewhat wild-looking *coiffure* made her look like the personification of thirst. The beautiful Melusine, a German fairy-tale figure, is said to be sitting at the "Thirst Fountain" waiting for men. It would seem that Mme. Sagan was such a Melusine at the Thirst Fountain: forever in love, but never loving; forever drinking, but never satiated. In a letter Metternich subsequently wrote to Princess Lieven, the woman in whom he confided without restraint, the perennially loving State-Chancellor explained the strange association with icy precision. It is the tale of a love which, he claims, never was a love, and an indictment of the lady who had attracted him for ten years while never really captivating him. She had been married twice, the second time, as Metternich reports, to a man of her choice. But "the husband of her choice ceased to be her lover and ceased even to be her friend the day after the marriage."

After this dour experience she would have liked to have consoled herself with Metternich. "She wanted me as a lover, but I was unwilling," he tells his new mistress with a regrettable lack of chivalry. Then, Metternich continues, she became the sweetheart of an English agent by the name of King, the man whose secretary Metternich had had arrested by masked robbers, in 1813. This throws a strange light upon that political action, and also upon the machinations of the Princess who no doubt also dabbled in espionage. "A little while after this liaison," conscientiously continues the unconscientious reporter, "she wanted no more of him (meaning King) and returned to me." But again it was not an untroubled happiness; for, so reports the Keeper of the Records, "three days later she took a new lover," which was at least a bit precipitate. Nevertheless, the highly unsentimental love-affair took a rather surprising turn: "She was free and unhappy, I was free . . ."; being both free, they decided to join forces once more.

Metternich's justification is as curious as it is significant. It seems that this species of love—*"amour sans,"* to quote Stendhal—based on such sober premises, happily satisfied at least the female partner who evinced a desire for a stabilization of the affair, but without striking a responsive chord in the male breast. "I did not want to enter into very definite relations," says Metternich. Not wishing to aggravate the affair, and being a diplomat both in and out of the conference room, "I proposed a compromise. I asked her for six months of fidelity." The lady declined; or rather, she did not even bother to decline, for you might as well have asked France to do without Paris.

Nevertheless, Metternich was deeply implicated in this rather repulsive affair, and his frivolous heart placed him in the hazardous position of the man who is ready beforehand to condone a breach of faith which he knows is sure to occur. Their association was all the more reprehensible since the woman in the case entertained equally liberal views and had no illusions as to Metternich's faithfulness. The latter's liberality, on the other hand, was more a matter of theory than of practice. Of his partner-in-love he demanded faithfulness in spite of everything, and was even inclined to demand it of himself—without, however, succeeding.

These two created violent scenes. During the Congress when the world revolved around Vienna and Vienna itself revolved in waltz-time, and at the nearby idyllic health resort of Baden where the State-Chancellor sought to recover from the rigors of making world-history, there occurred any number of fearful altercations which considerably jeopardized his reputation not only as a man and husband, but also as a public character. It was probably then that Gentz wrote in his diary: *"cette maudite femme."* But Metternich recovered his senses before it was too late and considered what he owed to his exalted position. He turned his back upon an affair which he realized was beneath him, and said good-bye to his thirsty Melusine who, he reports, wanted to kill herself of grief. She thought better of it, however, and slaked her thirst at another fountain. The Austrian Ambassador in London, Count Paul Esterházy, was his chief's successor or—to amend what may be a rash statement—the successor of one of his chief's successors.

Metternich, a man of forty-two at the zenith of his successes as a statesman, found himself loveless and with a ravaged heart. Sober judges of his mode of living will point out that, after all, he was a married man and the father of seven children. That is quite true, and though he was not an affectionate husband, he surely was an affectionate father. But his love for his children and whatever affection they felt for him could not make up for the other love which seemed so indispensable to him. No matter how good a mother, wife, and keeper of her husband's seals Eleonore Kaunitz may have been, she never had been his sweetheart. Theirs was an aristocratic and prudent match, and while it may be regrettable that there are such marriages, one ought not to be surprised at seeing the partners to them drift apart.

Loveless, but not altogether loveless, as was proved on a winter's day of the year 1816. On that day a liveried lackey with a mourning-band on his arm presented himself to Metternich and, in the name of his recently deceased mistress, the beautiful Countess Julie Zichy, handed him a little casket. A strange casket that could set a poet to dreaming. It was wound round with a black silk ribbon and contained nothing but ashes—the charred remains of his own letters; and in the midst of the ashes lay the pieces of a broken ring. As Schubert sang: "The little ring in twain!"

Countess Julie Zichy, née Festetics, of the foremost Hungarian nobility, had been one of the most beautiful women in Vienna. At the time of the Congress, she was labeled the *"beauté céleste,"* in contrast to one of her more earthly rivals who was known as the *"Beauté* who gave you a delicious chill." She had borne a striking resemblance to the late Queen Louise of Prussia, and the widowed King of Prussia must have felt many a pang as he sat in the Countess' drawing-room and became entangled in the maze of his categorical infinitives. None of her social intimacies, not even those with a crowned head (which are only too apt to leave a stain or two), were able to affect her unimpeachable reputation. It was spotless. And yet there were those letters? And the ring?

These questions may have led to inexorable conclusions: where there are ashes of letters, there must have been letters at one time; and where there is a ring, there must have been a finger to wear it. In spite of all this circumstantial evidence, Julie Zichy would have been unanimously acquitted of any guilt or suspicion of guilt. Not only because she was a devout Catholic, and bore a blameless reputation, but also because, as Metternich himself says of her, "she was an angel who passed through my life without touching the earth." It is certain that she loved and wanted to reform him. Then the angel suddenly died, leaving instead of a pair of charred wings the ashes of a package of love-letters. As for

Metternich, it is certain he had sighed for her, and had done so all the more ideally, since at the same time a sensual, and nothing but a sensual, association had tied him to another woman. According to the laws of love's counterpoint, which secretly rules discreet affairs of the heart, it is understandable that in the embrace of the Duchess he yearned for something better. What could have been more delightful than the heavenly Julie, who so fascinatingly resembled his first dancing-partner at the Coronation Ball? It is a unique fact in his life that this was a truly platonic love.

It is illuminating to read in Gentz' diaries how the tragic demise of one of Vienna's most beautiful and honored women, one so closely connected with the all-powerful State-Chancellor, affected Vienna's social set, as heartless as it is everywhere else. On November 18th, 1816, Gentz conscientiously records with whom he had dinner: Czerniczeff, Count Hardenberg, Prince Ruffo, and a Madame Fekete. Having brought these names off, Gentz continues that, on November 19th, Pillat had called at half-past nine in the morning and brought him *"la terrible nouvelle de la mort de Julie Zichy."* Gentz is moved to the depths of his soul, and continues his entry by recording: *"Nous sommes allés aux ramparts voir la grand éclipse de soleil."* Gentz goes on to record the weather: *"Le temps . . . clair et beau."* There follows an entry of November 20th: *Allé chez le Prince de Metternich* (a daily visit there was one of Gentz' official functions) . . . *"arrangé avec lui l'expédition de mon manuscript."* On November 21st—was it the day of the beloved woman's funeral or the day before the funeral? —*"Diné chez Metternich. Après . . . longue conversation avec lui et le Baron Bartenstein sur les objets de finance."* And finally, on November 24th: *'Allé chez le Prince de Met-*

ternich pour le féliciter à son jour de nom." Life goes on, and those who die prematurely do so at their own risk.

So, after all, Metternich's life in those years may well be called loveless. In the throes of both a sensual and a spiritual passion, floating in their midst like Mohammed's coffin between heaven and earth, the mind of the man who at forty-five had reached the full stature of his personality, subconsciously yearned for something that, as a matter of fact, was close at hand. Perhaps it was so close at hand because he yearned so much for it. He longed for a woman who would be his match in every respect, for a great lady in whose company he could show himself, or not show himself, as the case might be, and who would encompass his whole being—an experience he had not yet been privileged to have. In contrast to his earlier pictures he had, figuratively speaking, shown women only his profile, having loved them without looking at them, or in looking past them. Now he was longing to find one—and was destined to find her—who, worthy to be contemplated both with the sensual and the spiritual eye, could hold her ground under the double scrutiny, would be equally desirable as a woman and as a lady, and to whom he could turn his full face, with all that life had made of it and with all the potentialities still charted on it.

Fate had held such a woman in store for him. It was Dorothy Lieven.

Grande Passion

CARLYLE, the hero worshipper, once said that from the way a man sang it could be determined how he would fight. In the case of Metternich, who was not a hero, but a statesman and minister, it was the other way around: from the way he administered his office, deductions could be made as to the manner in which he conducted his love-affairs. While he was not a pedant, he was a systematizer. Grunwald conscientiously records with the pleasure in classifications characteristic of the historian, that nine women played a part in the life of the Austrian State-Chancellor and "House, Court, and Conference Minister." The latter title was conferred upon him only somewhat later. Three of them were Frenchwomen: Constance de Caumont, Caroline Murat, and Laure Junot; three Russians: Madame Bagration, Madame Sagan, and Dorothy Lieven; three Austrians: Eleonore Kaunitz, Antoinette Leykam, and Melanie Zichy, the last two being his second and third wives, respectively. If we add that, of the three Austrian women, one was of German origin; another, Antoinette Leykam, partly Italian; and the third, Melanie Zichy, wholly Hungarian, the balance of power which was as dear to the heart of the statesman as it seems to have been to that of the lover is strengthened by a still broader European foundation, including with an all-embracing catholicity almost every European nation. Princess Lieven, too, was a cross-breed, née Benckendorff, half German and half Russian, and according to her intellectual habitus and her social attitude, rather more of an Englishwoman, than either a Russian or a German. The fact that there were nine of them—just as there were also nine Muses—may be a source of satisfaction to the humanistic scholar, forming as it does a connecting link with the classical age. Julie Zichy, to be sure, is not included in the number. She was the Tenth Muse, as exceptional in this respect as, it will be remembered, she was in the other.

Speaking of Muses, the question arises: to which of them may Dorothy Lieven be compared? She was not a Terpsichore, nor was she a Polyhymnia. Having lived in London for a quarter of a century, and as the wife of the Russian Ambassador there, repeatedly having influenced historical developments, she might be compared most aptly to Clio, the Muse of history. Dorothy herself did a good deal of recording, although it was mostly in the form of marginal remarks in the book of history. Through her, posterity learned of some of the most malicious opinions concerning her contemporaries. But then, who has a better right to be malicious than Clio? Is she not condemned to witness all the nonsense perpetrated by great men and leading personages—to witness and preserve it in voluminous books for the delectation and enlightenment of later generations? "Kings are big children," said Madame Lieven on one occasion.

Metternich made her acquaintance at the Congress of Aix-La-Chapelle, in the autumn of 1818, when he was forty-six years old. It was two years after the conclusion of the Second Paris Peace, in which the Allies, grown wiser by experience, had determined upon a military occupation of

Northern France by a policing force of mixed nationality, recruited from the victorious Powers and commanded by the Duke of Wellington. Since then France had behaved unexceptionably and, like a good loser, dutifully paid the war indemnity imposed upon her. Napoleon, dictator of St. Helena, confined himself to dictating his journal. The time had come to think of lifting the sanctions, and therefore it was decided to meet peacefully in Aix-la-Chapelle, the historic city of Charlemagne.

Present at the Congress were the crowned heads of Austria, Russia, and Prussia, and delegations from a number of other countries, including their staffs and ladies. It would be cheerless, indeed, if such Congresses took place without the presence of ladies; "horrible," probably breathed Metternich, at the mere thought of it.

One of these ladies, not exactly the most beautiful, but as it appeared later, the most interesting, was Countess Dorothy Lieven, wife of the Russian Ambassador to London. She was one of the last to arrive in Aix-la-Chapelle, long after the sovereigns.

Of the latter, the King of Prussia had been the first to arrive in the old German coronation town. He had a rather cool reception. The town did not relish its new name of Aachen, and the population had not yet taken cognizance of its subsequent Prussianization. The King was displeased at the indifferent welcome, but in his autocratic way managed to put things right again on the following day. He drove to meet the Emperors of Russia and Austria, who had not yet arrived, and got into their carriage. Sitting at the side of these considerably more popular rulers, he made his second entry into the town, and affably acknowledged the cheers which he determined were for him also—a little trick arising out of Prussian over-sensitiveness and a desire for self-assertion.

Metternich, in high spirits, came over from Johannisburg, the new estate which Emperor Franz had but recently presented to him. The old Prince, Clemens' father, had died a short time before, and the new head of the house had been festively greeted by his subjects—there were such things in those days. He had set foot in his castle for the first time and for the first time had acted as host. His illustrious guest had been the Emperor of Austria who, being en route to Aix-la-Chapelle, had invited himself to dinner at Johannisburg.

As was his habit, Metternich traveled without his wife. At times it was her health that kept her at home, at times it was the children's. All of them suffered from the affection of the chest to which Princess Eleonore, too, was to succumb at a comparatively young age. In the first years of their married life, two of the seven children Eleonore had presented to him had died. The others died later, five of them before he had even reached his sixtieth year. The graveyard atmosphere of his home which continuously surrounded the vivacious man was now further aggravated by the death of his father. The bereavement may have been an added reason to prevent Princess Metternich from accompanying her husband, or for his not having asked her. Family mourning may have served as a reasonable excuse. As for Metternich himself, this mourning in no way prevented him from taking a most active part in the festivities and entertainments provided in Aachen. No doubt he would have pleaded that participation in these affairs was part of a diplomat's and statesman's official duties.

There was no dearth of such entertainments, nor did the town of Aachen fail to show its earnest intention to make

things as pleasant for its guests as possible. The famous Cata-
lani sang, the most popular bands dispensed music from the
early afternoon until far into the night, and two aerial acro-
bat ladies presented their sensational feats daily. There was
also a four-year-old child prodigy, playing—a most fetching
contrast—the bass-viol. "You can imagine the number of
wrong notes," Metternich wrote ironically to his wife. He
also mentioned, more or less tactfully, how boring social life
and activities were in the prominent diplomatic drawing-
rooms. "Nothing but women between fifty and sixty," he
stated peevishly.

He finally withdrew altogether from the official bustle,
preferring to play whist at home and to invite a few selected
guests who responded to his summons with alacrity. All this
was not particularly exciting; if the Congress of Aachen had
meant to rival that of Vienna, it was far from successful. At
last, however, Dorothy Lieven arrived in Aachen, and everything was changed. Not all at once, of course.

It is a strange fact, not lacking in piquancy, that this
world-famous pair of lovers disliked each other at the first
glance. The lady who was of the exacting type, as she herself admitted, found the Prince was putting on too many
airs and was not amiable enough. For his part, he took so
little notice of her that he did not even recall having met her
casually in London four years before, a fact of which she was
careful not to remind him—possibly she did not remember
the incident either. Dorothy Lieven was a great lady and a
great snob. The one does not necessarily preclude the other.
Used to intercourse with kings, lately acquired princely
titles must have failed to make a very deep impression on
her. On the other hand, she was not particularly attractive.
Everything in her appearance was somewhat too elongated:

her limbs, her neck, and her nose. Narrow, tall, and exces-sively slender—hopelessly thin, her plump contemporaries called her—she was outwardly what the North-Germans called a "split lath." Metternich did not seem at first to be greatly attracted by the lanky lady. But it turned out that the very novelty of her appearance, which in the beginning repelled him, was his undoing. The fact that they had dif-ficulties in finding the way to each other, cemented their friendship all the more securely in later days. An old experi-ence, this. Great passions have small beginnings.

Dorothy Lieven was not accustomed to being overlooked. She felt nettled about it and threw out a hint to Nesselrode, her compatriot and colleague of equal rank, to take Metter-nich to task. Nesselrode did not fail to remonstrate with Metternich, to ask for the reason for his lack of amiability, and to point out graciously that his behavior had been the subject of general comment. He said it without reproach and with a certain diplomatic smile on his lips. "Oh, really?" replied Metternich apologetically; he was very sorry and would be charmed to meet the Lievens more informally at the Nesselrode *ménage*.

The meeting took place. They actually became ac-quainted with each other only then, for now their conversa-tion had the background that had been lacking the first time. The background was furnished by the fact that Doro-thy Lieven *wished* to be noticed by Metternich. What she had done had been but a little snobbish maneuver, a co-quetry *par ricochet,* a pretended offense calculated to draw attention to herself. Metternich would not have been a dip-lomat had he not been able to see through it. The question was: for what purpose did she want to attract his attention? In her capacity of woman, or Ambassadress? In putting these questions to himself, he probably looked at her with different eyes and began to see her in a different light. No longer did he see her somewhat scrawny neck and generously proportioned ears, which the ladies of the diplomatic set never failed to mention when referring to the arrogant bean-pole. He looked more deeply into her eyes, which he noticed were quite beautiful, and more curiously upon her lips, which he decided were entirely kissable. The young woman—being thirty-three, she was young compared to him—began to occupy his mind. His imagination was not yet involved, but already his intellect and appetite. In the course of the conversation it soon became apparent that she was intelligent and witty, although her wit was not of the kindly variety. As for that, Metternich was also far from being a charitable man, though he was to develop along these lines during his association with this woman. He, too, had a poor opinion of his dear fellow-beings and was given to making sport of their weaknesses. More important was the fact that she had a sound judgment and knew how to express it in words. She was certainly a clever talker. But she was clever also in another and rarer art: she could be silent and listen attentively to what others had to say to her. Hers was not the disconcerting way of some ladies of the world who will ask a question and, without waiting for a reply, address another question to someone else. What her partner had to say was, on the contrary, of the utmost interest and importance to Dorothy Lieven; she absorbed it eagerly with her largish ears—perhaps it was that habit that had made them grow so generously. She certainly was no oyster, living self-sufficiently between its ossified valves, proudly content in the knowledge that it harbored a pearl.

In every affair of the heart there is a decisive moment

which most aptly may be compared to that fraction of a second when a plane, rushing and bumping along the ground, suddenly takes off and begins to fly. Nothing is more difficult to catch than this transition from one medium to another, and the pilot will be the last man to consult about it. His attention is riveted to his motors, and he neither hears or sees anything else. A disinterested passenger, however, provided his ears are sharp, may notice how between pulse-beats the miracle happens. The landing-wheels suddenly turn in empty space, the world is left behind, and the ascent begins.

The Congress, whose sessions were little more than social gatherings, soon came to an end. The concerts became more boring all the time and, to escape them, excursions were made into the beautiful autumnal countryside. On one occasion the whole company drove to the nearby Spa and stayed over-night. Metternich, who was of the party, sat in one carriage and Countess Lieven—she was still a Countess then—in another. But at a certain moment—nobody knows exactly where and when—he climbed into hers, for no other reason probably than that he felt bored by his own princely company. On the return drive, the following morning, he invited her to share his coach, to reciprocate for having been permitted to ride in hers the day before. Sometime between these two drives, the landing-wheels left firm ground, a fact which is also verifiable indirectly. In a gaily-worded letter which Metternich wrote to his good Leonore on the following morning, he praised the magic of the autumnal landscape between Aachen and Spa. He grew quite rhapsodical about it and called it *"charmant."* "You old landscape enthusiast!" the clever Leonore may have thought to herself.

From then on things proceeded swiftly, as if they were

actually sped on wings. On October 28th he paid his first visit to the interesting lady, or, as he expressed it semi-jocularly in a confidential letter to her a month later in his best ministerial style, he sat at her feet for an hour and found he had chosen a good place. To speak more soberly, she pleased him and he decided to court her. Before he knew it, he was caught, ensnared, in love. The largish ears, the pointed nose, the scrawny neck, and the excessively high forehead no longer existed. He only saw the flattering look of the black eyes, the rich silky hair, and the kissable lips which so delighted him with their amusing talk. Her fundamentally uncharitable mind sparkled and scintillated for his benefit. She was amusing and caused him to be amusing, too. The great world, the world of the great ones, formed a link between them—the world they both knew, smiled at, and mastered. She told him tales of the old English King who had been mad for nine years. He was blind too and the happiest man in his kingdom. Restlessly he wandered through his old castle, held converse with shadows, played the organ, and—happy man!—immersed in his dreams, took no notice of the present. In the course of these nine years he had grown a beautiful white beard that reached far down over his chest. The Duke of York thought it made him look like a venerable rabbi. Metternich laughed. Then he ceased laughing and cast a sidelong, searching look at her. If the Duke of York used such comparisons in his conversations with her, he must have been paying court or perhaps even making love to her, he thought ruefully, while the elongated lady opposite him continued to prattle gaily. Metternich had not been born yesterday.

But he, too, was able to spin some tales. He recalled his visit with Napoleon at the Marcolini Palace in Dresden, in June, 1813, five years before. It was then that the talkative lady became silent all of a sudden. There was a light in her big eyes, and the mocking spirits that were forever hovering about her lips were at rest. Her whole spirit was crystallized in her lovely mouth. Never did she seem more kissable.

"She loved me for the dangers I had passed, and I loved her that she did pity them," says Othello.

There could be no question of pity on the part of Countess Lieven. Hers was too entertaining a spirit, and Metternich too much of a favorite of fortune to have any claim to pity. But otherwise, that was about how it happened. By his tales, he won her, as Othello won Desdemona, and Aeneas, Dido.

How did matters proceed? They proceeded as they were bound to and ought not to have proceeded. It became increasingly obvious that the Congress was nearing its end, and the Lievens who had been the last to arrive seemed among the first who wished to depart. They did not at first go beyond Brussels, where the Empress Dowager, Czar Alexander's mother, expected them. It was quite impossible to get out of the invitation which Maria Feodorovna had issued when passing through Aachen. Dorothy was her godchild, and Dorothy's mother had been her lady-in-waiting. When the latter died, the exalted lady had taken charge of the young orphan, had her educated at a convent, and finally married her to Count Lieven. Thanks to her, Dorothy was also in the good books of her son, Czar Alexander.

Metternich was loath to see his new-found friend—"my friend of eight days, my friend for life," as he soon apostrophized her—depart from a circle which had formed quickly, only to disintegrate as quickly. On the other hand, he was probably duly impressed by the fact that she was so clearly in the good graces of the Russian Court. Would the lady deign to return from her Imperial surroundings into the lowlands of the Congress of Aachen? In this dilemma, torn between the hope of winning her, and the fear of seeing her slip away from him—a situation, all in all, which for an experienced woman and a mature man in quest of love could hardly be more fraught with fascination and perspective—Metternich vented his feelings a few hours before her departure by writing her a letter—a midnight letter. How could there be a great love without a midnight letter?

"It is impossible to see you go away without telling you what I feel. The history of *our* life is centered in so few moments. I have found you but to lose you. The past, the present, and perhaps the future are contained in these few words. The day I see you again will be one of the most beautiful of my life.

"I have ended one period of that life in less than eight days. If I did not know myself I would say I was dreaming. For me, a person is either everything or nothing. My soul is not capable of entertaining a half sentiment or a half thought. I have passed several weeks near you. I have scarce spoken to you, and yet you are today part of my existence. That which tempts most men is without effect upon me. I do not know if I need more than others, but I do know that my needs are different. The day when I saw that my thoughts met yours, when I could no longer doubt that you understood me, that your mind and above all your heart proceeded in the direction I regard as mine, that day I felt I could become your friend, that day was enough to convince me that I was not deceiving myself in loving you. I feel constrained to confide to you what you have probably already guessed. I say nothing here that you do not already know, but I must say it again to you, my friend of eight days, my friend for life!

Perhaps we shall meet again some day. I shall be the same then as I am now. If there are but few associations that satisfy me, those that do never end. Remember me kindly, and perhaps more than kindly, and try to feel regrets, though they can never rise to the heights of mine. I have neither the hope nor the right to demand that one should give what I am ready to give. Permit me at least the consolation of saying that had you known me better your sentiments for me would have been different from those you are now entertaining. I am hanging on, you see, to whatever can save me from frightful pain. The shipwrecked man does not choose the plank that is to save him, but seizes what comes within his reach—and drowns!"

It is not known how Dorothy Lieven answered this rather diffuse letter. It is not unlikely that her reply was what diplomats call a "dilatory" reply; presumably she was still somewhat hesitant. Certain it is that after eight days in Brussels she did return to witness the Congress' conclusion in Aachen. Now was the time for the decisive sessions, presided over by the Czar. Metternich was the leading figure in the debates and suddenly had his hands full. That was like meat and drink to Countess Lieven. It will be seen repeatedly that she was almost powerless to resist such men. "I love historical events," she admitted in one of her letters. Before she knew it she had become such an historical event in Prince Metternich's life, and he in hers.

There is no room for doubt here. The Austrian State-Chancellor himself furnished whatever information might be desired in a letter he penned four weeks after his midnight epistle. He did it in his pedantic manner and with that touch of bureaucratic preciseness which affected even his love-affairs—he had to see it in the acts, black on white, before he was ready to believe it. When it had happened, and how she had come to him—"*Quand tu es venu dans ma loge. . . .*"—he assured her with seeming frankness, he could not recall (though surely he had not forgotten it). He continued to tease her in the manner usual between lovers: "*Tu as eu la fièvre, mon amie, tu m'as appartenue!*"

This "*loge*" in which she became his, has made writers of the past half century (Metternich's exchange of letters has not been known longer) shudder and dream. They thought of a *loge,* a box in a theater, and never grew tired of retailing the delectable story to their readers who crossed themselves lustfully before such an abyss of wantonness. Prince Metternich, Plenipotentiary of the Emperor of Austria, and the wife of the Russian Ambassador—in a box! As a matter of fact, it was not as bad as all that. Strachey in his excellent and enlightening essay on Princess Lieven stresses the fact that "*loge*" is used here in the sense of "*logement*," representing the somewhat antiquated and possibly incorrect French sometimes found in the letters of the Austrian statesman. What he meant, at any rate, was his apartments: the house he had rented in Aachen from Mademoiselle Brammertz for the duration of the Congress. That he paid for the magnificent *logement,* where he first received Countess Lieven's visit when she "had the fever," a rental of 20,000 francs, or rather permitted the Austrian State to pay it, is another matter and belongs to another chapter: the chapter containing the Rastatt expenditures of Metternich's father, late lamented but still very much alive in his son's blood. *Loge* or *logement:* no matter! The State bore the expense.

After that feverish first visit everything developed quite logically. While the Congressional clearing-off work in Aachen had already begun, the Lievens once more went to Brussels to see Empress Maria Feodorovna. It may be assumed that Dorothy had promised the Empress Dowager, who still held Court there, a second visit. Perhaps, too, she was prompted by her cleverness which made her shun unnecessary talk in Aachen and spare the feelings of her husband who fortunately had not noticed anything yet. The little maneuver no doubt also suited Metternich's book, as shown by a letter he wrote shortly thereafter. Nothing was farther from his mind, he declared with remarkable audacity, than to attempt to disturb a matrimonial peace. He gave his sweetheart the devilishly logical advice—which, to be sure, makes one wince a bit—to be good, very good, exceptionally good to her husband (*"sois bonne, douce, excellente pour lui."*) A woman like Dorothy Lieven, used to reading diplomatic correspondence, had no difficulty in understanding at once what he meant. She was the mother of two children by her husband. A few months later, from London, she advised him of the expected advent of a third.

On her second visit to Brussels, she did not remain alone very long. Four days, and her new Lothario found it impossible to stand the sudden solitude and bleakness of Mademoiselle Brammertz' house any longer. He therefore decided that a little excursion to Brussels would be just the thing. Perhaps there were some things he still had to discuss with his illustrious Russian colleague.

This trip naturally could not be kept secret. The conservative *Journal des Débats,* immediately reporting it to its readers, adding well-manneredly and conscientiously as behooved such a journal, that the reason for the Austrian chancellor's trip was not known.

Dorothy, who was fond of laughing and making others laugh—perhaps not including her husband—must have chuckled to herself as she read the brief item in the daily Congressional report. Nevertheless, her days in Brussels were unfortunately numbered. Her husband being meticulous about attending to his official duties, a week later found her back again in London, while Metternich accompanied the Duke of Wellington on a visit to the battle field of Waterloo. Out of a love-affair he found his way back to history.

A Diary in Letters

I F Metternich's affair with Countess Lieven had been no more than an escapade, there would not be so much to say about it now, so many years later; but it was much more and went much deeper. Metternich had not only won himself a charming sweetheart in Aachen; what is infinitely more, he had found a woman to whom he could wholly disclose himself and who, while she demanded all of his personality, also induced him wholly to develop his personality. He had a wife who was not a sweetheart to him, and a sweetheart whom he would not have wanted for a wife. Like every man at a certain stage of development, he longed for a synthesis of all that was most desirable, and to become wholly one with a woman.

His association with Julie Zichy was perhaps an attempt in that direction. But being a sensuous as well as a spiritual lover, like his fellow-countryman Faust, Metternich had lost a great deal of time and missed much happiness between longing for a distant love, and enjoying one that was all too near; between an angel who floated through his life "without touching the earth" and a beautiful Melusine, sitting forever yearningly at the "thirst fountain," who could not disengage herself from the earth. Now he had both, or could at least imagine a few years, that he had both: a partner who was humanly his equal and a charming mistress. Head and heart—or what is usually meant by the two terms—were united in a mystical marriage. All the censers sent forth their fragrance, all the candles were burning. It is significant that from the very beginning and throughout many years, they exchanged letters; it is still more significant that of Metternich's innumerable love-letters only those exchanged between him and Dorothy Lieven have been preserved. Chance had no share in this circumstance. An element of spirituality was one of the original admixtures of this association; and it was its spirituality that preserved it. It has come down to our day in the preserving alcohol of their correspondence.

The fascinating point about this written dialogue lies in the fact that it is really no dialogue; to be exact, it consists of two diaries, each one of which, to be sure, was intended for the eyes of but one person, before posterity was permitted to peruse them. Their character is further emphasized by the fact that the entries do not correspond chronologically; only when one party has finished does the other begin to talk.

Metternich had the first word. The hundred and more sheets that followed upon that very first midnight letter, when he threw himself at Dorothy's feet, all have been preserved. Metternich's letters extend until July, 1819; hers begin in January, 1820. Consequently, they differ greatly in tone. The lady is silent about the first phase of her love; the man's words are prompted almost wholly by it, by what he calls "the most important relationship of my life." Thus written on the 27th of April, 1819, at the Austrian State-Chancellery! Another straggling little sentence, written three months later by the man who in the meantime had been traveling and had just returned from Italy, is dated at Karlsbad: "I love you at Karlsbad as at the foot of Vesuvius; on the ruins of Paestum as on the Champs Élysées." The short eloquent sentence comprehensively tells us all that the preceding midnight effusions expressed more volubly. It is characteristic that almost all of them were actually written at the ghostly hour, when quiet reigned in the State-Chancellery and only its chief was at his desk, "working."

It is to be assumed that Dorothy Lieven's first-year letters were destroyed. Why preserve them, since the man's flaming passion continued to flow immortally in his letters? *Ne bis idem!* By expunging everything else she coolly restricted her epistolary diary to its matter-of-fact and chronological contents: a detailed description of English Court society in the twenties of the last century. She kept this up conscientiously to please the friend of her heart. Because of family considerations, publication was delayed until barely three years ago. As far as posterity was concerned, this fact placed her at a chronological disadvantage; Metternich's love-letters, as far as they have been preserved, have been known these fifty years, while hers limp unfeelingly after, as if they had nothing to tell us and were quite unimportant. Haughty beyond death, she quite disregarded this imputation and permitted her letters to speak for themselves. Her diary, in letters, is actually the more important of the two. It explains the woman, explains the relationship, and at the same time throws a spotlight upon the political and historical landscape within which the book—for a book it is—came into being.

Habent sua fata libelli is a truth well known to publishers; but at times even authors are conversant with it. When, in 1827, the former Countess Dorothy Lieven, advanced since to the rank of a Princess, again held in her hand the letters she had once or twice a week for seven years sent to the "Grand Inquisitor of Europe," she turned into a literary Grand-Inquisitress herself. The sentimental passages, and those that were not exactly intended for perusal by her husband, who either pretended to be or actually was quite unsuspecting, were ruthlessly expunged. Scissors in one hand and pencil in the other, she neatly transferred to a number of exercise-books, such as her children used at school, whatever she did not wish to keep from posterity; these politically dangerous exercise-books then were securely locked up in the family vault. They did not see the light of day again until ninety years later. It was in 1917, in the midst of the World War, when their grave yard peace at a castle in Livonia was suddenly disturbed. They were smuggled from the occupied territory to Berlin, whence they found their way to London, in 1936. Judging correctly that, far from endangering the reputation of the long-deceased seductive ancestress, the letters would rather tend to rehabilitate her in the eyes of posterity, permission was given by her descendants, Prince and Princess Lieven, for the publication of the yellowed documents. Thus the European literature of memoirs was enriched by a sparkling work which will be able honorably to maintain its place on the shelves of book-lovers, between the letters of Horace Walpole and those of Lord Lytton.

Dorothy Lieven, a clever woman, had correctly foreseen the fate of her book when she wrote down its many paragraphs for the man she loved.

"By their fruits shall ye know them," says the Bible. The fruits by which their love was to become known were their

letters. It was not before Clemens had reached Vienna, and
Dorothy, London, that we were told what caused these two
people to find the way to each other in Aachen. More than
anything else, it was a certain vivacious gaiety that formed
the original connecting link. She praises him in one of her
letters for his "inexhaustible fund of gaiety," adding mer-
rily: "You are the most good-humored man I have ever met;
and I am fond of laughing." There we have one of the
threads of the tapestry: the mutual enjoyment of a good
hearty laugh. That it was a mutual enjoyment will become
clear instantly even to those who merely thumb Dorothy's
letters. There is nothing more amusing than her manner of
observing with ever-watchful eyes, the Court and society in
which she moved, and her way of transforming into gay
words the message her eyes conveyed to her clever brain.
It must be considered, too, that her writing was done with
the hardly disguised intention of keeping the ruler of her
heart in good humor. In that mood she used to address him
half familiarly and half mockingly, and with an implied
Court curtsy, as: *"Mon Prince."*

Metternich, while inclined towards laughter, was by no
means a "laughing diplomat." To be sure, he had succeeded
at an audience granted him in Rome, in 1815, in making
even the Pope laugh—a fact on which, among other things,
he prided himself not a little. When Metternich had finished
laughing, however, he liked to get to the bottom of things
seriously. It was the German in him that prompted this
probing, and he was apt even to overdo his thoroughness.
"I am a singular being," he would meditate; or ponder:
"Love for me is conscience." In an attempt to fathom the
deeper meaning of their consonance he might declare: "You
are as a woman what I am as a man" (which, as a matter of

fact, was true); or, bordering upon the metaphysical: "What a field to explore—that of inner life!"; or, quite metaphysically: "Of all the realities, the strongest for me is love" —an expression which forms a pretty contrast to the aged Talleyrand's last definition of love: "A reality in the sphere of the unreal." Metternich also made the profoundly simple statement: "You are full of me"; he was naïve enough to admit it, and it was a fact he appreciated most of all in her.

Dorothy was not so thorough as Metternich; nor had she his warmth of feeling. It is a strange fact that in Metternich's love-letters a certain trait began to assert itself for the first time; a trait which otherwise came to the surface only by way of his paternity—he was the loving father of a large number of children—or in letters of condolence: his warmheartedness. As for Dorothy Lieven, she does not pretend to anything she does not possess. It is not unlikely that in the destroyed series of her first year's letters, while still much under the impression of what had happened in Aachen, her passion flamed up more hotly. In the second series, the one at our disposal, love has become little more than a faint echo, but a melodious one. Though she refuses to analyze and ponder like Metternich, preferring to relate and banter, there are nevertheless instances, few and far between, of faintly stirring memories; all the more charming when they do occur. A year after Aachen, for instance, she wrote to Metternich from the castle of some friends: "Last night again, upon re-entering my apartment, I remained for a while on the balcony of my bedroom. I heard footsteps in the room next to mine. I do not know to which of the party I have been assigned as neighbor. Had you come to Lady Jersey's, the room would probably have been yours. You would have been on my balcony, dear friend. We would have been saying sweet words to each other very softly. I closed my balcony door. I lay down. I dreamed, and the dream was delightful. I saw you; we talked, talked a great deal. Fearing that we might be overheard, you took me upon your knee so that you could whisper to me. I felt your heart beat, my dear Clemens. I felt it so strongly under my hand that I awoke. It was my heart responding to yours."

In this letter, which ought to adorn a collection of the world's most beautiful love-letters, one passage is highly significant: ". . . we talked, talked a great deal." From the beginning it was a love which indulged in a great deal of talking. That is why it was able to overcome years of separation.

The lines quoted are from Dorothy's only love-letter in an ocean of gossip. She sailed and fished in that sea endlessly. The law-suit of Queen Caroline, as unhappy as she was fat, whom George IV could not bear and wanted to divorce at any cost, furnished almost a year's material for her pen, for the disgraceful divorce suit which divided the whole of England into two hostile camps dragged on interminably. She sided with the King, an attitude which as the wife of the Russian Ambassador she felt in duty bound to assume. The people, however, to whom Dorothy referred only as "the mob," were in the other camp, and thus arose all kinds of untoward little incidents concerning which she reported good-humoredly to Vienna. Repeatedly when she went for a drive or to the House of Lords, where the infamous trial took place, her carriage was stopped by the "mob" giving "Three cheers for the Queen!" and demanding that her footmen take off their hats and she join in the cheering—which she bravely refused to do. Things finally came to such a pass that placards and handbills told the Londoners: "The Queen forever—the King in the river!" People who refused to join in the cheering were shot by the rabble. Nevertheless, the trial dragged on and on; and with all its tragedy, it finally became so boring that the fat Queen passed the time by playing backgammon in one of the rooms adjoining the trial hall where witnesses were examined. On another occasion she attended the court's session and at the examination of one of the Crown's witnesses uttered the words: "Oh, Theodore!"; that, and nothing else. In the end the autocratic King, much against the will even of his own Cabinet, succeeded in obtaining his longed-for divorce. The Queen's name was stricken from the Prayer Book. She died soon after.

Hardly had Princess Lieven finished describing for her friend's entertainment a religious procession to St. Paul's in honor of the Queen, which the King watched furiously from a hiding place behind a window-curtain of his palace, when she began to draw a word-picture of the fantastically ugly face of the new Spanish Ambassadress: an immense nose atop a huge mouth, making Dorothy wonder why the one had not long since swallowed the other. She continued by poking fun at the unfortunate woman's absent-minded dwarfish husband who at a party failed to recognize the Duke of York and asked him repeatedly and most affably to be seated, whereas the laws of Court etiquette demanded that he himself, get up from his seat and remain standing. There was also the Ambassador's sister, a Madame de Princeteau, one of Louis XVIII's discarded mistresses. Being at loose ends, she had developed a tendency towards fainting fits while at social gatherings. This made it necessary to cut the strings of her corsets, so that her beautiful shoulders could be duly admired. They were truly beautiful, stated matter-of-fact Dorothy, and fainting spells were rather becoming to her; but three in a row was overdoing the thing. In another letter she stirred him up against Naples where, for a change, a revolution had broken out. "Metternich must march!" she reports the Duke of Wellington as having said, while the words, of course, represented but her own opinion, and she had used the Duke merely as a shield. "Metternich *will* act!" she says her answer to the Austrian Ambassador, Count Paul Esterházy, had been; "he will act—and he will act energetically and promptly, I thought of saying, as your Ambassador should have said of his own accord."

She also tried to hurt the prestige of the Ambassador who, although he was her political rival, or perhaps because of it, tried to pay court to her. She said to him peremptorily: "I do not like to see men of thirty-four behave like boys!" Then again, she might try to flatter her distant lover by saying to him: "I aspire to the honor of being, for one moment, the rival of re-united Europe." Again, she contradicted him in a political controversy and closed her argument most charmingly with the words: "So it would seem that I am right and you are wrong—if it were not that you are always right, *mon Prince!*" Though enjoying references to "the mob," she was inclined to pose as a liberal on other occasions. Speaking in a serious vein and trying to envisage his and Europe's future, in the 19th century, she said: "In forty years' time the whole of Europe will be constitutional. You will hold out to the last; but you will be included!" If here she pretended to be more liberal than she actually was, Metternich, too, just to please her, occasionally made similar pretenses. In one of his letters he analyzed—he liked to analyze when talking to women, but not when it was a question of marching on Naples—the problem of society marriages as he saw it from the standpoint of his own experiences. A girl of eighteen is married, he explained, "starting at a point where she ought to end." But what was the poor thing to do, seeing that "she lived under an autocratic régime?" a fact which the letter-writing dictator, conscious of writing to Dorothy Lieven, deplored pharisaically. Satirizing himself, he added: "You see, I *am* a liberal!"

At such moments a certain devilry in Metternich's character came to the surface. The triple "f" of his school-days was in evidence. He was rather an amusing drawing-room devil, however, somewhat on the order of Molnar's "Devil," who talked to the world through Metternich's mouth. That is how the Italian, Benedetti, painted him in a portrait during the Lieven period: one eyebrow raised and one corner of his mouth drawn up; a painting that was possibly more an act of Italian revenge than a portrait. It quite suits that picture that Metternich, in the heyday of his love, and while another man's wife made him supremely happy, should parade solemnly like a devil in a priest's cassock, or like an Austrian Machiavelli by penning the words: "The principles of religion and of the family in Europe must be protected, and the moral authority with which Divine Providence has invested the governments, serves this exalted purpose."

Princess Lieven was a political woman, a fact attested to by the future course of her life. Metternich was not her last prime minister; there were others after him, and finally Guizot. She lived and loved for politics, as all the world knew. What was not known, however, until the publication of her letters, in 1938, and what throws an entirely new and illuminating light upon her association with Metternich, is the circumstance that this lady politician was also a writer of sorts—a writer of a special variety, to be sure, in which connection a few words may not be amiss.

There are literary writers and unliterary ones, just as some people are able to write quite correctly and to express themselves very learnedly in writing, without in the least being authors. One of these unliterary writers, perhaps the greatest of them all was St. Simon, the mirror of the era of Louis XIV. Another one was the Englishman, Pepys, author of diaries in the 17th century. St. Simon, who was a grand seigneur and who disliked intensely to be considered a professional author, said of himself in one of his writings and not without pride: "I write like a cheese-borer." He actually did at times, especially when he gave free rein to his pen. And yet, what a wealth of imagination, what sound judgment, and knowledge of humanity, lay underneath that badly dressed and frequently disarranged full-bottomed wig of his style.

It must not be assumed that the dainty and well-mannered Dorothy Lieven was of the same high rank. Nevertheless, she may be considered a skirted little St. Simon at the Court of George IV of England. She saw everything, she knew everything, and also knew how to write in words from which there breathed a very decided personality. That, however, makes a writer; the unliterary ones are at times the better of the two.

That Princess Lieven belonged in the category of the unliterary writers was further proved by the fact that she scarcely read anything, although she was not so inordinately proud of it as are some of the analphabets of the trade in our day. She had not read much, but at any rate the best. She knew her Shakespeare, Walter Scott, and she even knew the third canto of Byron's "Childe Harold" by heart. Metternich took this trick over from her later, and used it to dazzle his guests. She knew, above all, the letters of Madame de Sévigné, whom she held in great esteem throughout her life. She thus resembled, let us say, a writer of comedies who, of all comic literature, knew only Molière—by no means the worst schooling for a writer of comedies!

Of the few masters she had read, Madame Lieven learned only what was in tune with her own aristocratic character. Aristocracy in the noble sense of the word is, above all, simplicity. In this respect Dorothy Lieven, although considerably less of an adept in writing than Metternich, is much more literary than he, since he frequently becomes volubly entangled in the brambles of his phrases and metaphors.

How simply, for instance, does she tell her great friend the history of her marriage in one of her first letters. No use citing a passage or two of the little letter; best to quote it as a whole. It reads:

"I have been married eighteen years today. How joyfully I left my convent, how delighted I was with my beautiful clothes, how well my wedding-dress suited me, how pleased I was with my success when the Empress put some of her diamonds on me and took me in to see Emperor Paul, who in turn led me into his drawing-room to show me to his Court! I should have liked to get married every day, and I thought about everything except that I was taking a husband."

Not a word too much, and not one too little, which is proof of the born writer. At the same time the letter also contains an apology for what occurred later, and undoubtedly was meant to contain it. What can be the upshot of a marriage contracted so unsuspectingly? Children, at best, whose legitimacy is beyond any doubt.

Another such apology—an apology without commentary; and that, too, is aristocratic—is contained in a letter she wrote from Brighton, in March, 1822, in the fourth year of her love. She and a woman friend were invited to Court which was held for a short time in Brighton. The King was ill, the woman friend was bored to death, and voiced her surprise that Dorothy could stand it. Referring to it in a letter, she wrote: "But, really, the fact is that I observe scenes worthy of the finest comedy." (From these words speaks the writer who, when in company, has an entirely different idea of a good time than those who go into company simply to have a good time.)

Opening her heart to Metternich, she inserted a personal recollection. It had been here in Brighton, in the summer of 1818, that she had once wanted to take her own life. "My husband had brought me here for my health. I was quite well physically, but I was desperately depressed." The third canto of Byron's "Childe Harold" had just appeared, and accompanied her. In it Byron said "things of fearful beauty" about death by drowning. She read the book sitting on a rock in the ocean and waiting for the flood to come and submerge the rock. How about waiting long enough, thought the young woman, to prove to oneself whether or not Byron's poetical description was true? "I waited on the rock a good half hour, my mind made up; but the tide did not rise. When at last it did, my madness ebbed as the water advanced. In short, I did not wait long enough even to get my feet wet, and I did right. . . . Since then, whenever I am in trouble, I have only to think of my little adventure to put myself in good humor, or at least to make myself appreciate that pleasant thing—existence." What she did not mention, not even by a single word, is the fact that three months before going to Aachen she was in a state of mind so deplorable that it explained and justified everything—even Aachen.

On another occasion she covered four pages of a letter to tell him the story of a youthful love, which reads like one of Alfred de Musset's gaily-sad romantic comedies. She was only eleven years old and already someone wanted to marry her, a circumstance in keeping with common usage then. Her suitor was the young Count Elmpt. Dorothy's mother, then still alive, favored the match, and so the small girl felt obliged, as she writes, to fall in love with the little gentleman. She did it so thoroughly that she actually became ill with love. It seems therefore that even then, hers was a passionate nature, a fact which Metternich recognized twenty years later, when he wrote teasingly: *"Tu as eu la fièvre."* But her mother died, and the Empress who assumed her place had made quite another choice for little Dorothy. She was sent to a convent, while a quarrel the young Count had had with the Grand-Duke Constantine was used as a pretext for banishing him from Court and keeping him at a safe distance from Dorothy. The young girl, however, in a fever of love, was unwilling to give up her Romeo, and wrote him the tenderest of love letters, to which he answered with equal fervor. As always in such cases, an indulgent and conniving governess played the intermediary. One day, though, the Empress appeared unannounced in the room of the little convent-pupil, burst open cupboards and drawers, and found in the governess' clothes-press the love letters the latter had tenderly laid there. The unfortunate woman had to leave immediately. Following Russian custom—concerning which even Princess Lieven voices some surprise—she was put across the border by two policemen. Another, and stricter, supervisor took her place, and Dorothy's romance had come to an end. She wept for a time, continued by consoling herself, and finally forgot. Five years later she married Count Lieven. At the same time, young Count Elmpt died. "I knew that he had written to me, but I never got his letter; I have reason to suppose that my husband suppressed it."

The tale of this romance, to which music by Tschaikowsky would be eminently suitable, was invited by one of Metternich's letters. Having conscientiously told Dorothy about his various experiences, he laughingly also told her about his first love which came to him when he was nine and whose object was a married woman of thirty-four. Two stories, and two apologies. Dorothy, whenever she loved, had the misfortune of being seized with "the fever" and would probably continue to be subject to these attacks. As for Metternich, in the fifty years of his love-life he always had a weakness for women of thirty-four, which also had been Dorothy's age in Aachen. So it was their "destiny," as lovers will say when they transgress established laws.

These are exceptional romantic instances. As a general rule Dorothy very seldom wrote of love. Her great passion was politics. Even when she presented to the friend of her heart a new and ultramodern lamp to assist him in his midnight correspondence, and explained in the accompanying letter, that this newly invented English lamp was fueled with hydrogen gas, she added to this little excursion into chemistry in the next line: "Speaking of chemistry, there is much talk of a fusion of parties to form a new ministry. . . ."

A year before, Metternich also had made her a tender present in the form of a Paris *portefeuille à la Huret*. It had a secret lock which opened only when the number 1-8-1-8 were properly adjusted. *"Une serrure à combinaisons,"* these locks were called in Paris, and the 1-8-1-8 represented, of course, 1818, the year of their love. *"Cette année est la notre,"* said Metternich in his accompanying letter. *"Celle de notre hégire."* He continued by explaining to her in French the somewhat complicated manipulation of the lock; but she should not let that discourage her: *"Si une fois tu as ouvert, tu ouvrira toujours. Il n'y a que le premier pas qui coûte, au fait de cadenas comme en tout autre chose. . . ."* It may be seen that in everything there is a reference to Aachen; their love lived on delightful memories.

At other times she told him stories and storiettes of her surroundings, gay and sad, political and unpolitical, just as they occurred in her everyday life. Among the political ones were preparations for their first meeting in three years, in Hanover. For that purpose the King of England would have to go to Hanover and, for that, Dorothy pocketed her pride and paid a visit to the King's new favorite, the Marchioness of Conyngham. The Marchioness, who did not receive many visits from society, thought very highly of Dorothy's call—so highly, in fact, that the King actually journeyed to Hanover. It was, of course, all done for the sake of the Holy Alliance. Dorothy Lieven had preceded the King to Hanover. That is how history is made, say the French. The lovers' happiness was brief, as it always was. The King suspected something, bundled up his favorite, who could not get enough of Dorothy Lieven's company, and returned to England after a few days. Metternich, for his part, returned to his Chancellery in Vienna quite satis-

fied, and the first thing he did was to issue a *communiqué*
to the effect that the discussions between the King of England and the Austrian Chancellor took place in an atmosphere of entire harmony and mutual satisfaction. Terms
like "amicable relations" and "traditional friendship" also
may have been taken from the shelf and dusted off for the
occasion.

A similar meeting between the two lovers came about in
1822. The scene was Verona, the city of Romeo and Juliet,
where they were able to enjoy a brief political honeymoon.
Dorothy's happiness was at its zenith. Metternich was the
"Coachman of Europe," and she was blissfully installed in
the coach. Then came the end. Metternich no longer went
to Italy; the time for political journeys to watering-places
was over, his letters became fewer and finally stopped altogether. At one time Dorothy waited for him for months in
Florence and in Rome, but he failed to turn up. "Austria
will have to suffer for it," she wrote him, and there was a
real threat of her political influence behind the joking tone
of her remark. It was in vain; his presence in Vienna was
indispensable. Politics and love are rarely good bedfellows;
almost without exception it is politics that in the end ousts
love. The exchange of letters, however, continued for quite
some time but until—much later—politics separated them
definitely.

The authoress who emerged from her letters a century
after they were written, shows up to best advantage when
she indulged neither in politics nor lyrical effusions but
permitted her chronicling pen to run on without restraint.
How charming her account of disposing of the boring and
hard-to-please guest by making him suspect that his bedroom

was haunted. Or take the story of the mad Herr Harden-brot. He was a gentleman of German origin, a former member of the late Princess of Wales' household, and a man "remarkable for his enormous nose." One day he called on her and remarked in the course of their conversation that he was from time to time subject to fits of mental aberration, when he did not know what he was doing. It was like a scene from a French farce and developed accordingly. Dorothy, finding herself alone with the man, got up casually and posted herself at the bell cord, where she remained "like a sentry" until, after some time, the Duke of York saved her from her awkward situation. A few weeks later Herr Hardenbrot actually became a raving maniac and died in a lunatic asylum whither he had been hurriedly taken.

The Duke of York, who saved her from the man with the enormous nose, was also a rather curious bird in Dorothy's aviary, in which male birds exclusively flitted in and out. He called regularly once a week and usually stayed a few hours, during which time he talked incessantly and irresistibly so that—as she relates—she could hardly contribute ten words to the conversation. What was the reason for his calling, anyway? she asked herself and Metternich, to whom she wrote with secret satisfaction about the fatiguing visits of the King's brother: "He settles down; he chatters; he tells stories; and at the end of his visit he kisses my hands with tears of emotion and gratitude for the pleasure I have given him. I am charmed to give it, as it is so easy." The scene readily may be imagined. The delightful womanliness of the partly roguish, partly resigned Dorothy: "as it is so easy"!

A few years ago, when the world still had time for such

things, a rather voluminous collection of love-letters appeared in Germany under the title "The World's Most Beautiful Love-Letters." Which is the most beautiful among those Princess Lieven collected in exercise-books? Is it the last letter, in which she asked him once more and in vain to write? "Neumann gave me your No. 174 yesterday. You have done so little to spoil me for some time that that letter seemed quite an occasion. I hasten to thank you. Do unassuming manners make you more generous? They do me. If you are like me, you ought to write to me often. Let us start again from the beginning. We should be hard put to it, you and I, to find in the whole world people of our own caliber. Our hearts are well-matched, our minds too; and our letters are very pleasant. . . . I repeat; you will find no one better than me. If you meet your like, show him to me. Goodbye."

Or is that other letter the most beautiful in which in her dream she felt his heart beat and, awakening, found it was her own; or is it a third, and still briefer one in which, being once more a guest at some house-party, she described the two old trees outside her window? Nothing, she said, was more touching, more beautiful than two such trees towering into the air, their roots and branches intertwining. She closed the note with a charming question, such as only a woman or a poet could have asked: "Would you not like to be the other tree?"

Was theirs a frivolous association? It was thought so for an entire century. As a matter of fact it was not the meeting of two "worldlings" as Arthur Herman disparagingly says in his biography of Metternich, but that of two strong personalities who, each chained to an insufficient partner in matrimony, loved because they felt irresistibly drawn to each other. They both were made to suffer for having wilfully disregarded the laws of morality. The woman especially paid dearly for her moments of sweet satisfaction. Who is to judge her? To glorify her love would be too much; to acquit her would be just.

The Coachman of Europe

A LIFE of Metternich could be written in nicknames. After the "Adonis of the Drawing-Room," he became the "Comte de Balance," the "Minister of the Coalition," "Ministre Papillon," the "Knight of Europe," the "Grand-Inquisitor of Europe," the "Coachman of Europe," and many other things until finally, to use the beautiful words of the poet Hebbel, he ceased to strike as the "Clock of Europe." It will be seen that in the second half of his life the word Europe is his constant companion. The other descriptions pale, but this one remains.

In those years of Congresses and political journeys to watering-places in which Dorothy Lieven had a share, between Aachen and Verona, the transition from Knight to Coachman of Europe took place. The conqueror of Napoleon had reached his fiftieth year. Even darlings of Fate, provided God spares their life, inevitably arrive at that point, and must ruefully admit that their shining knightly armor has lost some of its youthful brilliance. Verona was the scene of the last Congress in which Madame Lieven participated either actively or passively. But even in her time, the scenes of the Congresses were not always so romantically named. At one time it was Karlsbad, at another Troppau, and then again Laibach. Aachen and Verona had been holidays of happiness; but in the end the workaday duties of his office claimed all of his time.

At each one of these Congresses another issue was ventilated and mulled over. At Troppau it was Naples, and at Laibach and Verona, Spain. At Aachen, France was received into the League of Great Powers, a realization of the European Pentarchy that Metternich had visualized. Everywhere, at Karlsbad and Verona, too, the adroit Metternich was able to attain his object. People thought they were complimenting him when calling him the Coachman of Europe. As a matter of fact he actually was. It was in those years of his mild dictatorship that his good and faithful, albeit at times somewhat stubborn, Emperor Franz said of him in his usual humorous way: "Whenever I hear the people sing: 'God save our Emperor Franz,' I always think to myself: 'God save Metternich for me'!"

The great power Metternich now wielded continually placed new tasks in his way. There was, to begin with, the German problem that gave him no peace of mind. It grew in importance after Napoleon's fall and, in a certain sense, may be said to have become acute because of that tremendous victory. As long as Germany was enchained it enjoyed the slave's privilege of not having to bother about its future, because it was not master of its own destiny. Now, however, it had risen, and with it rose the German problem which only in 1870, when the German Reich was founded, was partly solved. Present-day occurrences seem to indicate that the solution was but a temporary one. The problem of those days lay in the fact that a people which through its own strength had vanquished Napoleon now wanted to become an independent nation.

In the 18th century, Germany had consisted of a bundle

of States, above whose sovereignties stood an impotent Emperor forever at odds with the reigning princes. For four centuries the Emperor had been a Habsburg residing in Vienna and having little time for quarreling. Nevertheless, the German Reichstag did all in its power to make life miserable for the chosen of the electoral princes.

All this was to be changed now, according to what the German idealists thought, hoped, and dreamed. There was, foremost of all, Baron von Stein, from the Rhine like Metternich, but ideologically the latter's antithesis. Stein's arguments went back to the popular uprising that had been necessary to bring about Napoleon's overthrow. In the very fact that all the German tribes had found the way to one another lay convincing proof that they belonged together, and therefore they must remain together. A national Germany under a glorified Imperial Crown was to rise out of the dust and ashes of the brittle old assembly of States, and this time the nation itself would share in the government: the nation that had shed its blood on the battle field and thereby gained the right to have a voice in the Crown Council. It was the French Revolution that had given birth to the idea of a nation in that sense, the people sharing in the rule, instead of being ruled.

Emperor Franz saw the connection with the Revolution and, with innate cunning, declined with thanks. Again, he said something witty which in its sober matter-of-factness hit the nail on the head. Referring to his intended retransformation into a brand-new German Emperor, he said: "If they want to make me as I was before, I'd say 'Thank you, No!'; and if they want to make me different, I'd like to see how they'll manage it." Metternich never could have said that because, being by nature complex, he had neither the originality nor the simplicity of his Imperial master. No matter how it was expressed, however, it was fundamentally his opinion, too.

This opinion was not a pro-German one in the national sense, as became apparent when Franz declined the German Imperial Crown, but retained the presiding seat in the German League—without personally attending to his duties. The whole of Germany was lowered therefore to the level of a dependant of Austria, which it had been, more or less, throughout the past centuries. In that respect, too, Metternich was consciously a reactionary. An impotent Germany and a powerful Austria were in his opinion the best guarantee for the peaceful development of Europe.

There was Prussia, however, the ambitious Great Power; and there was also King Infinitive, Friedrich Wilhelm III, who, when he again took the field against Napoleon in May, 1815, had rashly promised his people a constitution. Constitution! The word itself gave the Emperor a headache. It was said in Vienna that when the Emperor's physician, Dr. Stift, once praised the monarch's strong constitution, the latter requested him with a wry face to say "bodily disposition" rather than "constitution."

There again, Metternich entirely shared his master's opinion. He wanted no part of any *"charte,"* no matter in what form—and especially not in his neighborhood! Nationalism was to him nothing but Jacobinism *avant la lettre,* in which respect he was not far from right, as was to be proved in Germany a century later.

It was now a question of inducing Friedrich Wilhelm to rescind his promise or, simpler still, not to keep it. That, however, was no easy matter. The obstinate King Infinitive had pledged his Royal word and was disposed to keep it.

In politics one has to take every advantage of an adversary's mistakes; that was Metternich's axiom, too, in the present instance. Nationalism being folly, it could be assumed that sooner or later it would be guilty of some act of foolishness. The deduction proved to be correct.

Within Germany, after the floodtide of "The Hundred Days" had ebbed, a liberty movement from time to time threw up its waves, on whose crest the country's excited youth liked to ride. There were the student members of the *Burschenschaften,* the more or less secret student fraternities, and the gymnastic associations, with their even then anti-Semitic tendencies, losing no opportunity to emphasize their yearning for "liberty." They swilled beer, bawled, and sang *"in tyrannos."* The national humbug becomes apparent through the fact that the so-called German Revolution permitted itself at first to be borne up and sustained by the educated, while in the next century it faced about and turned against them.

Among the educational institutions the universities were hotbeds of revolutionary activity. Foremost among them was the University of Giessen, where revolutionary songs were bellowed, and that of Jena, where the phrase "Blücher and Weimar" was given out and the song "Freedom, my beloved . . ." was most violently shouted out into the world. The students of Jena also arranged the so-called "Wartburg Festival" in October, 1817, which was to commemorate the Battle of Leipsic and at the same time be a tercentenary of the German Reformation. On that occasion the first public burning of books took place in Germany, so that National-Socialism cannot claim it as its own proud invention. Among the books that were burned were the works of Kotzebue, the writer of comedies, who was suspected of being a spy, in the

pay of Czar Alexander, and of obstructing the German liberty movement. In the midst of a national movement it is a
dangerous matter to be, or to have been, a writer of comedies. The mere fact that some of the shouters know his name
from the posters suffices to brand him as an enemy of the
people.

Poor Kotzebue was not to enjoy life long after the burning of his books had set the nationalist youth on his trail.
A young fanatic stabbed him to death in Mannheim, near
the house in which Schiller's "The Robbers" had been performed. A dagger for a writer of comedies! How far he was
overestimated when he was deemed worthy of Caesar's fate
and the pointed steel was plunged into his defenseless
breast! The points of his dialogue, brightly polished in the
glare of the footlights, never drew blood. At the most, they
but tickled the nose of human folly.

The youthful Brutus' name was Carl Sand. He was the
Horst Wessel of that era, a "black brother" from Giessen,
where forbidden songs were sung. Herman, the American
historian, has included one of them in his book on Metternich. It shows most eloquently the Bolshevist romanticism
of those days: a fermenting mixture of Eichendorff and the
Marseillaise:

> *Brothers in silk and gold,*
> *Brothers in tatters old,*
> *Clasp hand in hand!*
> *Answer our country's need,*
> *Unto the Lord give heed:*
> *Slaughter the tyrant breed,*
> *Save ye the land!*
> *Life will be as of old,*

If you give blood and gold;
If you your guns with lead,
Battle-axe with scythe do wed,
Bludgeon the despot's head!
Be ever bold!

Such songs of hatred never remain without a roaring echo. On the one side were the dissatisfied young people of the post-war period who furnished even then the motive power, while on the other side were deceived idealists who shouted and applauded. While the former were to be found mainly in the *Burschenschaften,* the latter, the idealists, were represented on the professorial staffs, both joining together on each and every occasion. The deed which, according to Metternich, "followed upon the teaching" bore fruit. Murderous attacks disturbed the lavender-scented peace of Congressional days. There was lightning in Germany and France; flashes were seen in Italy where the Carbonari were at work, and now and then lightning even struck. In Nassau, State-Minister von Ibell met his Brutus in the person of a certain Loening, while in Paris the Duc de Berri was stabbed to death at the theater by friends of liberty. Dorothy Lieven buried him in one of her letters to Metternich with a single merciless line: "He was a nobody, but he was assassinated!" At all events, it was the fourth murderous attack in the course of a few months.

Metternich, who kept a careful count, watched quietly at first like a spider in its web. It is significant that he had a special liking for spiders. He once made the statement that he could watch these insects for hours at a time. It is possible that now he followed their example. Soon after the murder of Kotzebue he had a meeting with "King Infinitive" at

Teplitz. Friedrich Wilhelm was all the more disconcerted because Giessen, the haunt of the "Black Brethren," was a Prussian university. What was to be done? The King complained that he had no ministers in whom he had confidence. Therefore he had come to Metternich for advice. Metternich immediately turned this un-royal attitude to his own advantage by presenting to the King the highly unpalatable fact that Hardenberg, Friedrich Wilhelm's minister, was old, deaf, and hopelessly passé. The frightened monarch did not at once abandon his minister, but said that he would lose no time in arranging a meeting between Metternich and Hardenberg, at which time the former could instruct and enlighten Hardenberg. There was but one thing to do, said Metternich inflexibly. "No Constitution!" The King yielded. He broke his sacred pledge to the people.

This is a most significant point in German history. Had the Prussian king granted a constitution in 1815, there is a possibility that the other German princes would have followed suit, and the unification of Germany would have resulted half a century earlier. The jealousy and religious differences between the German states, however, weakens this hypothesis, nor was Prussia in the dominant position in 1815 which she occupied in 1871. German unification was a direct threat to the position of Austria as the dominant Teutonic power, and this Metternich always recognized. The North-German historians, however, who have blamed Metternich for a century for having stood immovably in the way of German unification, fail to realize how great were the obstacles in the way of the establishment of a united Germany. Nor do they take into account the pernicious effect on the peace of the world of a strong united Germany, dominated by the ideals of Prussian militarism and anti-democracy. This, as much as Metternich stood in the way of a Constitution. It was only when the Junkers realized that Constitutionalism was a bad means to a great end, i. e., the establishment of a powerful German Reich, then, and only then, did they yield.

Metternich, reactionary as he was, saw, perhaps not very clearly, that a united Germany was not only a threat to the Austrian State, but even more to the peace of Europe. Whatever one may say of him, he was devoted to that.

(In the meantime Metternich drove his coach quietly and judiciously. He tightened the reins in Germany as well as in Italy and Spain, cleverly taking advantage of events here and there. Everywhere the kings lately had manifested a tendency to treat peoples like equals a *sequela* of the French Revolution. They had to be cured of their inclination to grant constitutions without further ado. Even armed intervention was necessary now and then to make them see reason.) They were easy and short wars, conducted on foreign soil and conferring honor upon a dictator. While he left it to France to intervene in Spain in the name of the Pentarchy, he took it upon himself to restore order in Naples and, immediately after, in Piedmont; best to kill two birds with one stone. Before being permitted to continue their rule, properly curbed, both Kings had to abrogate the constitutions solemnly affirmed by their oaths. Everything went like clock-work.

In other respects, too, everything went like clock-work, if one but refrained from reflecting on the fact that one grew older. But there were bewitching moments now and then that made one forget the ruthless fact; at Castle Herrenhausen in Hanover, for instance, where one day the King of England and his ladies, including Dorothy Lieven, arrived on one side, and Prince Metternich on the other. A Russo-Turkish war was to be prevented. Count Lieven, by the way, arrived eight days later, because he had been entrusted with the task of working upon the Czar's mind in the meantime. So it was a complete success for Metternich in every direction. At the evening reception, Dorothy sat next to the King on the royal divan, so that even princesses of the blood had to cede precedence to her. At leave-taking the King of England embraced Prince Metternich three times in succession—an occurrence, it is asserted, unheard of in the history of the English Court—whispering the while into his ear a long list of great names to which Metternich's own should be honorably added: Minos, Themistocles, Cato, Caesar, Gustavus Adolphus, Marlborough, Pitt, and Wellington. Metternich and Dorothy may have had a special laugh at Cato when, a few days later, they met in Frankfort once more and were entertained at the house of the Rothschilds.

Metternich was to be fêted similarly in Paris a few years later by Charles X. He was able now to boast of quite a nice collection of royal and imperial satellites, among whom was also Alexander of Russia. The man, who at the time of the Congress of Vienna had been on the point of challenging him to a duel, had become Metternich's creature altogether, passionately forswearing for his sake, his former principles of mystically exalted liberalism. When in the course of a conversation Metternich respectfully permitted himself to wonder about it, the Czar vaguely justified his complete change of front by pointing out that seven years had passed since 1813. His were seven-year convictions.

The first years of Metternich's dictatorship were his best.

The satisfactions derived from power were still cradled in a joy of life, the adept in the art of governing being matched by the adept in the art of living. The warning to the young Emperor which Goethe sounds in his "Faust": "To rule you want and taste the joys of life. . . ." (the words were originally Maria Theresa's in a letter to Marie Antoinette), was not heeded by the considerably older Metternich who actually succeeded at times, when politics and love went hand in hand, in both ruling and enjoying himself. "Epaphroditus," the ancient Romans flatteringly used to apostrophize the rose-garlanded Caesar. That is what Metternich was in those Anacreontic years and in the afterglow of his triumphs: "Epaphroditus."

All the same, politics and love are an ill-matched team, and politics always outruns love. The truth of this fact was to be brought home soon enough to this Prince of Life holding the reins over his "four-in-hand." The roses faded; disappointment lurked in the path of fulfillment.

Noon-day splendor one moment; shadows lengthening on Metternich's course the next. He who had been lucky in everything—"brazenly lucky," Madame de Rémusat had called him—began now to experience reverses in his own house, in his own family. Perhaps they came his way because he had been too busy hunting luck in other people's houses. Perhaps, too, it was the other way round: he went hunting so assiduously in strange hunting-grounds, because at home ill-fortune was waiting for him. Two of the seven children which Eleonore, she of the cork-screw curls and the bovine eyes—the latter term being used in the Homeric sense—had presented to him, died when quite young and in the early years of his married life; and now, when he was nearing his fifties, two of the grown-up children followed. First it was the 16-year-old Clementine—not to be confounded with that other Clementine of his Dresden days, the daughter of Madame Bagration—who went off quietly and charmingly, sadly meek and dreadfully sweet, like the gently fading chords in Schubert's "Death and the Maiden." The beautiful child had not yet learned to know how beautiful she was. With a show of emotion Metternich used to tell how, when they went walking together, the men would stare at his Clementine who had no other comment to make but: "These people must never have seen a hat like mine." Or she began to pull at her dress embarrassedly, lest everything was not quite in order. . . .

Clementine died in the month of May and was followed in July of the same year by the twenty-three-year-old Marie, Countess Esterházy. It was she with whom he had arranged *tableaux vivants* at the time of the Congress, while two Ambassadors waited in vain for him in the ante-chamber, a fact concerning which the Prussian Ambassador was so thoroughly wrought up. She was his favorite daughter, his comrade, his friend, his better self. No thought went through her little head that he might not himself have thought; no word passed her lips that he might not have uttered. On the occasion of her death he spoke words about her that vibrated with a deep-felt tenderness. It is in his relation to his children that we touch the warmest spot in Metternich's soul. He was a bad husband, a better lover, a good father, and, as far as Marie was concerned, the best father in the world. In the letter he wrote after she had died, he grew poetic. The same may be said of the letter of condolence he received from Dorothy Lieven who was also an excellent mother. It is true that already in the letter's fifth line she spoke of the uprising in Naples which her friend was about to quell; but at the conclusion of the letter she found the way back again to his heart, in the womanly and beautiful words: "Adieu, *mon Prince,* I suffer in your grief and I shall rejoice in your glory." By their letters of condolence may be measured worldlings' depth of soul. There are those who are not even able to sympathize.

In either case the cause of death was the inherited disease of the lungs. Eleonore, too, suffered from it. She was to succumb to it at a comparatively early age. Her frequent confinements also may have had their share in undermining her health. At the time of the girls' death she was already ill, and the three remaining children were likewise threatened by the insidious scourge that claimed as its victims half the children of the Vienna of those days. There was good reason for a medical school's calling tuberculosis the *morbus Viennensis,* the Vienna disease. The granite dust of the Vienna pavement favored its development as much as the lack of an adequate sanitary force and the ignorance of the physicians. Instead of fighting its causes, pulmonary tuberculosis was treated with cough-mixtures and whey-cures. In Metternich's somewhat more enlightened circles one had advanced a step further. The family physician recommended a change of air and life in a milder climate. In the course of the same year, the ailing Princess Eleonore, accompanied by her three children, moved to Paris where she remained until her death, which occurred a few years later.

Thus Metternich suddenly found himself alone. His wife was in Paris, his sweetheart in London; there was nothing left for him save his beloved State-Chancellery from which he must not be separated. Loneliness, a dictator's last companion, began to surround him, surviving friendship and love. In his case, though, at least it did not have the last word. It formed only a state of transition which brought to its ultimate maturity his virtues as a ruling statesman: his diligence, his watchfulness, his tenacity, and his consummate art of treating people. It safely may be asserted that they never flourished as well as in those quiet years, when he was about fifty, and when he administered noiselessly his enormous wealth of power. Now and then he wrote a midnight letter to Dorothy Lieven. Now he was actually the Coachman of Europe. But at what price? The Dictator of the Continent had at the same time become a slave to his desk.

Just as Talleyrand on his deathbed, as a man of eighty-four, still made a last political treaty—with God—Metternich, the rising sexagenarian, found a last sweetheart: politics. He remained true to her to the end, although finally she disappointed him bitterly.

He ruled, and did nothing else. Where were the times when he had been able to boast: "My head belongs to the world, but my heart belongs to me alone, and I can dispose of it as I see fit." Now he no longer had any private life. Even when he was about to journey to Paris to his wife's deathbed, he had to consider whether his going to Paris could not possibly be misinterpreted politically by Canning as an attempt at an English *rapprochement*. He postponed the journey "until it was imperative." Similarly, on the day when his dearly beloved daughter Marie died, he was obliged, according to his own written testimony, to preside for six hours at a Cabinet Council, followed by four hours at his desk where he elaborated the subject-matter. And his heart? It was eliminated.

At last the journey to Paris, which he proposed to undertake only in case of absolute necessity, could no longer be postponed. The necessity actually became absolute, for Eleonore to whom he had been married twenty-eight years and who had borne him seven children, was dying. A few days before she breathed her last, he arrived in Paris, where he had not been since 1815. He sat at her deathbed and, when he had closed her eyes, dedicated to her memory one of his poetic obituary letters. He called her a beautiful soul and the best of mothers. Facing death with Christian composure, she used what little breath was left in her to give her children advice for the future and to thank her husband for all "he had done or had not done for her." A touch of remorse, this, quickly suppressed, however, in a further calm account of her last hours. She had not complained but, guided by her firm belief in God, had found the way safely to the Father. He had suffered an irreparable loss; Providence had so willed it. He spoke as if he were addressing a Cabinet Council.

The last word in those difficult Paris days was spoken not by the husband nor by the father, but by the politician. His fears fortunately had not come true. His journey had on the contrary made an excellent impression—on Canning: *"Ma présence ici ne manquera pas d'avoir des bons résultats!"* We may breathe freely again. Soon he described with a prima donna's vanity how he was courted and sought out: "Ministers, job hunters, ultra-legitimists, Bonapartists, Jacobins, and Jesuits—a veritable vale of Jehoshaphat" crowded his ante-chamber. The Archbishop of Paris paid his respects to him. The King invited him to dinner and bestowed upon him the Order of the Holy Ghost; he assured him of his gratitude and offered him his friendship. *"Le Roi, le ministère, et tous les gens bien pensant sont venus devant de moi, d'une façon qui indique la position élevée que l'Autriche occupe aujourd'hui,"* he reported to Emperor Franz, identifying himself with Austria. On another occasion he used the significant phrase: *"Notre pays ou plutôt nos pays."* Already the Coachman of Europe, when he has decided or accomplished something, is using the word "we," like all dictators. Or ought we to say: like all coachmen?

Came the Second and the Third

AFTER Eleonore's death Metternich was an inconsolable widower. Nobody in Vienna doubted for a moment that he would soon marry again. No matter how paradoxical it may sound, Metternich was a born husband. The fact was that in the twenty-eight years he had spent more or less at Eleonore's side, he had never become quite conscious of it. What he demanded subconsciously of women during those years was that they be his wife. That the women of whom he made this demand changed so frequently was, in the majority of instances, not his fault. Fundamentally he had a certain leaning towards faithfulness, as he himself admitted ingenuously. "I was never unfaithful," the married man once wrote blandly to his inamorata. If he found it impossible to remain faithful to his inclinations towards faithfulness, it was the fault of the women who prevented his living up to his good intentions: some of those with whom he was associated gave him too much, while others gave him too little.

Dorothy had given him everything—for a time. In their oral and written intercourse they were one heart and one soul; they understood each other in the day-time and at night. Madame Lieven, as he once wrote, actually was as a woman what he was as a man. She was also just as matrimonially inclined as he. She proved it more than once, the last time with Guizot with whom she spent the last twenty years of her life. In the case of Metternich, however, it was an excessive congeniality of characters which sounded the doom of their association. It is the essence of matrimony that it demands a certain complementing of forces, and not a parallelism of the two individualities. This became obvious the moment when his and Princess Lieven's political paths began to run in different directions. It may sound like a joke but it is sad truth that their ideal *affaire du cœur* was wrecked by the Russo-Turkish question.

Politics had stood godmother at the cradle of their love. Dorothy came to Aachen as the Russian Ambassadress and Metternich as the Austrian Chancellor and Foreign Minister. They made each other's acquaintance and fell in love in a political drawing-room. Just as their relationship developed organically in the months and years that followed, politically, too, they were in complete harmony, both being convinced Europeans and aristocrats with inclinations to wield power. If, in the instance of Naples, Dorothy Lieven in London exhorted her friend in Vienna: "You must march!" he was already on his way to Naples of his own accord. So far everything was in perfect order. They overlooked the fact, though, that in spite of the full harmony of their views, the atmosphere surrounding them in London and Vienna respectively was totally different, smacking of a seasonable liberalism there, and of an obdurate feudalism here.

In time, however, the atmospheric difference of their surroundings began to make itself felt. Metternich, in his fear of conspiracies and his dread of constitutions, went to ever greater lengths and proposed in the end to intervene everywhere in Europe: in Portugal, in Spain, in Italy, and

finally even in Greece. England declined to play the part
of Europe's policeman, and France followed England's example. This point caused the disruption of the Pentarchy.
What was left was the Holy Alliance, the tyrannical union
between Austria, Russia, and the reactionary Prussia. Following the Congress of Verona there was a distinct demarca-
tion of the ideological fronts. The liberal West stood up
against the reactionary East of Europe, a contrast which
lasted a century and to this day sways the fate of a continent.

From that moment Dorothy and Clemens were in different camps. Once more she tried personally to bridge the
contrast by going to Italy and rambling about there to enjoy
the company of the Coachman of Europe, as he had promised she should. He kept her waiting for months in Florence
and Rome, and failed to put in an appearance. "It will do
Austria a great deal of harm in Rome!" she shook her finger
at him half jokingly. Metternich was willing to run the risk.
He had a sick wife in Paris and an overcrowded Chancellery
in Vienna that took up his time day and night; he was not
anxious to travel. To rule and enjoy oneself at the same
time was not possible in the long run. Metternich decided
definitely in favor of ruling.

Dorothy's letters grew fewer in numbers and bitterer in
tone. "Would you not like to be the other tree?" A question
without an answer. Then, suddenly, the Russo-Turkish
question created an unbridgeable chasm between their respective standpoints. Austria was opposed to Greece's striving for independence, although the Greeks were Christians
and the Turks, who administered the country so wretchedly,
heathen. England strongly favored the creation of an independent Greece, in spite of the fact that further intervention

on the Continent was not considered desirable. Contradictions everywhere. Canning, England's Prime Minister and Metternich's enemy, succeeded in bringing about an alliance between France, England, and Russia. Being Russia's Ambassadress, Dorothy took the part of that country as a matter of course, while Metternich was loath to give up his position. If he, the European, placed himself in opposition to the European Greeks and in favor of the Asiatic Turks (a double treachery in the eyes of his great friend and sweetheart), he did it because the Turkish rule was the "legitimate" one; out of pure doctrinairism. This finally led to a war in which the united Anglo-French navies put to rout the Austro-incited Turks at Navarino.

On the day that battle was fought, Metternich married a very young and extremely beautiful girl in Vienna, Antoinette Leykam. Now Dorothy burst out. "The Knight of the Holy Alliance has made a *mésalliance,*" she mocked from the other shore. In another letter she supposed that the former "clever Minister" Metternich no longer existed, having been supplanted by a dummy who mechanically continued to rule in his name and in his stead. Then she uttered a terrible word. She called him the greatest scoundrel of Europe, forgetting as almost any woman in her situation might that if under certain circumstances he was a scoundrel, under certain other circumstances the fact had been agreeable and even highly desirable to her.

Metternich, the newly wed, remained silent and continued in his silence for years and decades, until his end. Not a single word of censure or bitterness concerning the woman he once had loved so dearly! His deep affection for her bears upon its lips the aristocratic seal of every great love: silence!

Who were the Leykams, anyway? The question was asked in every political drawing-room in Europe. In the aristocratic circles of Vienna, where the family of the all-too-beautiful bride had been closely scrutinized, an answer was readily forthcoming. The father was a small clerk in the ministerial department, a man with artistic leanings; the ancestors on her father's side were employees of the Thurn and Taxis Post—"coachmen," the oh-so-kindly-disposed Vienna society said. The background of the mother was even worse. Imagine her having been an opera-singer! An Italian woman from Palermo, named Pedrella. Oh, yes, quite a handsome woman. She sang and entertained at her home. Gentlemen only, if you please, no ladies; "not a single one," said the old Princesses, secretly referring to themselves, of course. What was more, there were rumors that racially they were not quite unobjectionable: Jews, you know.

To repair the damage, even before her marriage, the Emperor made Antoinette Leykam, Countess Beilstein. Probably he had had a lengthy discussion with his "Court, House, and State Minister" who, in the usual manner of middle-aged gentlemen in similar circumstances, was not to be swayed from his purpose. Metternich's mother, who was still alive then, was strongly opposed to the match. She had in mind a bride of the Catholic nobility, in which direction she had once before successfully steered her son's life. This time it was the beautiful young Countess Melanie Zichy, daughter of the equally beautiful Countess Molly Zichy, of whom she was quite fond. Clemens said, No! He became engaged to Antoinette Leykam, and Melanie Zichy and her mother, so the story went in Vienna, departed on the same day for their Hungarian estates. A declaration of love in reverse and, besides, the cleverest thing Melanie could have done.

Antoinette Leykam was not quite so clever. In the eyes of her bridegroom, and in view of his recent experiences with the ultra-clever Princess Lieven, this was probably her greatest attraction. Possibly he may have sided with his favorite poet, Heine, in this respect, whom he caused to be persecuted politically, but whose poems he liked to read after dinner to his future spouse:

> *"When meeting stupid women I thought*
> *The dullards have little attraction;*
> *But what by clever ones I was taught*
> *Was fill'd with still less satisfaction."*

In Metternich's case, to be sure, the clever ones had come first. When and where the change took place is not easily ascertainable, documentarily. Strange, indeed! Though we are so thoroughly informed concerning Metternich's illegitimate relationships—by himself, in the majority of instances—we know next to nothing about the circumstances leading up to his three marriages. Even of his first one we only know that Eleonore had decided in his favor even before her father had made his decision—a proceeding quite unheard of in her straight-laced 18th-century circle. Regarding Antoinette, however, we are completely in the dark. There is hardly a single document extant referring to the days of her engagement, which took place at a time of political high tension. While the historiographer is able to follow from day to day the development of the Oriental question, there are no acts from which he could gain any knowledge con-

cerning the development of Metternich's affair of the heart.
The man of learning therefore will have to skip over this
point silently. He must fail, because his sources fail him.
Here, for want of a historian, it takes a poet, who needs no
sources because he is one himself.

At any rate it is possible to make some psychological deductions which are plausible also physiologically. Antoinette
was exceptionally handsome and hardly half as old as Metternich. She was much more beautiful than her predecessor,
and beautiful in an entirely different manner. A little doll's
face, a dainty mouth, ringlets over an infantile forehead,
and a dreamy forget-me-not-blue look from her cast-up eyes.
"Une grace lamartinienne," is the praise bestowed upon her
by Grunwald; Comte de St. Aulaire, the French Ambassador
at the Court of Vienna called her a beautiful odalisque; her
gentle insignificance, he added maliciously, came near winning all hearts for the Princess. However, the question arises:
how did Clemens get hold of his odalisque? As in all his
other experiences with women, society provided the medium
for making her acquaintance. Antoinette's mother, still bask-
ing in memories of the glory that once had been the share
of the member of the San Carlo Theater of Naples, liked to
have company at her house. The fact that her singing voice
was still quite good, attracted a number of aristocrats to
her receptions. While the ladies of that set seemed to be
considerably less eager to be entertained musically, gentlemen whose names were to be found in the Red Book were all
the more willing to be invited to the Leykam drawing-room.
Metternich was one of them, a fact which is to be placed to
his credit. One of the most attractive phases of his character
and personality was his attitude towards art—including literature, a subject to be touched upon later—and especially

towards music. He himself was a performer on the 'cello, and it is said that, when he was quite a young man, he once appeared publicly as a 'cello-player in Rastatt. As an old gentleman, he was apt to shed tears of emotion when listening to the overtures of Donizetti's operas, his special favorites. Princess Lieven, herself a splendid pianist, a fact of which Metternich may have convinced himself in Aachen, was the recipient once of the following letter by Metternich on the subject of music: "It has the power to move my whole being; it does me good, and causes me pain; but even the pain is pleasurable." While this avowal may be testimony of a rather sensuous relationship to music, his attachment was nevertheless deeply rooted and formed the bridge which led him to the home of the Leykams. There he sat, the handsome middle-aged man surrounded by the halo of many experiences, listening to the mother who soulfully warbled her songs and arias into the honeyed fragrance of the candle-lit music-room, while the daughter was lyrically silent. "My blessed silence," Caesar, in Shakespeare's drama, addresses his wife. As for Antoinette, she did not need to sing; she was a song herself.

The foregoing lays bare some of the tender threads that drew the Austrian State-Chancellor, Prince Metternich, towards the Leykam ménage where, to the chagrin of his envious contemporaries, he felt truly happy for a time. That it was not a house of the first rank, was perhaps an added reason for his feeling so contented there. It was a home filled with an intensely musical atmosphere, but rather quiet in other respects; therefore it was all the more attractive to him. Again he was able to say, even then, what his favorite poet, Heinrich Heine, was to write ten years later in his own behalf:

No longer young, bereft of power,
As I, alas! am at this hour,
I fain once more would love in quiet
And happy be,—without a riot.

The Prince's health, to be sure, left nothing to be desired. With the exception of a slight affliction which had permanently weakened the vision of his left eye, and an incipient deafness, he had nothing to complain of in that direction; and though he was no longer a young man, still he was young enough to attract and hold a very young girl. He was most willing to overlook the fact that she was fully thirty-three years younger than himself; that she looked up to him admiringly, and in the attitude of a docile pupil was an added attraction. Of politics, which had embittered the best years of his life, she knew nothing at all; she asked no questions, she gave no advice, and did not presume to have an opinion of her own. There was no danger of her peremptorily writing to him one day: "March upon Naples!" even before he had quite made up his own mind to march. She would, on the contrary, wait patiently, under such circumstances, to see whether he'd go, and then duly admire him for it. Nothing is so apt to turn the scales, when choosing a partner in love, as unfortunate experiences with one's predecessor. Disappointments often lead to the opposite camp.

All in all, Metternich's relationship with Antoinette was one of those which die of boredom in the third year. Things did not go so far, however, for Antoinette died after a year and a half of married life, and after having given birth to a healthy boy, Richard. She died of puerperal fever, as was not unusual in those days. It was, along with tuberculosis, one of the scourges of humanity.

For the second time in his life Metternich found himself a widower. A Bluebeard of heartfelt obituaries, he wrote again a deeply felt letter in which he said of the deceased: "She was beautiful as an angel and had angelic qualities." Hardly, though, had the ink dried on the inscription to his second wife, when the third turned up again in Vienna. Her name was Melanie Zichy, who seemed simply to have waited for the moment when her predecessor would be gone.

Although Metternich's mother had died in the meantime, she may be said again to have had a part in his new marriage. A woman of importance in her quiet way, Metternich owed to her his character, while the world owed to her his existence. She died, very old, and was soon followed to the grave by her grandson Victor, Metternich's only son of his first marriage, who had spent his last years in Paris. Like his father a great friend of the ladies, he lacked his progenitor's robust health. Being in the last stages of consumption, he eloped from Paris with a beautiful Duchess who nursed him to death in Italy. To elope to Italy, and float on the bosom of the Venetian lagoon in love-sick gondolas was the accepted expression of Parisian romanticism of those days. Musset ran away with Georges Sand, Liszt with Marie D'Agoult, and young Metternich with a delightful Duchess who, after his death, became the mother of his son Roger. Metternich's path at this period of his life, his sixth decade, was a veritable cemetery-walk: grave was succeeded by grave. Fortunately there was another son, the little Richard of the second marriage, who, sixty years later, was to collect his father's memoirs in countless volumes.

Once more the old tree, shaken by the blasts of autumnal winds, threw out new shoots; this happens with trees as well as with men. Melanie Zichy turned up again in Vienna, this time virtually engaged to a young Baron Hügel. That was no insurmountable obstacle, though; it simply meant that Metternich would have to make up his mind more quickly than two years before, and he did so with pleasure. By her sudden return to Vienna, he felt that Melanie loved him. This time, to be sure, the lady was only thirty-two years younger than he. Well, the one year would make no difference. He was then fifty-eight, and years were of small account to him.

Metternich's relationship to the world of women is again worthy of a few moments' smiling contemplation. When he was young, women desired him for their lover; now when he began to get old they were satisfied to marry him. His was not an every-day case. Metternich attracted to himself a great deal of enmity, both during his life and after. There must have been something to him, though, since the female, and we may say the better, half of humanity took his part so emphatically.

At that time, when Melanie's wooing—the expression seems justified—took place, Richard, Metternich's little son and heir, was one or two years old. A scene from that epoch of Metternich's life has come down to our day. It depicts him and his old friend and assistant, Gentz, in Richard's nursery, bent over a little pot of soapsuds and using straws to blow bubbles that float past little Richard's gaily waving pudgy paws. Is any further proof needed of the innate charm and kindness of the man's heart? In a long-forgotten comedy, a young woman, apostrophizing the world of men, says: "What makes the likes of you lovable—we women darkly guess it; the children know it."

Melanie Zichy, too, knew it, or at least darkly guessed it. She was a beauty, a racy Magyar thoroughbred, passionate, impetuous both when she restrained herself, and when she bolted, just like an unbridled horse of the Hungarian steppe, She compared with her immediate predecessor with regard to disposition, tone, and tempo, approximately as a rhapsody by Liszt compares with a nocturne by Chopin. Outwardly, Melanie was the very antithesis of Antoinette. She had a fleshy face, a general tendency towards plumpness, raven hair, and blue eyes, like Constance Caumont of blessed memory. One of her eyes is said to have been greenish-brown, forming a variety and also a difference that ought not to be overlooked.

The matter developed in the manner Melanie deemed proper. The semi-engaged Herr von Hügel was sent to Paris on a diplomatic mission and stayed away for quite some time. Meanwhile she became engaged to Clemens Metternich. The worthy Baron Hügel, who later developed into Metternich's staunch friend, did not take the matter amiss. He only wrote to his impetuous Melanie from Paris that he would not return to Vienna before he was cured of his love. "He will never return," the beautiful girl said with composure.

These very words show that Melanie Zichy was not lacking in self-assurance. Her haughtiness, called pride by her admirers, was known everywhere. The Zichys were of the oldest Hungarian aristocracy, having in their veins the blood of Turks, Huns, and Avars. To cap the climax, she was to become the wife of Prince Metternich, then the mightiest man in Europe. No wonder, then, that directly she had established herself firmly in the saddle she made others thoroughly sensible of her superiority. Using her riding-crop and spurs freely, the beautiful young woman took every hurdle.

For many years the Viennese were in the habit of telling tales of Melanie's unbelievable conceit and despotic lack of tact. On one occasion, to oblige Clemens, she was compelled to dine at the house of the banker Eskeles, who was of Jewish origin. She brought her own gold knives, forks, and spoons, and shoving those of the banker to one side, put hers next to her plate. The Milan archaeologist, Labus, was honored with an invitation to tea, and turned up sans the white kid-gloves demanded by etiquette. Thereupon the Princess ordered one of her lackeys to present Labus with a pair of these gloves on a silver salver. The learned man fortunately was not a whit abashed. He took the gloves and under the Princess' very eyes placed three silver coins on the tray, the usual price for gloves of that kind. Another anecdote, showing Liszt's gift of repartee, is also rather amusing. The great composer-pianist wove his magic spell at a charity concert in Vienna. After the concert the beautiful Princess walked up to the artist and, in French of course, found nothing else to say to him but: "You must be making a lot of money, Herr Liszt." "No, Madame, I make music," was the quick reply. The worst incident of all, however, one which brought about a diplomatic *démarche* on the part of the French Government, was that in which Count St. Aulaire the Ambassador of Louis Philippe in Vienna, was implicated. Louis Philippe, who after the deposition of his incompetent cousin, Charles X, had caused himself to be elected "King of the French," was generally considered by reactionary Vienna Court society to be nothing but a usurper, who had practically stolen the throne of France. At a ball, when Princess Metternich wore in her hair a magnificent diamond tiara, the Ambassador admired it greatly and, thinking to pay her a compliment in the manner of the gallant French, said to her: "Your tiara, Princess,—why, it's almost a crown!" "Well, at least I have not stolen it!" the irritated belle retorted acidly. A few days later Metternich had to tender a formal apology to Ambassador St. Aulaire who called at the chancellery for that purpose. Being a dictator of consummate good taste, Metternich managed the affair splendidly by apologizing with a smile, and the words: "I am not responsible for the up-bringing of my wife."

In this phrase, no matter how well chosen it may have been, lay the first admission of his own weakness, a weakness which Grillparzer, Austria's greatest poet, the contemporary and opponent of the eminent statesman, cast in his teeth. Pointing out the disparity of years between the princely couple, he maliciously remarked that because of his advanced age, Metternich, no longer able to satisfy the "robust Hungarian lady" in any other way, had to compensate her by making little presents to her. Thus he had made her a birthday present by admitting the Jesuits to the country, and a New-Year's gift by prohibiting marriages between Catholics and non-Catholics. Disregarding their political aspect, these are ticklish questions which are best side-tracked by pointing out the fact that Metternich's third marriage produced four children in its first five years. The family physician, Dr. Jaeger, finally felt induced to remonstrate with the young woman, because she put too heavy a strain upon the Prince. Melanie's life-long enmity was the reward and probably also the honorarium of the all-too-considerate doctor.

It goes without saying that there was no lack of the usual calumnious remarks. The difference in years was really too great. People felt justified in commenting upon the fact that the fiancé of former days, Baron Hügel, later accompanied the Metternichs on all their travels and, when in society, always stood behind her *fauteuil* or sat close by; but the deductions they drew were certainly quite unfounded. Baron Hügel may have returned to Vienna entirely cured, or only partly so, again to take up his duties at the State Chancellery. Princess Metternich, at any rate, was Princess Metternich, body and soul, and nothing else. In the initial stages of their married life she was hopelessly in love with her Clemens. She always wanted to stand at the side of his writing-desk, when he attended to his dispatches, "because it was so frightfully interesting" to watch him write. In the early days of August, 1830, a few months before her wedding, news of the outbreak of the July revolution was unexpectedly received at Castle Königswart, obviously moving the State-Chancellor very deeply; the young Countess, according to the testimony of an eyewitness, knelt down at the side of his arm-chair and kissed his hands upon which her tears fell freely. Such actions speak volumes and save us the trouble of reading volumes—including the many ample diaries written by the Princess herself, in which she refers to her husband only as *"ce pauvre Clement."* This too, in so far as it did not spring from her impulse to be a gracious dispenser of favors, is further proof of her being in love. Married to just about the happiest man in Europe, and to the one who had perhaps been more pampered by Fortune than any other being, she felt impelled to pity him in the bargain, and to make him appear a sort of martyr of his high office. She exaggeratedly attributed to him a crown of thorns in order that she might add a few more brilliants to his Prince's crown. To draw other conclusions from the repeatedly occurring *"ce pauvre Clement"* would be improper. In love with him at first, she later idolized him, and continued to do so to her very last breath; but this does not preclude the fact that theirs was at times a rather stormy married life, and that her unbridled character occasionally caused him a great deal of trouble and embarrassment. She was apt to remark maliciously, upon returning from a visit to old Baron von Rothschild, that the financier had shown her his vault, by all means "the most interesting piece of furniture in his house." This was not so serious a matter; but her imported Hungarian, and somewhat noisy ideas of social behavior, were accompanied by an equally Hungarian liberality in money matters, which at times involved him in serious unpleasantness. She would run up accounts with the Vienna tradespeople who dared not dun for their money, settling only when considerably more than the permissible time had elapsed; she tried to procure some of her adornments a little cheaper, by having shawls and laces smuggled to Vienna, by the diplomatic courier without passing them through the customs-house. Metternich certainly objected to such practices most strenuously, but it is equally certain that Melanie made light of his objections.

Disregarding the erotic element (if in the case of a man like Metternich it can be disregarded), the biographer is confronted with the question of how far the "public character" of the statesman was influenced by the dangerous disparity in ages in this third matrimonial venture. It is true that in the seventh decade of his life clerical tendencies became clearly visible, due undoubtedly to Melanie's influence. She came from those bigoted aristocratic circles which are on terms of equal familiarity with the catechism, and with the *Almanach de Gotha*. Devoted, with a mixture of meekness and despotism, to a highly dogmatic church creed from their early youth, their lust for ruling made them

pious, and their piety made them want to rule. Thus she succeeded, as Grillparzer's evil eye correctly discovered, in inducing the somewhat weakened man to tolerate the "Society
of Jesus." She also accustomed him in his advanced years to
hearing mass daily—he, the son of enlightenment, who, ten
years before she became his wife, had raised his head and
uttered the authentic words: "I mistrust the lamplight of
the sacristy!" For this very reason his seeming change for the
sake of domestic peace is not to be taken too seriously. Metternich was too much the son of the 18th century, with its
reasonable beliefs, to become clerical by conviction, though
he exposed himself to that suspicion from time to time. He
always rejected the idea of domination by the Church over
the State, which conception was shared by Emperor Franz,
and the latter's successor on the Austrian Imperial throne.
Emperor Franz Joseph, at the age of eighty-four, showed the
door to the Archbishop of Trient who, in the second year
of the World War, tried to induce him voluntarily to cede
Southern Tyrol to Italy. The primate's counsel nevertheless
was the very best any non-clerical politician could have
given the aged Emperor.

On the other hand, Metternich's third and last wife cannot be absolved from the charge that, though he had never
suffered from any excess of popularity, she wholly estranged
him from the people, and finally secluded him entirely
within his caste. Her drawing-room, which was now Metternich's drawing-room, was frequented exclusively by the
nobility, and if as happened very seldom an untitled visitor
should stray in he was in the manner of the Viennese ac-
costed as "Herr von. . . ." Thus the lowest and cheapest
title of nobility was gratuitously bestowed upon him to
deprive him, at least for the time being, of his presence

among noble surroundings, of the bourgeois atmosphere he had brought with him. This intolerant attitude was to have dire consequences when the waves of the Revolution of '48 engulfed the old statesman. Then, and in the following years of his exile, the bill was presented to him, and again it was a highly inconvenient bill for Princess Melanie, although she herself had been the cause of it. In justice to a woman with so utter a lack of restraint it must be admitted, nevertheless, that only at this period did she fully deserve the place of honor at Metternich's side. A great problem to her non-aristocratic contemporaries in the years of her good fortune and a constant source of anxiety to her husband whose patience she sorely tried, she showed her real worth only when misfortune had overtaken him. She would have carried him out of a burning house in her arms, or jumped into the sea to save him or prevent his drowning; literally she would have permitted herself to be drawn and quartered for *"ce pauvre Clement."* The more she was able to pity him, the fonder she grew of him.

A sequence of three marriages, all blessed with progeny, fill sixty years in the life of this ladies' man. Three women who, as far as their characterization is concerned, have little more in common than the mere fact that they were women. With which of them was he happiest? With the second, probably. Which was the best woman of the three? The first, by all means. She had an advantage over the others—and over those, also, to whom he had not been married. They all knew what they were able to give him; and they gave it. Only she, the noble Eleonore, knew one more thing. She also knew what she could *not* give him. She withdrew in good season; and when the time came, she quietly stole away.

Perpetuum Immobile

B<small>EING</small> naturally methodical, Metternich, in retrospect, divided his life into two great halves, the year 1815 being the dividing line. One he called the political half, the other, numbering almost as many years, the social half. What he meant by "social" is not quite clear, but one would hardly go wrong in assuming that he had in mind chiefly the maintenance of social order, as he saw it; in other words: the existing system of society. That, of course, was again politics, though politics using different means. If the first half had occupied itself mainly with the map of Europe, the idea of Europe was henceforth the guiding thought. To defend it, Metternich had developed a defensive system, the famous "Metternich System." It was a sort of Maginot Line of his policy, having no other task but to prevent an invasion by the hostile forces of revolution, an event which similarly in the end it was quite powerless to prevent.

The "System" has caused a great deal of conjecture and talk. Metternich's most exhaustive biographer, Srbik, whose book has been read by many, and finished by none, devotes to it a whole chapter, which in itself is a book. If one finally succeeds in reeling up the tape-worm, one finds that after all in the endless chain of the learnedly involved links, the head is missing, that is: an explanation of what the System really is. It is all and everything; as Grillparzer, satirizing the monster, expresses it wittily in a few droll verses:

> *I know a word brim-full of force,*
> *The deaf can hear it plainly;*
> *It's never still, therefore, of course,*
> *They think it's magic mainly.*
>
> *Nowhere and ev'rywhere at once*
> *They use it to assist them;*
> *It fits the wise man and the dunce,*
> *The little word is—system.*

In many respects this political system is a suitable counterpart of the "Holy Alliance" which, if we inspect it closely, was neither so holy nor so mysteriously allied as it sounded. It is almost the same today with the swastika, and the fasces. Part of a healthy deception is a deceiving name. The abracadabra of the magician and the "dalli-dalli" of the Egyptian prestidigitator are essentially the same as the dictators' party cry. He who believes in it is blest; he who does not is shot.

Important for a proper understanding of the system and its operator are two characteristics: the intertwining of interior and foreign politics and, consequently, the convergence and almost total interlocking of politics and police. Etymologically the words are of the same origin; they are both derived from the Greek word "polis," meaning city, or municipality. Certainly the Greeks, in their happy days, would have objected strenuously had anyone attempted to put the cultivation of their civic ideals—politics in an intellectual and moral sense—on a level with police super-vision. Americans would object as strenuously, but the Germans had no right to object to anything; and the Austrians, as far as they actually existed, were not asked. That, essentially, was the system which Metternich put into operation during the second half of his public activity. He called it the social half; he should have called it the police half. After Napoleon's overthrow Metternich had only one task: to fight revolutionary ideas, in which he saw the root of all evil—including Napoleon. These ideas, being of an evanescent nature, "nowhere and ev'rywhere at once," obviously were not to be fought in open battle. They could neither be deposed at Fontainebleau nor banished at St. Helena; like bacteria they had to be attenuated. It was a question not so much of "do" as of "prevent"; and in prevention lay Metternich's essential strength, a strength that had its roots in his character; more clever than passionate: passion opposes, cleverness prevents. The former "does," while the latter culminates in "not doing"—which of course should not be confounded with "doing nothing." No one can deny that Metternich was a diligent man. He worked fifteen hours a day, for no other purpose than to admonish others to keep quiet. Secretly, his real heraldic motto was not "Might by Right," which served very well for history, but a soothing and hortatory "Be still!" To preserve for his continent the resultant quiet, which he considered the cure, never in all his life did he shrink from a display of force, no matter how stormy it was.

This strenuous supervisory activity brought in its wake a highly desirable concomitant in the strengthening of Austria's hegemony. Somewhere in Germany a movement would flare up; let us say: the Hambach Demonstration in favor of a European Republic, or the so-called "Frankfort Putsch," both consequent upon the July Revolt in Paris. Austria, which presided over the German League, undertook the obligation of suppressing these ebullitions, and attended to that obligation with disproportionate rigor. It is true that if we compared these methods to those used by modern dictators they would appear disproportionately lenient. Or, Switzerland would humanely grant the Polish refugees a right of sanctuary; Metternich's ubiquitous police took a hand, with the result that many of the fugitives had to pay with their lives for the wicked attempt to find a haven of refuge. Or, the Carbonari Movement would once more show signs of life in Italy; the system's *sbirri* forced their way into the "charcoal-burners' hut" (the Carbonari pretended to be coal dealers so as to mislead the police), no matter whether this hut had established its black headquarters in Naples or Turin, in Bologna or Milan. Metternich's secret police, especially in Italy, was distinctly a precursor of our day's Gestapo. Once they had a person in their clutches, they made short work of him; he was sentenced to a term of imprisonment on the Spielberg, ranging from ten to thirty years, or else was executed without further ado—the latter consummation actually being in the nature of a lucky development. On one occasion Metternich had a personal meeting with one of these unfortunates, the Italian Count, Gonfalonieri. He visited him at the police-prison of Vienna, and an exchange of views developed between him, and the conspirator under death-sentence, within the sinister shadows of musty prison walls. "There is a good deal of talk now among liberals," said Metternich, "of patriotism and love of mankind. It is the patriotism that parts the fatherland from its sovereign. As soon as you assume this standpoint, it becomes understandable that you feel innocent. We others, however, confirmed monarchists that we are, cannot separate these three words: God, Emperor, and Fatherland. For us they represent an indissoluble trinity. . . ." Here we have the entire Metternich, with his mystic trinity, which seems also to be one of the secrets of his dictatorship. All magicians try to convince us that three is one; that's how they bewitch the world. Metternich, at least, believed it himself, since he was neither a charlatan nor a Machiavelli, no matter if from time to time he used Machiavellian methods. Even his cruelty was not unconditional. Gonfalonieri was not executed. Twenty years later, on the occasion of Emperor Ferdinand's visit to Milan, he was even pardoned.

The question arises why Metternich had his two-hours' conversation with the Italian revolutionist, of whose conviction he approved. "You have sinned against the law," he said explicitly, "and you are being punished according to the law. But," he added, "the affair has also its political side or, if you prefer, its European side." This "if you prefer," spoken to a condemned man between prison walls, is indeed charming. It serves to put into the foreground a new quality of our hero: his extreme politeness. It is significant, too, for the "Knight of Europe" that even in the prison-cell he thought of Europe.

Speaking of Europe, such as it was, Metternich had his own troubles with it. One time there was a storm in Portugal, another in Spain. Then again it was Poland, or Turkey, to say nothing of France which, a year after the July Revolution, drew up her army in Belgium against Holland. On every one of these occasions Austria took up her position in favor of the old and in opposition to the new, and she succeeded in almost every instance in maintaining her position.

Not even Metternich, however, with all his reactionary tendencies, was able to prevent the formation of two States. One
of these States was Greece, and the other Belgium, "England's sentinel in Europe" as they called it in those days
without considering that sentinels, too, are apt to turn tail.
. . . Scarcely any of the day's developments are actually
new, a fact which may up to a certain degree excuse Metternich's reactionary attitude. There was, after all, in his noise-
less dictatorship, a good deal of sound common sense.

Only occasionally did Metternich become entangled in
the ideological maze of doctrinal dogmatism; as for instance
when he gave his support to the usurper against the legitimate royal power in the Portuguese as well as in the Spanish
struggles for the throne—he the legitimist! And why his support? Because the usurper was the more reactionary of the
two. Thus, in the case of Spain, for example, he claimed as
his justification Charles V's last will, which excluded women
(in this instance Isabella) from succession to the throne. In
the Orient, again, Metternich artificially kept alive the
"Sick Man," i. e., Turkey, for no other reason than to prevent the birth of a new State. This, in fact, was the tragic
guilt of Austria's foreign policy for which a terrible penalty
was to be paid in the 20th century. If the Austro-Hungarian
Monarchy, in the First Balkan War of 1912, had aligned
itself with the young Balkan States instead of against them,
it could have prevented the World War, and all that followed in its wake. It was the tragic fate of Austria, just as
it had been that of the social—not the political—Metternich that, in trying to prevent anything from happening, in
the end it made everything come to pass.

In these years of his life, between sixty and seventy, when
the shadows began to lengthen, he was still able to pluck

a few toothsome fruits in the field of foreign politics. One of these fruits was Cracow which, less cleverly handled, might have become the Danzig of those days. Ever since the Congress of Vienna, Cracow, the old Polish coronation-city, represented a sort of vermiform process of the former Polish independence and developed quite logically into an inflammatory center of revolutionary movements in Poland. Metternich had foreseen this, without however being able to carry his point in the face of Alexander's romantically liberal dreams of liberty; he was forced to acquiesce in the establishment of a Free State of Cracow, although he feared the freedom and mistrusted the State. There was nothing to be done as long as Alexander lived. Then, in 1825, this liberal despot died suddenly—so suddenly, in fact, that it was frequently asserted that he had not died at all, but had been spirited into a monastery. Nicholas, a much more outspoken autocrat, became his successor. When Metternich received the news of the Czar's death, he said calmly: "This is the end of fiction and the beginning of history." From the very first he got along quite well with the new Czar. After the establishment of the Kingdom of Greece and the defeat of the Turks by Russia in the Thirties, he drew him ever closer to his side. It seems that autocrats always pull together.

After the French July Revolution, which filled the Polish sails with a hopeful breeze, the situation in Cracow became impossible. The obvious drift was towards Austria, but Metternich was anxious to save appearances. For him it was not a question of annexing Cracow—as Hitler annexed Danzig, in 1939; he was content to permit himself to be compelled to annex it. To sin guiltlessly had now become his aim under circumstances such as the ones now confronting him. In this instance, at least, he still achieved it, although by devious detours. To begin with, in 1836, he managed to bring about a collective military occupation of Cracow by Russia, Prussia, and Austria, the group of Powers created by him and called the Holy Alliance. In the course of the occupation which lasted until 1841, a trade agreement between Cracow and Austria was ratified. This quite naturally led to an inclusion of the former State in the Austrian customs districts. The right moment came in 1846. Revolution again raised its head, the flames quickly spread and penetrated into the neighboring countries. Austria being one of them, the two other neighbors called upon her to restore order. Metternich was still reluctant to annex; the peach did not yet seem ripe enough for him to sink his teeth into it. At last the Czar was at the end of his patience. He threatened to do the annexing himself if Austria did not. What was left for Metternich but to do him the little favor? What good will of liberal Western Europe he had still held, was now forfeited. A storm of indignation swept through France and England because of this obvious disregard of existing agreements, the sanctity of which for many years had been solemnly affirmed by Metternich. It seems that his conscience actually bothered him about it, for it is said he sat for a long time after the signing of the act of annexation, his head thoughtfully cupped in his hands, staring silently in front of him. He could, after all, console himself with the thought that Austria had gained a nice piece of territory and prevented a war. Not every dictator in a similar position is able to advance this argument.

That during this period of his life, lasting from 1815 to 1848, Metternich actually was a dictator—at all times in Austria, and most of the time in Europe—cannot be doubted, although he probably would have objected to the label. So little value did he place on being taken for a dictator, that at times he actually ridiculed his own impotence. At one time he wrote to his son, whom he was to lose soon after, using one of the witty comparisons which formed the charm as well as the danger of a style reveling in circumlocutions: "My position is that of one crucified. One arm is nailed fast in Constantinople, the other in Lisbon, while the body is shaken by internal convulsions. It is Canning who has crucified me, and the Hungarian Diet is the sponge steeped in vinegar and tendered to me on a pole." Metternich presents himself as a rare and almost unique species of dictator, one with a sense of humor. There were times, however, when it deserted him. On such occasions he sighed and moaned and lamented or, as he did in 1839, feigning a stroke of apoplexy, kept to his bed for a few weeks and cursed his life. In the joy of power he, like every autocrat, had to recognize finally that power is not always joy.

In March, 1835, at the age of sixty-eight, Emperor Franz died, leaving a last will. In it he graciously bequeathed to the people he had ruled "his love." "I leave you my love," became the good-humored greeting of the satirically inclined Viennese. He made over the Crown to his feeble-minded eldest son Ferdinand, who was to have the benefit, however, of a Regency Council composed of Archduke Ludwig and Metternich, the all-powerful and indispensable grand-vizier of the far-flung Empire. Thus, from then on until 1848, Metternich was no longer a dictator, but only a regent. The "only" is justified; for although he was now privileged to enter a city to the thunder of cannon like any crowned head, the actual extent of his power, thanks to the unfortunate Regency Council, had become smaller rather than larger.

The era of Emperor Franz, called the "Vienna Biedermeier era" by art-historians and symbolized by a blue beehive, also wore the political imprint of the blue beehive (the
distinguishing mark of the old Vienna porcelain), while the
Emperor himself was a Biedermeier despot. The governmental system practised by him was called with good-
humored hypocrisy "patriarchal." The Emperor was the
father, nay, more than that, the tenderly beloved "papa" of
the many peoples he ruled, just as the householders in
Vienna watched over their various pieces of property, which
often were at a considerable distance one from the other.
He was the head of the firm, and Metternich the managing
director of the business and of the financial administration.
Things went along well in that way for several decades. In
the evening the employer and his manager met regularly
and locked themselves in for a few hours. It was whispered
that they were "working," and the children, meaning the
peoples, walked about on tip-toe so as not to disturb them.
In addition, the two also played in the quartet once a week.
The Emperor played the first violin, and Metternich the
'cello. He bowed low over his instrument to disguise the
fact that his head towered above those of the other players.

The Biedermeier style made everything small and charming, or as they said in Vienna: *lieb.* Fond of laughter and a
good time, the Viennese turned everything into a nice little
joke. They'd ask a visitor to sit down on a little stool which,
under the pressure from above, would immediately give
forth the tinkling melody: *"Du du liegst mir am Herzen!"*
"My lips are pressed against thy cheeks!" The Biedermeier
era had a touch of infantility, which just about fits the
"papa" ideology. As the period grew older and more childish, the infantility was quite apt to turn into imbecility.

This actually happened when the good Emperor was carried off by pneumonia—"a cute little case of pneumonia," the Viennese probably called it. The subsequent imbecility on the throne was called Ferdinand.

Even the Biedermeier-Emperor Franz who, after all, was still a real Emperor, confined his ruling during the last decades of his reign almost entirely to giving audiences. The audience is a special invention of Spanish-Habsburg-Austrian origin. Anyone, by stating a reasonable cause, may petition to be received in audience, and if the petitioner is a loyal citizen without any black marks against him, his request is usually granted. He is then permitted into his Emperor's august presence and is expected to give mannerly answers to whatever questions he is asked. That makes the humble petitioner feel good and serves to make the Emperor tremendously popular in the course of years. Emperor Franz Joseph's ultimate popularity, which he enjoyed only at the end of his reign of sixty-eight years, was mainly due to the fact that in his many years on the throne he granted innumerable audiences. Emperor Franz' case was quite similar, although sixty-eight denotes the entire span of his life. To make up for it, he laboriously went through a long round of daily audiences, beginning at seven in the morning. The hour was due to the fact that the Emperor was an early riser, partly because that was a Habsburg tradition and partly because elderly people usually wake up in the early morning hours. Those to be received were required to assemble in the Imperial ante-chamber an hour before the start of the audiences. They were given a number, just as if they had come to a busy barber-shop, and were summoned at any time between 7 A. M. and 3 P. M. It may be imagined that a good deal of confusion reigned in His Majesty's ante-chamber, especially on a bleak winter morning, when people had hardly had time to rub the sleep from their eyes. A writer of that period told the story of a distracted friend who, having overslept, presented himself in the ante-chamber unshaved, and had the misfortune of being called first. Stroking his stubbly chin in utter confusion, he was ushered into the Emperor's presence and stammered a few words of apology for his sprouting beard. The Emperor smiled graciously and said: "Ah, don't worry. Just step across to the Court barber's and get shaved. As for me, I'll be here, anyway, when you get back."

That's the way it went, and it would have continued that way had not Emperor Franz' sudden death prevented him from giving any further audiences. Who was to give them after him? According to the family law it would have been the deceased Emperor's eldest son, Ferdinand, who was barred, however, because of his splendidly developed imbecility. When Franz' pneumonia took a turn for the worse, the patriarchally ruled Viennese shook their heads apprehensively, speculating as to who would rule them patriarchally in a day or two. This was not without its dire influence upon the Government Bonds which declined sharply, the stock exchange, as usual, being a step ahead of the general apprehension. The House of Rothschild was a notable exception, buying while everyone else was selling. Rothschild staked his whole fortune on the continuance of the Habsburg Empire. This was all the more notable since it was an open secret that Baron Rothschild was a close friend of State Chancellor Metternich. Had they been Americans of our day, the Viennese might have asked: "So what?"

They were much too excited, however, to come to the correct conclusion at once. Three days later they all knew what had gone on behind their backs.

The Emperor had made a last will. If Metternich did not actually draw it up, certainly he counseled the Emperor. The first-born, Ferdinand, was to succeed to the throne after all, in spite of his well-known imbecility which in no way interfered with his popularity. Perhaps it even enhanced it. His defenseless kindness of heart had some of the charm of Dostoievski's "Idiot." At one time he had a hairbreadth escape from an attempt on his life. The unfortunate who had pointed a pistol at him was disarmed and the crowd wanted to lynch him. Ferdinand stepped between them and shielded the man with his own body. He insisted upon his complete exoneration, and even caused the State Exchequer to pay the man a life-long annuity to safeguard him for all time against the need and despair that had driven him to the deed. It was one of those instances in which imbecility and sanity are not greatly divergent.

At any rate, however, it was not possible to entrust to such a hand the sole guidance of the ship of State. For this reason Emperor Franz' last will and testament provided for the establishment of a Regency Council. It was to be composed of the phlegmatic and indolent Archduke Ludwig, a younger brother of the new Emperor, and Metternich. The Emperor had expressly stated in his will that the latter's judgment and advice were to be considered at all times. A subsequent member of this Regency Council was Count Kolowrat, a jealous rival of Metternich; he tried to obstruct as much as possible whatever Metternich wished, and whatever needed an early settlement, as far as Archduke Ludwig's persistent laziness had not already achieved this end. While in this manner the three men largely frustrated one another, things on the whole remained as they had been and Metternich was regent, after all—a sort of uncrowned emperor by his own grace. Rothschild, depending upon his personal information, had speculated wisely. The banking-firm made a handsome profit, and only Austria, somewhat later, became bankrupt.

What Metternich had created by this cleverly self-neutralizing Regency Council was, so to speak, a *perpetuum immobile* of his policy. Had his ambition made him conceive it? Hardly; for he was not ambitious. Rather it may have been due to his sense of duty. Who was to replace him and take up the reins, once the "Coachman of Europe" was forced to let them slip from his grasp? He believed correctly that there was no one in sight. As in every dictatorship, there was a distinct lack of eligible successors; like every dictator, he was surrounded by tools and creatures. The dictators, who are given to pointing regretfully to these facts, should be reminded that they are their own fault. By suppressing and crippling individualities, they prevent the development of personalities. Every growth presupposes freedom, fortunately. For if it were not so, there would be no limit to a dictatorship's expansion.

Two special events must not be omitted from a record of Metternich's later years of dictatorial reign. While the great statesman approached a patriarchal age, the Napoleonic legend came to a final conclusion through the early death of the Duke of Reichstadt, concerning whose touching fate more will be said anon. Then there was the diplomatic game of chess with the French Ambassador St. Aulaire, showing Metternich, master of politics at their best and worst, once more in full possession of his admirable gifts.

Young St. Aulaire had known Metternich at the end of the latter's brilliant days in Paris. It was he who, on the day of Metternich's arrival in Paris after the victory over Napoleon, on April 11th, 1814, had surprised him before the mirror, in a hair-dresser's wrapper. Twenty years later we find St. Aulaire again at the Court of Vienna where he represented Louis Philippe as Ambassador. Not a pleasant task, that, for Louis Philippe, the "King with the Umbrella," was highly unpopular in Vienna for two reasons. First, because as the illegal successor of the legitimate Charles X he had, as Princess Metternich expressed it, stolen the Crown; second, because his was a liberal government, the "King of the French" being supported by an ever-changing parliamentary majority. That, above all, he was successful and managed to avoid the collapse of this monstrous regime, in spite of Metternich's frequent predictions, was not designed to make him more popular.

St. Aulaire was an average diplomat and an excellent writer. In his latter capacity he has furnished a charming picture of Metternich's Vienna in French colors, the central theme being the Duke of Orléans' suit for the hand of the Austrian Archduchess Theresa. The Duke of Orléans, a strikingly handsome young man of twenty-six, was successor to the French throne, and the nineteen-year-old Archduchess the daughter of Archduke Karl who, victor over Napoleon, was considered a liberal at the Court of Vienna. This being a blemish in the eyes of Metternich, it made the Archduke and his daughter all the more eligible for St. Aulaire's purpose.

This marriage had been very deliberately planned by the Ambassador. Putting out a trial balloon, he had derived a great deal of satisfaction from the fact that on the occasion of a reception at the French Embassy the young Archduchess evinced considerable curiosity about the picture of the Duke of Orléans, from which could be deduced her inclination to become Queen of France at a distant date, in spite of the sad experience that had been the share of her two aunts, Marie Antoinette and Marie Louise. St. Aulaire, moreover, had had hours of conversation on the subject with the French royal couple. That it was considered desirable in Paris, to keep these conversations secret, was one more reason for Metternich's familiarity with their gist. It was usually so: he was better informed than the ones directly concerned. This went so far that there were times when he had knowledge of ambassadors' secret instructions before they themselves knew of them. To make this possible, almost all European postal connections were laid out in such manner that they had to pass through Austria. There the letters were carefully opened and closed again. The codes in which diplomatic messages were written were no obstacles either, since the head of that department, Eichenfeld, boasted possession of eighty-five keys to such codes. It had even been possible to solve the Russian code, the most puzzling of all, although it had taken fully four years of an expert's time (and he received a rather handsome yearly stipend for his efforts) to furnish a key. In the Austria of those days no less than in the Nazi Germany of ours, one did not mind spending money to obtain knowledge of other people's secrets. It paid. No matter how sadly depleted the State Exchequer was, there was always money for this honorable purpose. This, too, is a generic characteristic of a dictatorship.

The Duke of Orléans, accompanied by his younger brother, the Duke of Nemours, arrived in Vienna at the end of May. Hardly had the first half of June passed, when they returned to Paris without having attained their end. In the meantime the diplomatic game of chess had been played. Metternich had won it, although he seemed to be quite absent-minded, playing only with his left hand, as it were. One should have thought, too, that it was no great feat to decline a suitor inconvenient or not acceptable to the House of Habsburg. The matter was not quite as simple as it looked. The Duke of Orléans who had come to Vienna to take home a Habsburg bride was not only to be "given the bucket," but it was to be handed to him and he was to carry it back to Paris in such a manner that all the world would know of it. For that purpose it was necessary not only simply to reject him, but to encourage him at first and make him feel secure. In this, Metternich succeeded thanks to the lack of experience of those immediately involved, including Archduke Karl. The old war-horse rather liked the French Prince, and Theresa shared his feelings. So favorably impressed was the Archduke when the two young men called at romantic Castle Weilburg, in Baden near Vienna, that he readily consented! He was greatly embarrassed later when he had to take back consent, since the final decision was not up to him but to the Emperor—Metternich. Nobody, however, was able to prove that the latter had said No, or even thought of it. What was the use of a Regency Council, if one was not able to barricade oneself behind it? It is a fact, at any rate, that after having spent a couple of extremely pleasant June weeks in Vienna and its surroundings, the Duke of Orléans continued his journey in search of a bride in a southerly direction. His successor at Weilburg was the widowed King of Naples who succeeded in carrying off the bride. Poor little Archduchess Theresa who, we may assume, was somewhat smitten with the young Prince's charms found but little happiness in the unloved Naples; thoroughly embittered, she died there at a comparatively early age. The heir to the throne of France, on the other hand, soon married a Mecklenburg Princess who was not only clever and amiable, but liberal in the bargain.

In the end, what did it avail Austria that soon after the abortive wooing an attempt was made on the life of Louis Philippe, so that Metternich seemed justified when he declared one could have no dealings with a "King at whom people shoot"? The emphatic turning away from the liberal West, which took place quite patently at that time, was to seal Austria's doom a hundred years later, in the World War and afterwards, when the Austrian wreck was driven upon the Nazi coast. Metternich's temporary success must seem insignificant in comparison.

The years after 1830, when the happily married elegant State-Chancellor guided the destinies of Austria and thus influenced materially the whole Continent's destiny, do not represent the most attractive phase in his rich and widely ramified life. In spite of all his efforts to remain young, the picture of the sexagenarian naturally lacks the glamor of youth. What did he get in exchange for it? The kindly resignation of old age had not yet descended on him, and what he had always lacked in warmth of heart, was not yet replaced by a wisdom grown unselfish. Thus, between success and failure, we see him continue to play his old parts with the assurance and experience of an aged actor but not always with the driving forcefulness of the artist who lives the moments he portrays. It is Metternich's inherent lack of sympathy that strikes one most forcibly when contemplating the fate of the Duke of Reichstadt. Not that he drove Napoleon's son to his death; that he did *not* do. That his sympathies were not more profoundly stirred though, when he saw the premature end of this young life whose guardian he had been, is the guilt of which humanity will never be quite able to acquit Metternich. It was not cruelty on his part, but a want of feeling. It is not a deed we can mind, but we miss one tear. Politics, in this instance, should have been a little less than everything to him.

L'Aiglon

A FEW years ago, on the day marking the hundredth anniversary of the death of the Duke of Reichstadt, Napoleon's son, the romantic shadow of the ill-fated boy was called up by the stroke of history's clock and once more flitted ghost-like through the columns of the world's press. "King of Rome" in his cradle, he died in Vienna of consumption when barely twenty-one years old, surrounded by the serenity of the Biedermeier era. That epoch was called in France the "Musset Period," while in Vienna they gave it the less poetical but more palatable appellation of the "Fried-Chicken Period." In this respect, too, the little son of the great Napoleon is more the Frenchman than the Austrian, more the scion of Napoleon than that of the Habsburgs, so that the first of the two expressions comes to mind more readily than the second. He had something of Musset's girlish heroes in him, and it was therefore eminently fitting that when, as *L'Aiglon,* he started on his highly successful stage career while the nineteenth century was passing into the twentieth, a woman, Madame Sarah Bernhardt, lent him the charm of her femininity.

Quite in the spirit of Musset, he also was a veritable *enfant du siècle,* descended from that post-war generation, of which the poet says in the introduction to his world famous novel, *"L'Enfant du Siècle,"* that it was conceived between two battles and born to disaster. That is a generalization, and this young prince, too, was a poetical generalization. His personal misfortune became one with that of the epoch, which happened to be the romantic one. To be unhappy was then considered the height of fashion, and anyone living in moderately comfortable circumstances indulged in this luxury. *Weltschmerz* assumed the musk-odor of refined society, while the *"beau ténébreux"* became the drawing-room ideal of whom young ladies dreamed. The twenty-year-old Duke of Reichstadt, in the swan-white uniform the Austrians had provided for him, also mourned his sad, somber fate, and dismal thoughts dwelt behind the blue eyes and the boyish forehead which was so charmingly set off by a profusion of blond locks. To be sure, it was not an imaginary affliction in his case; though written by life itself, it bore all the earmarks of an artificially contrived tragedy, wherein there can be no other logical solution than death.

This tragedy has been often related and still oftener discussed. The last poet to lend it his talents was Rostand, who sentimentalized it in the beautiful pointed verses of his *"L'Aiglon."* Its course, however, was not so simple as would appear when viewed from the all-simplifying nationalistic angle. If nothing else were taken into consideration but the fantastic change of fortune with which it so tearfully toys, the result would be merely an emotional melodrama, a *comédie larmoyante,* never a tragedy. The truth is that in the case of Napoleon's son, Fortune took a fantastically retrograde course. The infant born at the Paris Tuileries was called "King of Rome" while still in his swaddling clothes, and His Tiny Majesty was surrounded by a princely household even before he could stand up and toddle. Then, before he had completed his fourth year, he was driven from his beautiful country, and the tenderest of fathers was replaced by a grumpy grandpapa who ruled over an Eastern Empire somewhere far away in a big yellow castle. Mamma was crying all the time; Papa was traveling abroad; and when the little tot stepped out of his nursery there was no longer anyone in attendance in the hall. The little four-year-old heaved his first tragic sigh: "I can well see that I am no longer a King, since I have no pages."

These pages, however, were but the first thing of which he was deprived. Soon his French nurse was dismissed, the stout-hearted Madame de Montesquiou to whom he was more attached than to his own mother; the French servants disappeared, and even his little French playfellow was gone. Invisible forces were at work to remodel the King of Rome into an Austrian princeling, a prince without a country. He was not even permitted to journey to Parma, where his mother had found the way in the company of a one-eyed *ersatz*-papa. Neither would they allow him to call himself Prince of Parma, because from it might be deduced hereditary claims which they were by no means willing to concede. At least, however, the child had to be given some name —the son of Napoleon! They thought of this and of that. Emperor Franz proposed "Duke of Mödling," which was the title used by the Babenbergs in Austria a thousand years before. But for that very reason the idea was dismissed, for the Babenbergs were the Habsburgs' predecessors in Austria; why invite comparisons? "Duke of Buschtiehrad" would not do either. It was Metternich's suggestion, and not a very kindly one, indeed; for it would sound ridiculous, especially to the Viennese who haughtily turned up their noses at the sound of the little provincial Czech town's name, as they did at everything that was "Bohemian." Finally they all agreed on "Duke of Reichstadt." It sounded well and, in the last analysis, meant nothing: the very thing! It was probably Metternich himself who invented the meaningless name. The name means nothing, but it sounds "as if."

There exists something that may well be called the Austrian "as if": the make-believe presentation of a reality which in truth conforms to no reality at all. We stumble upon it at every step in Austria's more recent history, from Metternich down. While the Emperor of Austria was no longer German Emperor, Austria still presided over the German League "as if" he still were. Metternich ruled "as if" he were Minister, while as a matter of fact he was the Regent. The Austrian currency was actually worth only one-fifth of its face value, a fact which led to the distinction between "in coin" and "in paper"; but everyone acted "as if" the currency were quite sound. Into this category belongs also the indiscriminate and exaggerated unofficial bestowal of titles: the "Your Worship" of the cabbies; and the "Herr von . . ." which the hostess of a drawing room used in talking to and introducing a guest "as if" the world were peopled only by aristocrats. As Melanie Metternich thought, humanity started only at the "vons." Even Metternich did not scorn to lavish this "as if" nobility upon untitled persons. All his life he spoke of a "Monsieur *de* Fouché," although Fouché had never in his life been a "de." The "I kiss your hand" of the Viennese, which may mean anything between "How do you do," "Thank you," "I am at your service," and "Good-bye," hails from the same quarter as Metternich's metaphorical style, the "as if" style of his communications which continued to be used by the Austrian Foreign Office until the very last. "There is an element of comfort in comparisons," said Schnitzler, Austria's most lovable and most biting satirist; and since there is comfort in them the easy-going Viennese loved them. Even in the World War, when it was a question of ceding the Italians Trentino to prevent Italy's entry into the war, a young Austrian diplomat of the Metternich school, in answer to a remark favoring the cession, made the clever-sounding but senseless reply: "A country cannot be plucked to pieces like an artichoke!" There is something fictional in the phrase, just as there was fiction in Austria as long as she existed. She lived in fictions—the last of which was the so-called "Guild State," abracadabra of the Schuschnigg dictatorship—and was after all but a fiction herself.

Another one of these fictions was the "Duke of Reichstadt," so cleverly invented by Metternich—a "title without means," as they say in Vienna. Behind it, however, stood a very-much-alive young man not content to play the part of a "Herr von . . ." on a somewhat higher and plush-covered pedestal. He desired sooner or later to materialize the ambitions he had inherited from his father. He was in earnest in the midst of a playfully make-believe world. This was his tragedy, or at least one half of his tragedy; the tragedy of a not-experienced glory. No one, including Metternich, would have begrudged his being a beautiful picture in the glorious frame of Vienna's Court society. Metternich was never small-minded in his "as if"-dealings with human vanity, as long as it had no inclination towards becoming serious. It was therefore a pity that the young lad, the "silly boy," as Marie Louise might have said and thought, had visions of glory and had brought from Paris the very seriousness to which Metternich objected. He had inherited it from his father, more was the pity. When the strangely handsome young man of twenty, girlishly slender and boyishly wild, clad in the handsome white tunic of a "supernumerary" Austrian colonel and mounted on the Arabian steed his kind grandpapa had given him, galloped through the streets of Vienna, as he did from time to time, the muslin curtains at the windows began to stir under the touch of coyly peeping maidens and the fuchsias and pelargoniums in their window boxes shook dangerously. Had he been satisfied with that kind of life, he could have grown old or remained young in Vienna until he was eighty, and would have been to the end a little "as if"-*Napoleon en biscuit,* romantically idealized by women. The youth, however, possessed by an inherent plutarchic longing for glory, was secretly determined not only to play the hero but to become one. It was from this typically Viennese contrast between pretense and truth, between "as if" and reality, that he finally perished in Vienna.

Accusations have been made, and accusations have been refuted. Frequently it has been asserted, and proof has been offered, that the Duke perished of Austria. That is correct; but it is equally correct that, had the Duke of Reichstadt been born in Vienna and been forced at the age of four to take up a new life in a victorious France, partly a stranger and a dangerous pretender, he would have perished of France. Politics in every country are wholly unsusceptible to pity. That one in a high position is apt to fall far, and that the higher the position the greater the fall, is unfortunately a physical law which even the cleverest statesmanship is unable to change; and certainly Metternich's statesmanship was not the most humane under the circumstances. That, too, has been asserted, and his reactionary cojurors (as for instance Jean de Bourgoing lately) like to offer proof

in wordy Metternichian sentences that the Napoleonic
Prince received the very best education—a fact which, not
even Bibl in the opposite camp, tries to deny. They say that
no attempt was made to remodel him into an Austrian Archduke, adducing as proof the contents of the secret archives
which have but lately become available. All the memoranda, reports, and quotations from diaries, however, cannot alter the fact that the youth of fifteen was asked at one
of his examinations, for instance, to write a description of
the Battle of Leipsic in which his father was so decisively
beaten, and which could serve only to glorify indirectly the
military genius of the Austrian commander, Prince Schwarzenberg. What must have passed through the soul of the
prematurely tall, precocious, and excitable youth who
idolized his father and now saw himself magisterially compelled to crucify the god in his own breast? No wonder that
the poor breast was unequal to the strain!

Metternich, as well as all of Vienna, knew the Duke of
Reichstadt entertained great plans. He was after all his father's son, the "young eagle," the *"aiglon,"* a name first
given to him not by Rostand but by the handsome and coquettish contemporary Viennese Countess Lulu Thuerheim
in her diaries. Once, at a ball, she had a conversation with
the young man of twenty, which she recorded. "Do you
really think," he asked her to the strains of a waltz, "that I
shall have to choose between glory and love? And which of
the two shall I have to renounce?"—"Love, of course," replied the experienced coquette and cast up her eyes to him,
though she was old enough to be his mother. Whether that
was really her opinion or merely a hint, an "Invitation to
the Dance," must be left undecided. Certain it is that Metternich, too, would not have minded seeing the "historical

child" espouse love at a certain age and forget in the embraces and kisses of an experienced woman his unwholesome aspirations. As in the case of every young man, there was that possibility, and Vienna of those and later days was fond of discussing it thoroughly. One's dear friends' love affairs was a favorite society topic. This was a secondary success of Metternich's statesmanship, which required all subjects to refrain from political discussions.

In the present instance two names were prominently mentioned: that of Archduchess Sophie and of the dancer, Fanny Elssler. One is as nonsensical as the other. The famous dancer never even knew the Duke of Reichstadt; and the Archduchess, the handsome Prince's senior by a few years, was at best nothing to him but a sisterly friend who, in that capacity, was to render him both the best and the worst service imaginable. When the cough-racked Prince was lying on his deathbed, the Archduchess was far advanced in pregnancy, expecting a second child who was to become Emperor Maximilian of Mexico. She paid the dying young man a visit and, wishing to prepare herself for her ordeal, asked him to partake of the Lord's Supper with her. He assented; and while the sacrament was administered to him by the Archduchess' confessor, the doors leading to the adjoining room were flung open. He saw the entire Court on their knees, a ceremony dictated by Habsburg Court Etiquette in the event of an impending death, and the realization that he was about to die penetrated his fevered dreams. It was a scene of intensely moving beauty, one which Rostand did not fail to utilize in his theatrically effective play.

Metternich had nothing to do with all that; not even with the matters referring to women, though they would have been quite congenial to him. The Duke of Reichstadt died without his assistance and of entirely natural causes. He bore two opposite battle fields in his all-too-narrow chest: Aspern, where Austria had beaten Napoleon; and Wagram, where the rôles had been reversed. How were these conflicting emotions to be bridged, how was a balance to be struck between his most extraordinary father and his most ordinary mother? The latter had not once found the way to Vienna in the last six years of his short life; only when the flickering flame of his life threatened to die away did she "rush" to her child's deathbed. In spite of all this, she, too, the Habsburg, lived in his blood. For while he wanted to become Napoleon II, Emperor of the French, he wished to achieve his ends in a legitimate way and on no account by means of a *coup d'état,* though after the July Revolution, it might have been possible to bring one about. His scrupulous leaning towards the legitimate revealed the scion of the Habsburgs, whose appropriate burial-place was the Capuchin Crypt in Vienna rather than the Panthéon in Paris. His fate exemplifies the interlocking of two tragedies: the unfulfilled dream of the pretender who, though born for the throne, will never reign; and the tragedy of a genius' son who, since genius is so rare, of necessity must be overshadowed by his father. Fortune is a calculating goddess who likes to deduct from the following generation what she has lavished upon the preceding one. How true this is was discovered to his sorrow by the "historical child," as Varnhagen called the Duke of Reichstadt; and the sorrow grew until it broke his heart. Between his cradle and his coffin, both of which were to be seen in Vienna until lately, the story of his life reads like a melancholy and lovely fairy-tale; the fairy-tale of the Emperor's son who was shunned by everyone. It is a subject almost too tender for matter-of-fact history, but just the thing for a legend. Musset ought to have fashioned a ballad of it, with Schubert writing the music. There actually exists only one mediocre poem: *"Le Fils de l'Homme,"* by Berthélemy, whose pompous rolling of the drums found an effective echo, seventy years later, in Rostand's *"Historie."* It is quite obviously the poet's task and not the historian's to sing of the pale immortality of this frail youth; but he must be a true poet, and not a hot-headed nationalist of either side.

The Duke of Reichstadt's early death played about the same part in Metternich's life as the shooting of the chivalrous Duke d'Enghien did in Napoleon's. Even those who are ready to condone everything cannot forgive him in this one instance. Rightly so. But whenever Metternich's accusers are asked to state their case, they have little to say. The young Prince was a consumptive, and yet was asked to command a body of soldiers at a temperature "considerably below zero." This "below zero" is not nearly so terrifying for Russians or Austrians as it is for Frenchmen or Italians, who are used to a milder climate. Besides, Metternich was not the military commander of Vienna. That the Duke was not permitted to go South, i. e. to Italy, there to cure his lung affliction, should not be laid at Metternich's door, either. He himself had to sacrifice three grown-up children to the "Vienna Disease," and only one of them, Victor, died in Italy. There remains the white tunic into which they put, or rather had to put, the young Duke, seeing that after all he served in the Austrian army. It is true that he was excluded from the succession in Parma—true but understandable, since a pretendership could not be allowed to germinate, of all places, in the hot soil of Italy. Cruel? Possibly. But what is the fate today of inconvenient pretenders of age-old ruling families? They are pursued by warrants of apprehension and threatened with shooting. At any rate it is a fact that at a certain moment Metternich even encouraged the Duke of Reichstadt's pretensions to the throne of France, or at least played diplomatically upon the possibility just to keep Louis Philippe in check. The only thing with which Metternich actually can be reproached in this sad family affair is the very thing which his adherents seem only too anxious to use in invalidating any charges aimed at him. How could he have hated and persecuted the Duke of Reichstadt? they ask; he hardly knew him, had seen him all of five times in his whole life, and had had only one lengthy conversation with the unfortunate youth in the last year of his life, a conversation which had no tangible results. That is true, but therein really lies Metternich's guilt. That he who had time for so many things had so little, so very little, to spare for an unfortunate child, must always be held against this man of many activities. He was a better dictator than he was a guardian.

A Refined Old Gentleman in His Arm-chair

THIS caption would fittingly describe Metternich's two last portraits between which there is a span of about ten years. The one shows a man of sixty-eight, while in the other he is nearly eighty. On the former he still wears the full-dress coat of the Minister, which fits his person like a glittering snakeskin, and his neck is still swathed in knightly cordons and the collar of the Golden Fleece. In the latter picture he is somberly but comfortably clad in elegant black: black coat and heavy black silk tie. Stripped of all outward honors, he still retains his own dignity. Tranquilly he holds a book on his crossed knees. In the last ministerial painting, he is seen surrounded by petitions, newspapers, and a group of mythological dancing girls in flowing Greek garments depicted in shadowy outlines on a piece of furniture in the background. Are they Graces? Or Muses? On the later picture, at any rate, they are seen no longer. The aged man looks bitterly into space. With head inclined to one side, and a tragical, composed, sullen expression on his face, how strangely he now resembles the old Grillparzer, his stubborn antagonist. Antagonist? At the end of their days both great Austrians were bitterly disappointed men.

Between these two portraits, lies the Revolution of 1848, the greatest event in the life of Metternich—his St. Helena.

Nevertheless, the importance of its influence on his character and fate should not be overestimated, the very same being true of Napoleon and St. Helena. The final island had no more power to change the great Bonaparte, than the year 1848 had to change the great Austrian statesman. The only difference was that he now confined himself to words where formerly his actions had spoken. Even that, though, made no appreciable difference, seeing that in the last ten years of the regency, he had done little more than talk. His jealous rival, Count Kolowrat, was heard to say with ill-humored wit that the daily performance in the Regency Council should be entitled: "He Alone Speaks!" This might be said of every dictator, as it seems to be a characteristic of the species. A dictatorship is a monologue and for that very reason, if for no other, must be sterile. Only dialogue, and clash of characters, can produce logically developed action.

The Regency Council, the *perpetuum immobile,* precluded every such possibility. That, after all, with the active co-operation of Metternich himself, was what it had been created for. His basically unimpassioned and deliberate nature was better suited to the defensive than to the offensive. Passion actively opposes, while wisdom prevents. Metternich was at all times a master of prevention; he had even forestalled Napoleon in the end. With advancing years this went so far that, always anxious to prevent, he ultimately forestalled himself. Sitting in his last arm-chair, he once said retrospectively and sorrowfully: "I may have ruled Europe, but never Austria." While still reclining in his Minister's *fauteuil* he sighed: "I am not even able to appoint a porter!" This inability was due probably to the fact that, porters being a domestic affair, came within the province of the Home Department headed by Count Kolowrat.

The uneventfulness artificially contrived by Metternich at least had the advantage of preventing war, which was as imminent in the summer of 1840 as it was in the summer of 1939, and for a similarly Eastern reason. The Poland of 1840 was Egypt, where a dynamic rebel, Ibrahim Pasha, and his no less dynamic son, Mehemet Ali, proposed to fashion out of the fragments of the moribund Ottoman Empire an Eastern Empire of their own, which was to include Syria and threatened to devour Constantinople. This was purely an oriental affair. Suddenly, however, and not without Palmerston's connivance, it turned into a West-European affair; all at once it was claimed that Egypt's frontiers lay on the banks of the Rhine. French nationalism, vanquished in 1815, blazed up once more, exactly as German nationalism did twenty-five years after Versailles. Public opinion in France, encouraged by the bellicose attitude of Thiers, peremptorily demanded the left bank of the Rhine. At about the same time Napoleon's ashes were transferred from St. Helena to Paris and interred in the *Cathédrale des Invalides*. Once more the Bonaparte legend raised its head. Louis Philippe, knowing that Louis Napoleon, the subsequent Napoleon III, was lurking in the background and recognizing the danger threatening him and his dynasty, resolutely shouldered his umbrella, dismissed the warmongering Thiers Cabinet, and appointed the peaceable Guizot. Metternich was on excellent terms with the latter who, in the meantime, had become his successor in the affections of Princess Lieven. Once more, through tactical cleverness and after months of finesse, the aging dictator succeeded in forestalling war. As this time it was a big war, there may be justification in the statement that Metternich's obstructionism terminated satisfactorily. There was no gainsaying the fact, however, that while the jealous claims of all Great Powers, including Austria, to the "Sick Man's" inheritance were kept alive, the peace thus obtained bore within itself the seeds of future wars. That, however, is true of every peace, always excepting the one about to be concluded.

In connection with internal politics, also, the indefatigable man in the arm-chair had accomplished something that looked like a specific action, although, strictly speaking, it was not. *Ut aliquid fieri videatur*—so that it may look as though something had happened, the physicians call it. One of Metternich's favorite comparisons was the obvious parallel between the art of the physician and that of the statesman. In the present instance he prescribed a mild sedative for Austria's ailing liberty and called it the "Academy of Sciences." Twelve drops of valerian on a lump of sugar. The patient, Austria by name, suffered from recurrent excitable conditions, tossed restlessly upon her couch, and demanded with increasing vehemence to be granted liberty of the press, and abolishment of the irksome censorship. "Well," said Metternich deliberately, "you shall have both; but we'll give it only to intellectual Austria's brightest flower: the Academy created by us." It is a matter of course that the members of this institute considered worthy of the prerogative, had been appointed by the Government, i. e. by Metternich, and not chosen by the corporation freely. The dictator even succeeded in forcing into the Academy his grumpy antagonist, Grillparzer who, being a civil servant, was powerless to decline the appointment. The poet's diary reveals the fact that he was clever enough to realize he was but to serve as a liberal screen for the Academy's reactionary President.

Gnashing his teeth, he had to submit and to suffer the inclusion of his name in the list of those glorifying Metternich's creation.

These methods of the refined old gentleman in the armchair were more distasteful to the populace—Metternich could never quite bring himself to say "people"—than acts of violence would have been. They stirred, they grumbled, they demanded, and at times even succeeded in attaining their object. In Germany the King of Prussia, by granting a sort of constitution, set a bad example. An amnesty had to be proclaimed in Italy, so as to make possible the Emperor's visit to Milan. In Vienna, the Juridico-Political Reading Society made a nuisance of itself by continually presenting petitions. Why, at one time it even had the temerity to propose that a committee be received by Metternich. Metternich declined. He would be pleased to receive each one of the gentlemen singly; but he was at a loss to understand the meaning of a committee—in Austria! Once more the old fox had avoided the trap set for him, and things remained as they had been: liberty of the press was a beautiful dream, and censorship remained a fact, as grotesque as it was painful.

Because of the pranks perpetrated by old Lady Censorship—the French called her *"Tante Anastasie"*—the Viennese wept tears of merriment for more than half a century. Here are a few examples. Schiller's *"Kaballe und Liebe"* was being performed at the Burgtheater. At the end of the second act, after a violent scene, the juvenile, Ferdinand, has to utter the words: "There is a place in my heart, where the name of father has never yet been heard." At the Burgtheater he was required to replace the word "father" by "uncle." There is a chorus in Mozart's *"Don Giovanni"* in which the words occur: "All hail to liberty!" In Vienna the choristers had to sing: "All hail to gaiety!" The words of the greatly censured Schiller in his drama *"Die Raüber"*: "The serpent's name is Franz," had to be omitted on the stage even after Emperor Franz' death; and the outcry: "O Jesus!" which in tragedies is not easily avoidable, had to be replaced by "O Heavens!" When in a contemporary work, Cossacks were mentioned, and the fact alluded to that they rode on small horses, the word "small" had to be left out so as not to hurt the feelings of allied Russia.

It must be stated to Metternich's credit that in a special instance he acted with considerably greater liberality. The matter referred to a new play by Bauernfeld, who was to the Vienna of those days about what Sacha Guitry was to the Paris of yesterday, and what Behrman is to the New York of today. He was a daring fellow, this democratic Bauernfeld, who refused to be awed even by the System. When he signed an etching by Kriehuber, he added to his name the motto: "Rather imprudent, than untrue!" His play was called "Majority." This in itself was an allusion to the suppressed wishes of under-age Austria. The play told the story of a young Baron who was not permitted to take over and manage his neglected country estate, because his bumptious guardian was unwilling to concede him that privilege. This guardian was not lacking in self-assurance. He considered himself indispensable and maintained: "If I were to go, everything would collapse. . . . Am I not doing more work than anyone else? Why, just now I had to sign my name twenty times." The roof of one of the farm buildings had been in bad condition for a long time, and it was suggested to the guardian that the long-overdue job of replacing it with a new one be tackled. "No innovations, mind!", he protested. "The system upon which the structure of the universe rests is conservative. God in person is conservative. The firmament remains the same, the planets travel in their appointed courses . . . ," and so on. It was to be seen at the first glance, what the author was aiming at. The refined old gentleman in the arm-chair naturally saw it, too, but looked the other way. He suffered the performance of the suggestive comedy to take place, after Kolowrat had succeeded in getting it into the Burgtheater under the very noses of the censors. Count Kolowrat was Minister of the Interior, and was backed by Archduchess Sophie, the mother of the Emperor-to-be Franz Joseph. She was a beautiful woman of splendid physique and was generally referred to as "the only man at Court." The refined old gentleman knew all that, and was fully aware of the various undercurrents. He was not small-minded, but his general attitude was unyielding.

Even on March 13th—March 13th was a critical day for Austria, in 1848 as well as in 1938—he was the only one in the Cabinet Council to oppose any and every concession. He talked and talked, and denied the possibility of an uprising in Austria, while shots were already being fired in the streets. Finally someone had to shout in his ear that the only thing to prevent a revolution was his immediate resignation, the only concession upon which the populace, now called people, insisted.

He withdrew at once, and immediately it became apparent that this "only" concession was but the first. On this point, Metternich had once more been right. What good did it do him? He was pretty nearly the last man alive who still had personal recollections of the French Revolution, while the others knew of it only by hearsay. He was seventy-five years old, and his weary prophetic warnings fell on deaf ears.

Looking back upon his forty-eight years of service, the refined old gentleman in his arm-chair was hard put to it to resist the temptation to pronounce his own obituary oration, an impulse readily appreciated. Such orations during one's life-time are the only ones that give pleasure. They also have a most soothing effect. The last word, the very last one, has not been spoken yet, but it may be foreseen. No great changes are to be expected between seventy-five and eighty-five. Virtually, one is dead already and so may lay claim to a modicum of posthumous fame.

There was, to begin with, Austria which he had helped rule for half a century, and exclusively governed for about forty years—although, under Franz, the Emperor had officially played the first violin, while Metternich was bowed over his 'cello. How had Austria fared under his rule? That was the question of paramount importance, for, as the Bible says: "By their fruits shall ye know them." The aged Metternich had turned into an assiduous reader of the Bible, the old writer of letters having a predilection for the Epistles of St. Paul.

Politically, Austria had flourished and grown mightily since the French wars. It played the dominant rôle in Germany and Italy, and beat the time in the European concert. No small achievement, indeed, especially when one takes into consideration the preceding humiliations and the difficulties that had to be overcome. Napoleon had been but one of these difficulties; a passing one. The other and permanent difficulty lay in the fact that one had to deal with Austrians: a people that was no people, and a nation that was no nation. In spite of this, and perhaps even because of it—the Austrian is a paradoxical being—it was a people, a country, "worthy of e'en a prince's work and patience," as Grillparzer says in his "Ottokar." It was a beautiful country, with a southern bloom on it, warmly animated, frivolous and gifted, pious and ungrateful, Muse-like and foolish, childish and wise, simple-minded and profound, composed of nothing but contradictions, like mountain and valley. But what a charm upon the mountains and in the valleys! What a wealth of possibilities with all its impossibility, what an assurance of vital instincts between Nature and God, what charming dizziness above yawning chasms, accompanied by a profound sense of moderation, of dignity, and of humanity. Austria: the Greece of Germany, the heart of Europe, the Europe of Central Europe! Metternich had not invented it any more than he, the Rhinelander, had invented the Austrian; the latter, however, an independent species in the European family of peoples, may be said to have achieved his full stature only under him, and in the presence of a mild climate which in spite of everything, was favorable to his growth. Under Metternich, the Austrian character became of age and assumed a decided attitude.

This character is mirrored in Austrian art, and especially in music and literature. One of these mirrors wanders from hand to hand, and from country to country, covering the whole earth. Anyone listening, no matter where, to Schubert's "Cradle Song," or to Haydn's Oxford Symphony, or absorbing into his mind the creations of Mozart and Beethoven, or those of Dvořák and Mahler, must have the instinctive feeling, no matter whether it be in New York, in Paris, or in Buenos Aires, that he is enjoying the hospitality of Austria and that this national organism is indestructible, at least ideologically.

The mirror of literature, on the other hand, rests in a locked cabinet, accessible to but few. To whom in the wide world do the names of Grillparzer, Raimund, Stifter, Lenau, Nestroy, Bauernfeld, and Feuchtersleben mean anything? They mean everything to the Austrian. It is significant, at any rate, that all of them lived in the era of Metternich. It was an era, although with typically Austrian moderation it was content to call itself an epoch: the so-called Biedermeier epoch.

There is, for instance, the "Hobellied" by Raimund, which may be called Austria's second National Hymn, the National Hymn of the Austrian character:

> *How often foolish folks dispute*
> *About good luck. What stuff!*
> *The poor man can't the rich refute,*
> *For neither knows enough.*
>
> *The poor man, he is much too poor,*
> *The rich is much too rich;*
> *But Fate planes both so nicely o'er*
> *You can't know which is which.*

This popular wisdom is typically Austrian.
There are also the verses from Grillparzer's "Medea":

> *What is man's fortune? A shadow.*
> *What is man's glory? A dream.*
> *Oh fool, thou who has dreamed of shadows!*

This adagio of resignation is also Austria. And how ultra-Austrian is the same poet's practical avowal of life, the anti-heroic one, in his "The Dream, a Life!"

> *One thing only makes contented!*
> *One: When hate has been prevented*
> *And the heart relieved of guilt.*
> *Greatness e'er is fraught with danger,*
> *Glory's lure is nought but dross;*
> *What it gives is oh! so little,*
> *What it takes is grievous loss.*

Here again we have a renunciation of the deed, a quality which Guizot, who considered it a political defect, scored against Metternich in later years, flight into contemplation, wisdom in place of action; once more the attempt to save man in the whirl of events, to preserve and restore man within the man. Therein, perhaps, lay Austria's mission. Here, too, we have the proud cultural consciousness that the course of the world is determined not so much by noisy deeds as by the still soft voice which, though out-screamed by the former, will in the end have the last word:

> *What—they cried with shouts unchastened,*
> *What has happened, what's been done?*
> *While the great thing grew and hastened*
> *Softly on.*
>
> *No one sees it while the masses*
> *Raise their clamor and their cry;*
> *And with modest mien it passes*
> *Softly by.*

These lines are by Feuchtersleben, the great physician of Metternich's days who, eighty years before Freud, wrote a classical "Dietetics of the Soul," as well as a few immortal poems, among them the widely known one beginning with the quaint lines: "If thee a flower given was, Go place it in a water-glass. . . ." This, too, is Austrian: gratitude for the little joys of life and, generally, greatness in little things.

Hunting out the greatness in little things, and the littleness in usurped greatness—in short, the establishment of the relativity of greatness—is one of the fundamental functions of what is known as humor. One of the characteristic features in the face of Austrian literature of Metternich's days is a well-defined "laughing crease." Bauernfeld, whose subdued laughter was more like a smile, was a most refined writer of German comedies; not one of those who occasionally writes a comedy, but one who again and again, and throughout his life, wrote comedies. Such a man was also Nestroy, the greater genius of the two, a large caliber satirist, a diabolical scoffer, and an Aristophanes who reminded one somewhat of Aretino. Being a self-conscious Viennese, he once said to himself: "I believe the worst of every man, myself included—and I have seldom been mistaken." Here we have, condensed into an epigram, the satiric game of the Austrian tragedy, the nihilistic negation of the Austrian character, as it ambiguously flourished in Metternich's days between suspicion and suppression.

What was said about literature and music is valid also in the realms of architecture and painting; and it is valid still more emphatically in connection with science, which had always been basically more congenial to Metternich's arithmetical mind than the domain of the fine arts. The assertion that the architectural endeavors of the Metternich period succeeded in adding to the City of Vienna some of its finest representative buildings needs no further proof. "Dictators are good for architects," said Dorothy Thompson. That, too, is a generic symptom, although Metternich's Bramante bore the prosaic Viennese name of Kornhäusl. As far as his personal taste was concerned, the aging State-Chancellor inclined more and more towards the Gothic, but he refrained at least from having artificial ruins erected on his estates, as his contemporary, Prince Liechtenstein, did. Everything that smacked of the historical, was greatly esteemed in the Vienna of those days, a fact responsible for the high rank accorded to historiography, which Metternich greatly favored. The other faculties, too, bore an excellent reputation. Jurisprudence, and especially medical science, as taught at the Vienna University, were held in high esteem throughout Germany and Europe. Technical science also made tremendous progress. Metternich himself, no matter how reactionary—or rather immovable—he may have been, kept step with new developments even at a greatly advanced age. He was the first Austrian to take notice approvingly of Daguerre's invention, readily recognizing its importance. He was also one of the first to have illuminating gas introduced into his newly-built villa. The Danube Steam Navigation Company was founded during his era, while the Northern Railway came into existence with the aid of Rothschild capital, in spite of all the attempts at dissuasion on the part of faint-hearted professors who warned against the disastrous consequences of the new invention. When the curious world traveler, Prince Pückler-Muskau, was staying in Vienna, with the black slave girl he had brought with him from the South, he invited Princess Metternich to accompany him to the Northern Railway Station to watch the arrival of the first cattle transport. Three hundred oxen, drawn by a puffing and snorting steam engine, arrived, the spectacle being duly admired by a few privileged members of Vienna society. It was a miraculous event, conscientiously recorded by Melanie in her diary.

As far as the cultural progress of the country under his care was concerned, Metternich had no reason to be dissatisfied with what had been accomplished. How much more satisfied he would have been, had he lived a hundred years later! All that is needed to make Vienna witness a Periclean age, and make of Metternich himself a Pericles, is possibly to have a Metternich follow the Hitler era.

Between politics and culture, society acted in an intermediary capacity. Metternich, who liked to refer to himself as the man of ways and means, was quite in his element as a mediator.

His three wives were society women. The first, Eleonore, was an Ambassadress of the old style, to which she had been accustomed all her life. The second and most lovely of the three, Antoinette, brought to his home a music-loving atmosphere in which the fine arts flourished. The Muses were happy and dispensed happiness, though that happiness was unfortunately of but short duration. The third, a Hungarian, was unable to conceive life except as a whirl of humanity and succeeded in infecting her husband, too, with this conception. While married to her, Metternich was virtually always in company. If he did not receive callers at the State-Chancellery he received them at home, and if they were not callers they were guests. It started right after the wedding, when the newly-weds were surrounded by a ball crowd that did not begin to disperse until long past midnight. That is how things went on, even when he was in exile, until the death of his insatiably social Melanie. If ever a widower was left lonely, it was the eighty year old Metternich.

What was Metternich's relationship to this society which, in spite of its great crowds, was never indiscriminate? How did he influence it? How did it thank him for this influence? Three questions, these, that demand three answers.

Society began with the Imperial House. There, with the exception of Emperor Franz' lasting friendship and a few pleasant attentions from the young Emperor Franz Joseph, Metternich always met with ingratitude. In March 1848, Archduchess Sophie brought about his downfall through an artfully contrived intrigue, while Archduke Ludwig, his collaborator of many years, was the first one who at the final Regency Council uttered the word "resignation."

What was said of the Imperial House applies in almost the same degree to the nobility. They cringed before him as long as he was in power, and revenged themselves later for benefits received. It certainly cannot be said that they remained loyal to him; rather the contrary was the truth. The Schwarzenbergs and Starhembergs, to say nothing of the Kolowrats, had never been well disposed towards him. What remained was what the Viennese called the second society. It, in turn, was prevented from becoming unduly familiar by the excessive haughtiness of the Princess. The middle classes, on the other hand, were wholly out of the question, and found themselves pushed into a corner. The same was true of bourgeois created literature, as far as it was of domestic origin. Members of the foreign literary set, on the other hand, were treated with the utmost kindness by Metternich; and socially prominent travelers passing through

Vienna were enchanted with him. Here, too, he was more European than Austrian.

It was Metternich's principle, observed long after he had gone, to appear more liberal abroad than at home. Foreign literary lights, therefore, were always most kindly received, partly because they had just arrived and partly because they were soon to leave again. There was therefore no danger of a permanent association. Like every dictator, he knew the value of foreign propaganda and was quite willing to pay an adequate price for it. It was worth his while to be amiable; and he was amiable. With Balzac, who had arranged to meet Madame Hanska in Vienna and who lived at the "Golden Pear" in the *Landstrasse* district, the sixty year old and extremely busy State-Chancellor conversed for hours at a time, and these conversations even inspired the Frenchman to write some sketches. The idea of Balzac's *"La Paix du Ménage"* is Metternich's. Stendhal was an enthusiastic admirer of Metternich. He worshipped him with the adoration of a boarding-school miss and, in the manner of these half-grown girls, had in his imagination fashioned a picture of him which did not quite correspond to actuality. Stendhal has handed down to posterity a rather flattering picture of Metternich in the character of "Count Mosca," who sleeps with a duchess and wears on his wrist the bracelet woven from his sweetheart's hair. With the pedantic Varnhagen, who could be depended upon to preserve in writing whatever he was told, he conducted meditative conversations on love and matrimony. He had meetings with Goethe at the Bohemian watering-places, and wrote the great poet letters in a Goethe-esque style, which Goethe in turn answered in the Metternich style, as he was chiefly concerned about the Austrian copyrights of his works. The best portrait, the most speaking likeness, and the least retouched of these literary reflections as they have been handed down to us on the sensitive plates of impressionable visitors' minds, we owe to the American, George Ticknor. He reveals to us most plainly how Metternich, the European, was judged outside of Europe during his life-time. The verdict was not unfavorable, as the gentleman in the arm-chair no doubt observed with considerable satisfaction.

Professor Ticknor, of Harvard, represented a somewhat prosaic transatlantic edition of the romantic travel-author of those days. He traveled about in the wide world, meeting famous personages whom he suitably bedecked with anecdotes and described in a most attractive manner. His writings are a veritable museum, in which one show-case is devoted to Metternich.

Ticknor came to Vienna in the summer of 1836, shortly after the young Duke of Orléans had departed with his "bucket." When he drove to Schönbrunn to call on Metternich, he noticed that the guest-wing of the palace was brightly lighted. King Ferdinand of Naples had just arrived, he was told. Ferdinand was the clerical successor to the liberal Duke of Orléans and succeeded in carrying off Archduchess Theresa as his bride. Neither the world at large, however, nor Ticknor had an inkling of how the wheels were working. He saw only brightly illuminated windows: a king had arrived.

Ticknor's first step had been to send Metternich a letter of introduction from Humboldt. Since in an authoritarian State like the Austria of that time, a good introduction makes almost as great an impression as in a democratic republic, the American was soon received by the man of many affairs. He kept him waiting in the ante-chamber of the

State-Chancellery hardly more than twenty minutes, during which time the keen-eyed traveler lost no time in making observations. What first struck the American was the number of superfluous servants (he did not know that some of them were probably detectives); but many other things too, were strange. In one of the corners of the spacious room sat a delegation from the City of Milan, waiting patiently and whispering furtively to one another. It seemed to him that everyone whispered. Two ministers were shown into the audience-room, but went out again presently. The Milanese, too, were quickly dispatched. In the meantime, a few Cabinet secretaries, holding documents in their hands, had hastened busily through the room; doors clicked open and closed noiselessly. Suddenly one of the doors, the middle one, opened and Prince Metternich advanced to the threshold to greet his visitor with a smile; it was made to look as if he had been waiting for him all the time. The Prince conducted Ticknor through the adjoining library—25,000 volumes, the American judged—to his writing-desk. When they got there, Metternich offered to his visitor the better of two chairs, seated himself opposite in the other one, and only then let his gaze rest on the face of the American, not to take it off again throughout the audience. Close attention and the ability to maintain it were among Metternich's most laudable characteristics. The conversation, a pseudo-conversation, was as a matter of fact but an examination veiled by pleasant phrases.

Ticknor, who after a few minutes tactfully rose to leave, apparently had passed the examination well, for it was not long before he was asked to an evening reception at Metternich's summer residence at the edge of the Imperial Park at Schönbrunn. The Bavarian Ambassador drove him out in his carriage. Again the American observed a whole flock of liveried servants. He also noticed that Metternich, who advanced to meet each of his guests with measured civility, would whisperingly retire again and again into window-recesses with certain persons, where apparently he received reports. It seemed that he was working even when socially engaged. At times he also advanced to the center of the room, engaging one or the other of his guests in a brief conversation; he chose the theme and carried it on. To his American visitor he spoke about the Vienna Polytechnical Institute. Why he chose that subject remained a secret to the curious traveler. He spoke well, however, "with the natural superiority of a man to whom the exercise of power is a matter of course." As soon as he started talking, a circle formed around him, the ladies and gentlemen approaching on tip-toe and listening raptly.

Ticknor also was privileged to be presented to the Princess on that occasion, which was a rather intimate one and did not last much beyond midnight. She was young and beautiful, but depressed and sad, so it seemed to the observant visitor. On the return drive he remarked about it to his companion, who nodded his assent to the American's observation. The Princess, he was able to report, only two weeks before had buried a child of hers, the second or the third with which she had presented the sexagenarian in quick succession. Social activities were in no way curtailed, though. It also seems that the guest from overseas made a favorable impression, for a few days later, shortly before he was to have started on his return journey, he was honored by an invitation to dinner at the State-Chancellery on the Ballhausplatz. This prompted the most remarkable part of the description by our eye-witness, who was as clear-sighted as he was unbiased.

The American was asked this time to appear at the Kaunitz Palace at 3 o'clock in the afternoon, for Metternich, who had time for everything—one of the secrets of amiability—wanted to have an hour's chat with him before dinner-time. Again he was kept waiting a few minutes in the nobly proportioned ante-chamber and was able to make some observations, as on the first occasion. The Police President was the first one to emerge from the door, which noiselessly devoured the callers and as noiselessly disgorged them again. It was then the Sardinian Minister of Finances' turn, but the white-and-gold door spewed him forth again almost immediately. A Hungarian Count in the picturesque uniform of an officer of hussars was next in line. He held in both of his hands an enormous letter with black edges, carrying it into the presence of the Chancellor. It was a letter of thanks from the King of Saxony for a message of condolence. Hardly had he been attended to, when the Prince himself appeared, and conducted his observant visitor through the splendid library, and into his study where, as he had done the first time, he smilingly offered him the better chair. Without pause, and as if he had had nothing else on his mind all day long, he launched into a conversation about democracy. It was a highly enlightening conversation.

Metternich was well aware, he started by saying pleasantly, that the world considered him a strict autocrat. Well, he was not. To be sure, he was no friend of democracy; that he had to admit. That form of government was all right for the New World, but would hardly do for the Old. In America, certainly. There it was a truth, *"une vérité"*; who could doubt it? But not here; here it was an untruth, *"un men-songe";* that was why he, Metternich, a friend and defender of truth as he claimed to be, must be against it. Democracy dissolved, divided, and disintegrated the elements of the State; the Monarchy, on the other hand, united. It brought the people in contact with one another, it formed a connecting link, and made possible a more liberal exertion of strength. He was, by the way, quite ready to admit that democracy might be more advantageous to the individual; it also produced more individualities, challenging individual accomplishments by giving free rein to initiative. Its most striking disadvantage lay in the fact that it could not stop; it had to go on and on. America, he said—in 1836!—would become more democratic as time went on. "I don't see how or where it will end, but I am sure it will not live to a quiet ripe old age." Here we have from Metternich's own lips the profession of the Old World's faith. All it wanted was to grow old in beauty. Not the rising of the sun, but its setting, signified the meaning of the day. A sentimental and highly Austrian conception, this.

After all, this was but a conversation before dinner, a sophisticated dialogue which here and there bordered upon nonsense; for the contrary of some of the statements is true. Democracy, in equalizing everything, has a tendency towards the standardization of man. It created fewer individualities by far than the monarchy, which makes everything unequal. Nature and history, moreover, have arranged it so that the Golden Age lies behind and not in front of us. Life is not an asylum for the old, nor is history an insurance policy. These objections, however, which Ticknor made firmly but with all due respect, changed nothing in the beautiful intellectual flow of Metternich's speech, the individual utterances of a man who occupied himself with the mental side of his task because he felt in duty bound to do so. It sometimes happened—and especially in his last years —that Metternich's eloquence became a source of danger to him, but this was another matter. Round the corner of Metternich's oratory always lurked the chatterer, and round the next the babbler.

The conversation had to be interrupted because the Princess sent a lackey to ask the gentlemen into the drawing-room. While Metternich asked to be excused for the moment, Ticknor started in the way indicated to him. He passed again through the magnificent library, through a second hall-like ante-chamber, and through a series of state-rooms. As he did not see a soul anywhere he had the awkward feeling of having lost his way and wanted to retrace his steps; but suddenly a servant materialized from somewhere and smilingly conducted him further along the indicated way, from drawing-room to drawing-room, until they finally reached the Princess' private salon. He found the Princess seated and surrounded by a few old ladies and gentlemen, four or five altogether, who like himself had been asked to dinner. The room appeared to him exceedingly splendid and large enough to require the light of five ormolu chandeliers. Dinner was announced, and the beautiful hostess accepted the arm of the American, who was obviously considered the guest of honor. The way led back through the succession of rooms he had lately passed, until the second ante-chamber was reached, where suddenly a magnificently laid table had made its appearance. There were eight covers altogether, and high, straight-backed chairs in which the occupants had to sit bolt upright in a dignified attitude. Behind each chair stood a servant who

moved it forward as the diners seated themselves. Only two
of the servants were liveried. The dinner itself was delicious,
but not sumptuous according to the standards of that epicurean epoch. There were twelve or fourteen courses altogether. The wines were quite excellent, and well chosen;
Johannisburger was followed by Tokay. The Johannisburger was of a particular vintage, to which the Princess
called special attention when clinking glasses. She mentioned, quite by the way, that Ticknor could procure the
wine even in New York as they had an agent there. Ticknor
duly made a note of it—for his diary.

The conversation at table was undoubtedly conducted
exclusively in French, a fact the reporter failed to mention,
because in the Austria of those days it was a matter of course.
The Government kept aloof from the people, and society
naturally followed suit. The conversation was interrupted
at one time by a secretary who brought a dispatch and a
bundle of foreign newspapers. Metternich opened the dispatch and seemed to be unpleasantly affected, although he
did not move a muscle of his face. A member of the Whig
Cabinet in London, whose overthrow Metternich would
have liked to witness, had been put on trial but had been
acquitted. Well, things don't always go as they should. The
Prince handed the deplorable news to the Princess together
with the newspapers, which ordinary mortals in Austria
probably were forbidden to read. The Princess was quite
chagrined, also. She read first the report of the ending of the
trial and then put the sheet to one side. She saw to it, however, that the Prince had opportunities later for an excited
whispered discussion of the case in a window recess, while,
to occupy the guest's attention, she showed him a newly-
arrived present from the Russian Czar: a magnificent pedes-

taled vase adorned with the elongated enameled face of the recently deceased Austrian Emperor. Thus the time passed; it got to be eight o'clock, and the State-Chancellor had devoted fully five hours to his guest, when he finally saw him to the door and took leave of him most graciously. The American knew how to appreciate this attention, but at the same time had no doubts as to its real worth. With that classic American matter-of-factness which never imposes upon anybody but refuses to be imposed upon, he closed his report by stating that Metternich, while they were standing in the door, was still overwhelming him with attentions— although, as Ticknor expressed it, in five minutes he would forget him as one forgets last year's clouds. At any rate, condensing his judgment after three visits, he called Metternich "the most consummate statesman of his kind"; which is the truth.

All this is glamor, and power, and vanity, and the gilded reflection of success; but what about the lasting accomplishments of the refined old gentleman in his arm-chair, and of what did they consist? What was it that justified him to say of himself: "I say to you that in a hundred years writers will judge me differently from those who deal with me to-day"? The century is over, and the accounting is due.

What is most to Metternich's historical credit is the very act which German historians for a century have claimed his most unforgivable fault; his resolute turning away from German nationalism. The charge came to his ears during his life-time, and once, at the zenith of his power, he replied to it. "There is nothing to prove that the National State is essentially better than the Juridical State," he wrote to Prokesch-Osten. Here we have his political concept, including his negation of the masses which, according to his idea, were amorphous. It is strange how in this respect he falls in with the views of Goethe, who shelved the popular commotion of the Wars of Liberty, with the declaration that the outburst was nothing but the "still innocent precursor of something terrible which one day will manifest itself among the Germans as the most unmitigated folly ever perpetrated, and before which, if a sound of it should reach you, you would turn in your grave." Thomas Mann cited the passage in his "Lotte of Weimar." The similarity of the prophetic discontent caused by the unleashing of the national movement is unmistakable. It would serve at least as an excuse for Metternich's alleged prejudice against the people. The great poet requires no apology. He proved himself a veritable prophet.

The means the far-sighted Austrian statesman proposed to use, hoping to prevent a national devastation, was the Feudal State. He dreamed of a European order which would hold down the national confusion through a "balance of power" assured by far-flung alliances. That is the autocratic solution of the question. But is it not at the same time the national one, also? By proclaiming nationalism, it does so also for the other nations; for, after all, they are all nations, and that one of the twenty is the masterful and dominating race is a claim that will not be conceded easily by the other nineteen in Europe. It follows that they must be subdued. To subdue them, however, is a negation of the national solution which had been so urgently recommended as the only possible one. Thus, if we follow the labyrinth of nationalism to its end, it becomes apparent that it was madness from the beginning. The European solution can be only a supernational one. Instead of setting the nations together by the ears they should be reminded of the fact that they are something else besides nations: human beings. When the element of humanity will be put to the fore, the continent will be saved.

That is the Metternich concept. It is of greater topical interest and more justified today than ever. A national Europe is a world danger, while an international Europe has come to mean world hope. History is indebted to Metternich for consciously having striven towards such a solution. Austria was equally indebted to him; for in Austria, which by its life and collapse clearly showed Europe its own future, the problem of a nationally mixed State was first to arise, and it was Austria, too, which was first to fall victim to an inflamed nationalism. Its last victim was Czecho-Slovakia, another State of mixed nationalities that went up in flames. Today all of Europe is in flames, a condition concerning which the gentleman in the arm-chair had always sounded a warning. To him nationalism had never been anything but Jacobinism or, to use a more up-to-date expression: Bolshevism. His contemporaries called the comparison a doctrinal whim. A century later, however, the awful truth began to dawn upon the beholder. "From humanity, by way of nationality, to bestiality," was Grillparzer's description of the way. Back to the Juridical State, therefore, and back to humanity! We have no other choice if we want "to save Europe," as Metternich did through the Battle of Leipsic. Then it was the demi-god Napoleon; today it is the machine-gun-gods of the totalitarian State. The recipe remains the same.

A Europe shot to ruins, groans today in bloody torment. Should we, therefore, give it up and throw it on the dustheap with the words of the cultural pessimist, Spengler, who only a few years ago said: "Europe, as an entity, perished in the World War stupidly and undignifiedly"? Even Spengler, whose pessimism later showed an alarming leaning toward the national resurrection, will hardly deny that this "entity" has gone to the ruin even more stupidly and undignifiedly in World War II, which an accursed nationalism had loosed to the applause of certain cultural pessimists.

Three hundred years ago, the peoples of Europe warred against one another and tore each other to pieces, because one half espoused the opinion that the wine in the chalice *was* the Blood of the Savior, while the other half thought that it merely *signified* the Blood of Christ. Today we smile incredulously at the thought that such a difference of opinion could have brought about so sanguinary a development. It is likely that at the end of the current century, men will think similarly of nationalistic differences, as the cause of a bloody war, and will smile just as incredulously. For, what does it mean in the last analysis to be "national"? To be proud of the fact that one was born in a certain place which, to quote Grillparzer again, "is rather a matter of course." Metternich correctly recognized the danger to the German character of this very "matter-of-factness." Mix it with a bit of philosophy, and it acts like gun-cotton.

The German is both choleric and judicious. When he is judicious he may produce great inventions; when he is choleric, he perpetrates his great pieces of stupidity, and the very worst was neo-German nationalism. It was a choleric excess which Metternich, the historical sedative, had managed to defer fully a century. All of us who experienced a measure of happiness in the nineteenth century and expect to experience it again in a remoulded Europe, should think highly of the service rendered to humanity by the refined old gentleman in his arm-chair. He was a pioneer of anti-nationalism. National State or Juridical State? He was in favor of the Juridical State; and he was right.

BOOK FOUR

The Wise Man with the Thousand Recollections

Vienna Illuminated

WHEN Metternich was overthrown on March 13th, 1848, turned out like a thieving servant after a continuous period of forty-seven years of public service, Vienna celebrated the occasion by a festive illumination. There is not much in that. In the course of her history the inflammable city has had a number of these illuminations, the last of them on March 13th, 1938. In almost every instance it was penitently admitted, a short time later, that it was a pity to have wasted so many fine candles.

The illumination of the year 1848 had carefully been prepared beforehand, and it was particularly announced that it would take place. After the February Revolution in Paris, an upheaval in Vienna was expected to occur any hour. This may best be deduced from a number of anecdotes handed down to posterity. Vienna anecdotes have always furnished a clear-cut reflection of world events. A few days before the ominous 13th of March, the Hungarian Count Szechenyi paid a visit to his compatriot and compeer, Princess Melanie Metternich. As it was customary in their social set to take nothing seriously, he was ironically greeted by his hostess with a salutation borrowed from the vocabulary of the French Revolution: *"Bonjour, citoyen!"*; to which with ready repartee and the spicy gallantry of the Hungarian, he quickly replied: *"Bonjour, délicieuse sans-culotte."* This was rather harmless. Countess Felicie Esterházy's act in the Metternich drawing-room was considerably less innocent. On the day preceding the Revolution she entered the room, saying: "Is it true that you are leaving Vienna? We have been asked to buy candles because of your departure to-morrow." The man who had given this hint to the notoriously stupid and guileless Countess Felicie was the Lord Steward of the Household of Archduchess Sophie, who a week later sent Metternich a letter in French, in which she expressed her admiration for him, and the deep regret his resignation had caused her. She had done her share, however, to help bring about his downfall.

When the same Archduchess Sophie, on the arm of her husband, walked from the Bastion to the Imperial Palace at the noon hour, she was enthusiastically cheered by the people; she acknowledged the ovation affably, though proudly. Metternich, who passed a little later, was greeted with catcalls. It happened on the same spot where, in the year 1813 after the Battle of Leipsic, the cantata "All Hail to Thee" had been sung, when Metternich was extolled as *"le vainqueur du temps et le modèle des grands hommes."* How strange it must have seemed to the old man's philosophically trained mind, that suddenly, as by preconcerted arrangement, they were all against him: the Imperial House, the nobility, the people, the students, and the rabble. There could be no doubt in his mind that the Vienna Revolution of 1848 was first of all a revolution against Metternich.

His own fault? Perhaps it was rather the fault of the government machinery, the *perpetuum immobile* of the wretched Regency Council—though, to be sure, he had been the prime mover in its installation. It consisted of two

forces pulling in opposite directions: Metternich and Kolowrat. The third man, Archduke Ludwig, acted like a lead
weight suspended from the cross piece of the scales, im-
peding every movement. Instead of doing away with this
weight, Metternich's driving force was eliminated, and the
feeble-minded Emperor thus deprived of his staunchest sup-
porter. It is a fact that this good-natured pseudo-Emperor,
who on the day of the revolution was seen standing at the
window counting the number of busses passing through the
Outer Gate of the Palace, was the man who stood by his
State-Chancellor longest and most loyally. He even instructed Kolowrat to dissuade Metternich from heeding the
advice of those who counseled flight. Kolowrat, however,
took his time so that he no longer found his ousted rival at
home, either at the State-Chancellery or at his beautiful
house on the Rennweg which bore the inscription *"Parva
domus magna quies,"* and which the mob had already begun to ransack. It was not entirely destroyed, only because
the students of Vienna, although they supported the Revolution enthusiastically, did not wish to see it degenerate into
plunder and pillage. The time had not yet come when the
standard bearers of education joined forces with the education deriding mob; that was reserved for a later period of
national uplift, when stupidity and brutality were united
in an all pervading "bond of popular union"; the brutality
of a degraded mob, and the stupidity of the *élite* of citizens
who, despairing of themselves, voluntarily and servilely
helped demolish the protecting walls of the intellect.

It was an altogether Viennese revolution, a fact clearly
and amusingly demonstrated by a number of accompanying
circumstances. The bearded professors and the rising generation, lustily waving their slouch-hats (it was then con-

sidered a sign of especial political depravity to wear a full
beard and a slouch-hat, a so-called "Calabrian"), were anxious above all to assure themselves of the support and approval of the Imperial House in their doings. The Viennese,
unable to conceive of a public-spirited undertaking without
the honorary protection of at least one archduke, instinc-
tively desired to realize their republican aspirations as far
as possible under the Habsburg aegis. The House of Habsburg was quite ready to meet them half-way, the archdukes
making common cause with the revolution at least up to a
certain point. Archduke Ludwig especially, whose ante-
chamber at the Palace was turned into revolutionary headquarters on that 13th of March, received everyone and
promised to do whatever was in his power. He benev-
olently declared his readiness to further the overthrow of
Metternich; he would presently talk to his brother about
it, as soon as the latter was through with his lunch. "How
can a man have lunch on a day like this?", cheekily exclaimed Bauernfeld, the writer of comedies, acting as spokesman. The pert remark probably was considered no more
than laughable, especially since it fitted in so well with
Bauernfeld's outward appearance. In his hand he held a
knotty stick, and his broad-brimmed Calabrian, a neglected
moustache covered his lip, and a glib and biting tongue was
forever ready for pointed sallies which no one took quite
seriously. If he succeeded, nevertheless, in enforcing his demands for an abolishment of the censorship and the immediate dismissal of the State-Chancellor, it was probably
partly due to the fact that the wine-merchants of Vienna
had allied themselves with him. They were fearless and likewise full-bearded men who saw to it that the wine of the
Vienna Revolution was suitably watered. Metternich must

go, they shouted; that was the least they could expect. In the end and with the support of the Imperial House they achieved their exalted goal. The comedy and the wine of Vienna caused the downfall of the all-powerful Chancellor and conquered Napoleon's conqueror. It was enough to make one laugh; but the honest Viennese suppressed their laughter for the time being, for a revolution must at least take itself seriously.

Before relinquishing his post, the old State-Chancellor once more, and for the last time, strode through his ante-chamber which was filled with excited people; he was saluted by everyone and spoken to by none. He wore a pea-green tight-fitting dress-coat, pearl-grey tightly-stretched pantaloons, and carried in his gloved hand a gold-headed cane and a high silk hat. Thus he strode haughtily past the full beards, and the knotty sticks, the personified eighteenth century passing the nineteenth, and disappeared through the archducal door, a wry and wintry smile on the smoothly shaven lips of his aged actor's face. A few hours later the Viennese placed lighted candles in their windows.

On the following day Metternich and his wife left Vienna. It was a wretched and disgraceful flight, forced on him because the Imperial House had refused to guarantee the safety of his life. There was hardly time to pack, and at the last moment he was short of money. The State Exchequer declined to pay his salary, and if his friend Rothschild had not sent him a thousand Ducats at the very last, Melanie and *"ce pauvre Clement"* would have been greatly embarrassed. How strange that the word *"pauvre"* suddenly assumed its original meaning: no longer was he the "poor fellow"; he was actually poor.

In an ordinary hackney coach, squeezed in between his brave Melanie who occupied the dangerous window-seat, and the faithful Baron Hügel, the seventy-five-year-old man rode dolefully through the gray March evening. They had waited for twilight to fall, partly to avoid recognition, and partly because it had not been easy to agree on a destination. Where in Austria was Metternich still sure of his life? Least of all on his own Bohemian estates, which would have been the most obvious place of retirement. At last Prince Liechtenstein had placed at Metternich's disposal his Castle Feldberg. It was a day's journey from Vienna, in a northerly direction and at the Moravian frontier. When the little party, consisting of Prince and Princess Metternich and their four children, had reached an outlying section of the city, they were whisked into a waiting traveling-coach and the journey proceeded at a labored trot throughout the night over high-roads that were in wretched repair. The tortured Chancellor may have wondered why under his government, the roads had not been kept in better condition. Finally, when every bone in their bodies seemed to be shaken loose, the party arrived at Feldberg at five in the morning. The castle which had long been unoccupied was as icy cold as only an ancient castle can be at the winter's end. In only one room a wretched little fire had been lit. The hunted man was assisted to a couch, shaking with cold; his wife and children covered him with their shawls and coats. It was a touching family scene, which for the moment, however, he did not greatly appreciate.

It was about six o'clock of a March morning, still quite dark. A single candle fitfully lit the room, in which four half-grown children, ranging in age from eleven to nineteen, and an already matronly wife busied themselves about the old man. They dared not light a second candle until the castellan had carefully fastened the curtains across the windows. There was no relying any longer on the estate-peasants who of late looked at their scythes and flails with strangely wild eyes when mention was made of the "masters." Thus it seemed best to let the visit attract as little attention as possible. To attract no attention had ever been Metternich's principle. . . .

What a contrast! This poorly lighted room in the icy cold forsaken castle, and the illuminated Vienna at the coming of the spring. Life provides antitheses which no dramatist could devise more ingeniously—not even Hans Sassmann, whose Metternich trilogy was performed during the last years of Austria's existence.

The great sea of Fate has its tides. The tide of fortune rises or falls, swells and ebbs, and either state lasts for some time. The fugitive must continue to flee, the banished must hasten from place to place, and there is no more taking root once a man has lost his "roots." The dethroned Metternich, too, was forced to undergo this inexorable experience, no matter how stubbornly he fought against it. After Feldberg had been made the choice in Vienna, the good Baron Hügel presented a petition to Archduke Ludwig, praying that the garrison stationed near Feldberg be instructed to protect the former State-Chancellor. He received no answer, and as it was impossible to remain for any length of time at Feldberg amongst rebellious peasants, the fugitives turned their faces towards Olmütz, increasing the distance from Vienna. Again they made off in the dark of night. When the former head of the Austrian Government and his companions knocked at the carefully locked gates of the fortress, Olmütz, at four in the morning, both the officer commanding the fortress and the archbishop ruling over the city made it known that the visit was not desirable at the time. The unspoken reason was, of course, that both the high church dignitary and the military commander were afraid of the mob which seems to be the most irresistible form of human cowardice. It is a well-known fact that no one dares to stand up for one who is pursued by the crowd; even his best friends will leave him, although this will not prevent them, once the persecuted man has found a haven of refuge, and they can do so without danger to themselves, eloquently expressing in words and letters their joy at the lucky escape.

Turned away at Olmütz, the journey, which had now become highly dangerous, was continued in still another direction, with the idea of reaching the line of the Prague Railway which was already in operation. Another hunted drive over bottomless roads, past threatening groups of peasants and grumbling postboys whose gaze followed the travelers venomously and who mumbled curses under their breath. They followed the railway journey which took up the whole of the night. Finally the family of six arrived in Prague, and the fragile old gentleman clambered painfully down the high steps of the railway carriage. It was the start of another sad chapter: the farewell from the children who were to be taken back to Vienna, according to a decision which the heavy-hearted parents had reached en route. The Prince and the Princess themselves intended to go to England, an undertaking which was easier planned than executed. The relentless flight became more perilous the closer it approached the German frontier, for the name of Metternich was even more hated in Germany than in the so-called "hereditary lands." There was no alternative but to disown the world-famous name and to hide disgracefully under an assumed one. As a Monsieur and Madame Matteux, the French-speaking couple arrived in Dresden. There they were not molested, although not everyone seemed convinced that their name was really Matteux. At the Austrian frontier the postmaster looked long and suspiciously at the shaky old gentleman and his pretentious spouse and at last mumbled to himself in the uncertain feeling that there might have been something wrong about the affair: "Who knows but what that was a king in flight." The partly deaf man with the snowy hair would not have turned round even if the remark had reached his ears. He was glad to have the Austrian frontier behind him.

There were the German, the Dutch, and the English frontiers still to be crossed. Finally, on April 20th, 1848, London was reached, and Monsieur and Madame Matteux were once more able to assume the name of Metternich. As soon as this was done, the bearer of the name was in safety. No matter what Palmerston might have had to say, and did say, against the old gentleman—and there is not much from which an emigrant can escape—he was yet the conqueror of Napoleon; he and Wellington, who was still alive, shared the honor. He was also benefited by the fact that once before—it was a matter of fifty-five years—he had spent some time in London and had, consciously or unconsciously, allowed England to contribute to his education. To translate himself into English was therefore not particularly difficult for him. He had always been half an Englishman, anyway. His dry idealism was English; so was his way of dressing, his Tory mentality, the detachment with which he spoke, either of improvements made on his estates, or of his meetings with Napoleon, his phlegmatic disposition, and his philosophy unshakably resting upon a foundation of classical quotations. At moments he might almost have been taken for an Oxonian.

English Society immediately swooped down upon the interesting fugitive and assigned to him the graceful part of the Great Old Man. The unceasingly talking old martyr saw himself pampered at house-parties and in drawing-rooms, as of yore. The Princess had nothing to complain of either. She entertained and was received; it was almost as it had been in Vienna. Only the Court and the Government remained aloof at first. There was also another little and rather embarrassing difficulty, money. In a wealthy country like England it was assumed as a matter of course that the Great Old Man was blessed with this world's goods. Unfortunately that was not so in Metternich's case. Even the pension to which he was entitled as a former State-Minister was kept from him. To save money by withholding pensions is the ultimate and deeper sense of all revolutions; they break with the past so as to avoid the obligation to pay. London, on the other hand, was an expensive place; therefore the Metternichs first moved to Richmond and then, in September, noiselessly to Brighton. These moves were prompted by the very prosaic reason that life was cheaper in these places.

"The Old Man of the Mountain," as Metternich was now called, had made a conquest in London which gave him a good deal of pleasure. Young Disraeli was completely enchanted with the *doyen* of European statesmanship and wrote him glowing letters in his flowery style. He called him the greatest statesman and the kindest man in the world; he apostrophized him as his "revered teacher" and referred to himself as Metternich's "grateful pupil." Or he sketched with an eloquent pen, this little instantaneous picture of a visit he paid his new-found friend: "He started in at a gallop and began to speak like a god. I have never heard such divine talk." How charmingly Victorian is this juxtaposition of two incommensurable pictures: a racehorse, and a divine chat; excellent style for an editorial! "He gave a masterly survey of present conditions in Europe and said more witty and wise things than I could recall. His eye shone with the brilliant thoughts he uttered." In passing, the ex-Chancellor also encouraged his pupil somewhat in the fight against his old adversary Palmerston. It was one of the satisfactions he derived from his English exile that, though he was no longer able to listen to it, he could at least read in the *Times,* on the following morning, what Disraeli had said against Palmerston in the House of Commons. In the end the two, master and pupil, jointly issued a conservative monthly, the *"Spectateur de Londres"* which, unfortunately, was discontinued three months later because of lack of funds.

Plans for this publication had their inception the very first days after the illumination of Vienna. At Castle Feldberg, when he caught his first breath on his flight, Metternich wrote down the basic plans of the contemplated periodical. This reminds us of Napoleon who, while Moscow burned, sketched the statutes of the *Comédie Française.* The parallel is obvious. Not that the two men were of even approximately the same stature; but there was after all something of the Napoleonic spark in Metternich. Greatness is greatness; and it is above all the gift, amplified by self-discipline, entirely to disregard one's own situation.

Perhaps this is as good an opportunity as any to contemplate once more Metternich's relation to the written word. He was a prodigious reader and writer. The former is espe-

cially noteworthy; for a statesman having time to read seems
to us today like a figure out of a fairy-tale. Neither did Metternich restrict himself to literature dealing with his own
field, as is the habit of pedants. His reading was not done
solely for the sake of enlightenment, but also for the sake of
pleasure. He was a genuine reader who felt an urge to fly
from the trivialities of the day and cross the fairy bridge into
the great open spaces of the imagination. He even read
novels, and managed to finish them. At one time he came
back from a journey, carrying a book which he had read
while en route. An important report was made to him and
his decision was urgently requested. He replied: "First of
all I shall finish my novel; perhaps I shall then be able to
think of the right decision." Not a bad method, this, for a
"master of the next step."

It would be going too far, perhaps, to call Metternich a
literary man, although he had to a high degree the gift of
the Plutarchic word, of the appropriate expression, of what
the French call *le mot heureux*. At any rate, even if he
was not a creative author, he was an eminent journalist, having had the best schooling possible in Paris and Vienna. His
master in the latter city was Gentz. For many decades Metternich's style continued to predominate in that city, being
accepted as the model for writers of editorials and especially
of *feuilletons*. The metaphorical journalistic style of Vienna,
taking a special delight in more or less ingenious comparisons, was lastingly influenced by Metternich, whose shadow
fell far even into the Franz-Josephinian twilight. It was
therefore by no means an accident that, no sooner had the
active politician ceased to be active, than the writing politician asked to be heard. Even when the printed page was
no longer available to him, he confided to beautifully fin-

ished letters what he wanted to say. The writing of letters had from the first been his very own gift: the letter was his domain. The difference was that where formerly his letters were addressed mainly to women, they were now generally directed to kings. In London, Brighton, and finally in Brussels, he corresponded uninterruptedly for years with almost all the crowned heads, and their State ministers, endeavoring to inculcate his thoughts in their minds, and pointing the way to their realization. What was most difficult of all, he even began to correspond with Vienna again after a time, not only with the Court, but also with the State-Chancellery where another man now ruled. This went so far that malicious tongues were beginning to call his third emigrant home in Brussels "the second Chancellery." It should be mentioned that Metternich, at Feldberg, had been circumspect enough to send a word of hearty congratulation to his successor Fiquelmont upon his appointment. At the same time, and again from Feldberg, he sent out previously prepared farewell letters, resigning all his honorary positions, the trusteeship of the Academy of Sciences, and the Chancellorship of the Order of Maria Theresa. He resigned his office like a king.

Paléologue, who owed it to himself to write about Metternich, called his great colleague of the 19th century a "romantic statesman." It would be quite natural for a Frenchman to call a man romantic because he had had love-affairs, though it should be considered that love-affairs need not necessarily be romantic. In this as in many other respects the central figure of our contemplations was anything but a romanticist; he ought rather to be called a classical statesman and lover. His conception of the State, as revealed to us

through his political testament, written while in exile, pre-
supposed a "cosmic order." Nature and truth were its sup-
ports. It is almost as if we were reading aesthetics of the
time of Goethe and Schiller. What in their case was called
the "eternal human" was to him the equality before the law,
the only equality he was ready to admit. All this is classical;
for that is classical that rests immutably in the immutable;
the static is classical.

At Brighton, to be sure, where he was given to contemplation *sub specie aeternitatis,* he was still the center of a few
tenderly reminiscent but none the less mundane comic
scenes. One of his dancing-partners at the Frankfort Coronation Ball, thirty-four then and ninety-two now, paid him a
visit. Soon all the others came, too: the Duchess de Sagan,
Madame Bagration, and the Princess Lieven; all, so far as they
were still alive, who had once been dear to him came again
into his presence. His granddaughter of eighteen, Princess
Pauline, who sat near at hand when grandpapa received
callers, described them to us in her memory-book: Madame
Bagration, the *"bel ange nu,"* who "has forgotten to grow
old" and still dressed exactly as she had done when Lawrence put her on canvas forty years before, "swathed in airy
veils and crowned with garlands of roses"; the Duchess of
Sagan, handsomely dressed and charming to look at, who in
spite of her paltry seventy-six years and all her faithlessness,
was still hopelessly in love with her old friend; and then of
course Princess Lieven, a solemnly treading, magnificent
old lady with a giant fan, a huge hat, and a gigantic green
eye-shade which she wore probably because she suffered
from cataract. Everything about her was large, even her
Fate which, invisible, stalked before her. Sent home to
Petersburg an overthrown Ambassadress, within a few days

of each other she had buried two sons in the prime of their youth. Horror-stricken, she had fled to Paris and there, a Niobe of fifty and widowed in the bargain, begun a new love-life at the side of Guizot. That he, too, had buried a son had brought them together in the beginning. Shared sorrows are half sorrows. She became the important man's friend in a beautiful sense of the word, and ultimately even in the most beautiful sense. The love letters he wrote her were almost as clever as hers. One of those which have been preserved begins with the legendary words: *"Le Cardinal de Retz dit quelquepart. . . ."* He did not always cite Cardinal de Retz, though. On one occasion, it was recounted in Paris, Dorothy Lieven entertained quite a number of people at her house. Guizot, who was then the chief of the French Government, was among the invited guests. He wore the grand cordon of the Legion of Honor on a blue ribbon. Merimée was standing on the edge of affairs, watching everything. He did not fail to notice that when the other guests left at about midnight, Guizot remained behind. Presumably there was still some political matter he wished to discuss with his hostess. When he reached the street, Merimée suddenly noticed that he had left a manuscript lying in the drawing-room. He rushed back and entered the deserted room unannounced. He heard voices in the adjoining bedroom; and on the sofa, keeping company with the script left behind by the author, lay neatly folded Minister Guizot's grand cordon which the statesman, noted for his tidiness, had taken off before starting his political discussion.

It was a pity that this little story which went the round of the Paris salons could no longer be whispered into Metternich's ear. Even if it had been shouted he could not have heard. All the same, he remained the amiable host and still

knew how to do the honors of the house charmingly. The
old ladies rewarded him for the attention he showed them
with withered smiles. Only Princess Lieven, whose "cold
and mundane heart" remained young solely by the greedy
absorption of gossip, gave written testimony of the impression the aged former friend of her heart had made upon her
by stating flatly that he was "boring when he talked of himself, and charming when he talked of Napoleon." It will be
seen that the Graeco-Turkish question which had caused
the severance of their relations was still unsolved and remained so until after her death. "I am surprised she did not
die before," was the only remark the octogenarian made
when receiving the news.

Brighton was the scene of a sort of farewell parade of
Metternich's love-life. What a picture it was, suffused by the
dim twilight of a fading autumn: the aged Paris and the
three goddesses who, in the meantime, had changed into
three Parcae of Love. A ghostly dance, he may have thought,
emerging from the fog and being swallowed up by it again.
But, let us see! Had he not always been inordinately fond of
the long-gone-by? His predilection for what was old came
home now to the aged man with force.

"Rejoice and Be Merry"

THE tender and soulful Biedermeier melody, "Rejoice and be merry," which, thirty years after the war-like *Marseillaise*, typified the peaceful Metternich era, is said to have made a deep impression upon Rossini when on one of his journeys he passed through Zurich. The celebrated operatic composer asked that the sugary tune be played to him again and again, while he hummed the words to it:

> *Rejoice and be merry*
> *While bright shines the sun;*
> *Gather the roses*
> *Ere they are gone.*

Finally the old confectioner of melodies, who even then was more devoted to culinary art than to music, said: "I'll remember that for my new opera." "And in what form, maestro, will you use the melody?" "As a funeral march, of course," was the composer's quick-witted reply. As a matter of fact, he did use it in the overture to his opera *"Semiramis."*

Such a funeral march, written to the "Rejoice and be merry" stanza, might have aptly formed the musical accompaniment to the last part of Metternich's life-journey, from

325

eighty down to the pit. It would have been in keeping, too, with his taste. Rossini was his favorite composer, and unfortunately there is no doubt that he preferred him to Beethoven. In this connection it is significant that, for instance, he preferred the hills to the Alps; he had no use for the Alps at all. The opera *"Semiramis,"* on the other hand, he liked inordinately; and whenever the reminiscent strains of the "Rejoice and be merry" dimly reached his ear, so far as he was able to hear it at all, he drank it in thankfully while a mournful smile played on his lips.

The exile dragged on interminably. What so many notable examples have illustrated became apparent also in Metternich's case; a finished personality remains the same, exile or no exile, and after a while is bound to be accorded the position which is his due. It would seem that an exile must once more go through the examinations he thinks he has passed once and for all. If he is successful, Fate is usually seen to relent, graciously conceding a second time what it had once before granted. Generally speaking, emigration is the inexorable testing-block of a man's worth, and reveals what measure of respect and esteem ought to be accorded him. After all, the only change is in the address, and not in the place in life the person occupies. Everyone lives again exactly how he has lived before. The haughty ones will keep to one side, while the efficient ones will unite in a common front. Drones will remain drones, and workers will work.

The exiled dictator's next station after Brighton was Brussels, where he rented the house of the virtuoso Blériot. In the turn of a hand, kindled by the flame of his spirit, it became the focal point of conservative Europe. A year after '48, the reaction had set in simultaneously in all countries. Almost all the heads of governments who were gravely concerned in the matter, turned for counsel and aid to the pensioned medical wizard of the Humanity Hospital, as he, joking once more, liked to call himself now. He made diagnoses and wrote prescriptions as he had done again and again in the past. The only difference was that everything was attended to by correspondence. Nevertheless, he also received a large number of callers. Thiers, who was working on his famous "History of the Consulate and the Empire," came to see him to make use of his invaluable reminiscences. Metternich readily placed them at the author's disposal, telling him first-hand stories about Napoleon, which no one else was any longer able to do; he also wrote to Vienna so as to make the archives available to his caller, just as he had opened them years before to the German historian, Ranke. Another time, he received a visit from the socialist, Louis Blanc, whose writings he had just then begun to study. He still read a great deal, partly because he was of the opinion that at eighty his education was not yet complete, partly from curiosity, and partly also for hygienic reasons, since at a certain age reading is perhaps the surest prophylactic against sclerosis both of the heart and the soul. The socialistic theories, no matter how abysmally they differed from his own, occupied his mind, and he had no objection whatever to the visit of the man who knew how to develop them so ingeniously. Melanie was beside herself. In her diary she copiously reviled the strange guest behind his back, though her husband did not permit her rage to affect him. He had class prejudices which to him were a matter of course; but he refused to be narrow-minded.

Although the political horizon in Austria looked increasingly black, unfortunately there was no chance yet for

Metternich's return. This was due principally to the suit brought against him by the people, whose sovereignty, though it was not to last, was still undisputed. He was accused of having violated his official authority. The journeys to watering-places and Congresses came home to him now thirty years later. Aachen, Verona, Laibach, and others; especially, however, Aachen, where he had actually been somewhat imprudent by paying from public funds a disproportionately high rental for Mademoiselle Brammertz' premises, the famous *"loge"* in which he had been so happy with Dorothy. The sovereign people were of the opinion, and not quite illogically, that such expenses should not under all circumstances be borne by the tax-payers. Starting at that point, long-forgotten bills were unearthed and examined, a process which took many months. Finally a round sum of 102,000 gulden was compiled, in the sum of which the expensive "House, Court, and State Minister" had damaged the State, if the matter had not actually been fraudulent. The amount was later reduced to one-fifth of its size, and finally canceled altogether at the direction of the young Emperor Franz Joseph. A decree, formulated by Prince Schwarzenberg, Metternich's successor in office, was issued stating that it would be disgraceful to make a petty and wretched examination of the accounts of the great man who had rendered to Austria such inestimable services. The proceedings were discontinued, the investigating commission was discharged, and the sequestration of the beautiful house on the Rennweg was nullified. Rejoice and be merry.

The sad part of it was that all this took so much time, and that meanwhile beautiful life ebbed away so inexorably. Like most emigrants, Metternich had to realize that an exile usually lasts much longer than was at first anticipated. When he had turned his back upon Vienna, he had estimated that his absence would last three months. Three years were to pass before he was allowed to make his way home again. *Quand on est mort, c'est pour longtemps,* say the French who remain philosophic even in adversity. The same is true of those who are buried alive on a foreign shore.

In the second year the corpse began to show signs of restlessness. "That's all very well and good," he may have thought; "I am a great man and a great Austrian, especially in a foreign country; here in Brussels they all show their respect by bowing low before me—from the King down. Well, the King has reason to be thankful, for he has learned more than a little from me, as far as speaking and writing is concerned. But where is my own country? Where is Vienna which, unless I am entirely mistaken, made me an Honorary Citizen, once upon a time?"

Vexation and disgust engendered by such thoughts even made him slightly ill. He remembered all at once that he was seventy-eight years old, and went to bed pettishly. His daughter Leontine immediately and without his knowledge addressed a letter to Archduchess Sophie in Vienna, saying that her father's health gave her a great deal of concern and hinting that the old man would prefer to die in Vienna, rather than in Brussels. Obviously the women, even those of his own family, would not let him down.

Archduchess Sophie who, it was known, had considerable influence on her son, Emperor Franz Joseph, came forth with a hypocritical and jesuitical advice: let Prince Metternich return, but not to Vienna right away: Let him first go to Königswart, his estate in Bohemia, and from there, at a later date, in course of time, perhaps . . . The old man was well again in a trice. He got up out of his bed, straightened himself once more to his full height, and let Vienna know that he refused to sneak home by a rear door like a thief. If they wanted him back, let them invite him to come. If he said "they" and "them," he meant of course the Emperor.

At last, on April 6th, 1851, the long-delayed Imperial message in the Emperor's own hand came. Franz Joseph with his unfailing instinct for tact and dignity did not say in so many words that the old gentleman should return to Vienna; but in an Imperial manner he expressed the wish to be able to thank Metternich personally for all he had done for Austria. That was enough. The exile was ready to return. It was not without purpose, probably, that he let another half year pass before he actually set out. In the meantime, at Castle Johannisburg, of which he had also taken possession again, he received the visit of Bismarck who was on his way to the Diet in Frankfort and paid his respects while passing. The Junker nobleman, and the old legitimist understood each other excellently. The fratricidal contrast between Austria and Prussia, which was to culminate in the war of 1866, made its fateful appearance only later, when dilettantic statesmen unwarrantedly forced matters to a head. Johannisburg could have prevented Königgrätz. In the same month, the King of Prussia, Friedrich Wilhelm IV, came to have dinner with Metternich. He was charming in his own way, and only at the very end did he become rough when he saw the table-cloth whose black-red-gold combination of colors, political reasons caused him to find "horrid."

Finally, in the autumn of the same year, the banished man started upon his homeward journey, into an Austria which in the meantime had thought better of it and re-

turned to reactionary standards. It was a triumphal procession. At every frontier station he was received by another minister, in every capital asked to table by another
king, and urged to spend the night. In Mannheim he was
the guest of the Grand Duchess of Baden, in Stuttgart of
the King of Württemberg. In Ulm he was taken in charge
by the Austrian Ambassador and the Chief of the Bavarian
Cabinet. He was asked to board a festively decorated ship
which was to take him by way of Regensburg and Linz to
Vienna. The mild September sun suffused with a gentle
glow the distant castles and abbeys, as Metternich's ship
slowly glided down the lovely Wachau valley, where rus-
set vineyard slopes may have reminded the Rhinelander of
his native Rhine. Thus Austria solemnly conducted him
home, as if he had been his own corpse. Rejoice and be
merry.

If no torch-light parade was arranged for Metternich's
home-coming to Vienna, it was probably due to the fact that
one wished to avoid painful recollections of a certain display of candles a few short years before. At any rate, Metternich seemed in an entirely too imperturbable frame of
mind for comparisons. His was not a vengeful spirit, and he
felt no grudge against Vienna because, after all, he had
never really cared for it. Try as they might, the Viennese
could not disappoint him. Again he was able to say both of
the good and of the evil spirit of that city what he had
once said of Napoleon: "I have never taken it quite seriously."

His mind reverted again and again to Napoleon, especially now when, after the Duke of Wellington's death, he
had become the only surviving contemporary of that heroic

epoch. The aged man's deafness forced him to confine his listening to the voices of his soul. At every step or turn he was reminded of his great adversary, all the more so because a similar fate had overtaken him. His St. Helena had been that, in the midst of a Europe which for thirty years had seen democrats only when they were fleeing from the authorities, one day had seen him forced to flee before the enraged democrats. In the end, and after a comparatively short period of affliction, however, Fate had set him free again, probably because, after all, he was no genius. The prominence of an historical personage may be measured by the depth of his fall. How much deeper and harder had Napoleon fallen, who on St. Helena had nothing but the memory of glorious days! To Metternich, on the other hand, it had been vouchsafed to outlive St. Helena and to gaze back upon it from scenes of renewed splendor. His comparatively mild fall had landed him again comfortably in an upholstered chair in Vienna. No tragedy, this; only an emotional melodrama with the mild glow of the evening sun at the end.

Instead of a one-volume "Memorial" he wrote eight volumes of memoirs, which he mulled over and over again in his conversations. One of his constantly recurring favorites was a recital of Napoleon's birthday celebrations which he had been obliged to attend as Austrian Ambassador. That had not always been convenient, and was for that very reason unforgettable. The ill-humored lord of the battlefield was particularly fond of picking a quarrel on such days, and it was then no laughing matter for his ministers and ambassadors—especially not for Metternich. As the years went by, how much he longed for a recurrence of those Imperial bursts of rage! How gladly would he have let Napoleon scold him day in and day out! He became wrapped in deep thought and silence. Because he kept silent so rarely, the others could gauge the depth of his love of Napoleon, and realize how unconditionally he acknowledged his genius.

Great age lives only in recollections. Perhaps it is to be envied for it, because in the reflection—as the poet, too, sees it—life is more beautiful than in reality; even exile becomes surrounded with a distant glow. When on some silvery autumn morning the returned man sedately walked in the garden of his villa on the Rennweg, thoughts went humming through his mind. Pensively he would stand still and see quite clearly all at once what had drawn him back to Vienna. It had been the stars of the autumn flowers in the border-beds, now lifting up their childlike gaze to his old and wrinkled face. It had been the earth on which he stood.

That, and nothing else.

There was one fact at any rate which Metternich had in common with the much greater Napoleon: misfortune had added to both men's stature. The post-revolutionary Metternich, as a wise man with a thousand recollections, did nothing any more but stroll leisurely in his garden—or in the high-vaulted passages of his State philosophy; in his kindness and amiability he was an almost venerable and, compared to his successors, a well-nigh ethical figure. Never, like one of these successors, Prince Schwarzenberg, would he have hoodwinked the people with a constitution which at the outset had firmly determined to rescind again at an early moment. Neither would he ever have been able to utter the words of Schwarzenberg who, when he was urged to pardon the revolutionary Hungarian generals, said: "An amnesty? Why, certainly, why not? But first we'll do a little hanging." That was the difference: Metternich was never cynical like Schwarzenberg; compared to him, he was almost liberal.

The human element of his character came more and more to the surface in these later years, as for instance when in a letter he drew a comparison between an aging and an old man. The aging man, he said, sees in a garden only the withered leaves, and sees them with aversion. The old man contemplates them with joy, because from them new life will sprout. Another picture takes us to the nursery of his two-year-old granddaughter, who later became Princess Öttingen. The man of eighty-four was sitting on the floor playing with the child, while the mother who had come in unawares looked on with emotion. When Metternich noticed her, he said gaily: "Well, it looks as though I was born to be a nursery maid." Must not all do now what formerly was the women's prerogative: love him?

There was no lack of honors for the old gentleman in the grandfather's chair. Once more Melanie was invited everywhere, just as she had been in London, Brighton, Brussels, and other places. Pleasure-bent as she was, she quite placidly attended a ball at the State-Chancellery where once she had been the hostess. Metternich, for his part, sent his excuses and did not again set foot in the venerable house on the Ballhausplatz until Schwarzenberg had gone and a successor took up residence there—a successor whose insignificance brought about a proportionate increase of Metternich's own influence. The young Emperor, who was now his own prime minister, repeatedly did his former teacher the honor to ask him his opinion. That he seldom acted upon it had its advantages, for it placed Metternich in the position of being able to say from time to time: "I told you so!" Sweet comfort for old age!

Among these I-told-you-so's was his old axiom that Austria must under no circumstances give up her alliance with Russia. When it was given up Austria's misfortunes commenced. In this category also belongs his old expression that "principles are the formulae of truth." To him these principles were the eternal ties between all governments. He did not only believe in a revealed religion, which every devout man must do and does, but also in a revealed philosophy which, to be sure, marked the beginning of his error. It was at any rate quite useless to try to make the entirely unphilosophically inclined young Emperor understand such things. On the other hand, the wise old man succeeded in the end by recognizing him as an Emperor in inducing Napoleon III to quiet down and forget his warlike desires, for the time being. Like the uncle, Metternich finally also defeated the nephew—and on the unbloody battle field of diplomacy, quite without a Leipsic. Thus it was a double victory; for not to unleash wars but to prevent them, is the task of diplomats.

With the Crimean War came Cavour, the new star, who together with Talleyrand, Bismarck, Disraeli, and Metternich formed the five-starred constellation of 19th-century European statesmanship; and came finally the increasingly unavoidable duel with the rising young Italy. "For Heaven's sake, no ultimatum!" said the eighty-six-year-old Metternich to the twenty-nine-year-old Emperor Franz Joseph. To which the latter answered drily: "It was dispatched yesterday." What was more, the young monarch who was so unamenable to advice soon assumed the supreme military command, which enabled him personally to lose the Battle of Solferino. It happened in a typically Austrian manner. The sanguinary battle as a matter of fact virtually had been won; but the Emperor, totally inexperienced in the profession of arms, lost his nerve at the sight of so many dead and wounded and ordered a precipitate retreat from a position which could have been held. The Italians stared in surprise. They had gained a victory without knowing it.

The unfortunate Italian campaign brought Metternich a last and singular honor, one which was never bestowed on any Austrian statesman before and after him. With a truly Imperial lack of consideration, Franz Joseph, about to start for the front, disturbed the morning slumber of the aged man and requested him to draw up his, the Emperor's, last will. Metternich, loyal servant of Habsburg to the last, did it. And so, an adept in the art of living to the end, he occupied himself with drawing up another man's last will, when quite unexpectedly the last summons came to him.

His very last days were a wonderful adagio, accompanied by the thunderous roar of a distant war whose painful conclusion he was spared to witness. No enemy penetrated into his presence any longer. Glorifying descriptions of his most loyal admirers, his granddaughter Pauline Metternich and Baron Hübner, tell of his passing into eternity.

Hübner, who was Austria's Ambassador in Paris, had been recalled at the outbreak of the war and paid a visit to the aged State-Chancellor. They took a walk in the park of the villa, the old man leaning on the arm of the younger one. The latter was pained to notice how light had become the arm which for half a century had ruled Europe. They talked of the past, the paradise of old people. To sum up, and probably for the thousandth time, Metternich said: "I was a rock of order." At this point, and for the time being, he dismissed his visitor, who was moved, however, by a sort of presentiment once more softly to open the door to the study, so as to snatch a last sight of the old man's waxy face. Metternich must have expected it, for, already seated at his writing table, pen in hand, he nodded to his young friend and, as an actor at the final rehearsal once more speaks the closing words of the act, repeated: "A rock of order." A ray of the May sun, so Hübner asserts, animated and beautified his face at that moment. Very touching. So as to provide an element of irony, which often lies in wait for sentimentality round the next corner, it ought to be mentioned that according to whispered comments, Hübner, who only later was raised to the rank of a Count, was supposed to be Metternich's illegitimate son. The assurance that he was a rock of order is therefore also placed in the glorifying light of the May sun, which we shall not begrudge the old fellow.

More matter-of-fact, and therefore more affecting, is Pauline Metternich's account of the moments of her grandfather's passing. She was an ingenious and spirited woman who became as old as he himself and, a true descendant of the Chancellor, held dictatorial sway over Vienna's social set of the Franz-Joseph era. A very young woman at the time, she was called to her grandfather's deathbed at eleven o'clock in the forenoon, on the 10th of June, 1859. Following his daily custom, grandfather had got up early in the morning, but had asked his valet to put him to bed again as he was not feeling quite well. The servant notified the physician, the faithful Dr. Jaeger, who came every day "to have a look"; the doctor in turn sent word to the father confessor. The latter was a Franciscan who used to read a daily mass at Metternich's private chapel at about that time. Metternich was fully conscious and was gladly willing to see the priest. The latest war news which he had read conscientiously may have made him somewhat less anxious to stay in this world. In the meantime the family-circle had closed round the bed. They were all there, with the exception of the society-loving Melanie who had dutifully preceded him in death, as had all his women friends. His elder son, Richard was absent. A few friends, too, had hurriedly arrived. Grandpapa lay in his bed, his blue eyes wide open, and nothing that took place in the room escaped him. When the face of his younger son, Lothar, who stood at the foot of the bed, was convulsed with suppressed sobs, the departing man softly motioned to him to compose himself. A little later, Dr. Jaeger felt for his pulse. "You will be looking in vain," the fluttering finger-tips of the apparently still jocularly inclined old man seemed to say. Then he considerately closed his eyes; and after a little while the shrunken chest moved no more.

It is said that a drowning man sees his whole life pass before him in a flash. Is not every death, though, occurring at full consciousness, the death of one who is sinking into the infinite? And does not everyone in such a position make a very tender final choice? What was it that had proved unforgettable to old Clemens? Was it his great conversation with Napoleon at the Marcolini Palace in Dresden? Was it Dorothy who from out of infinite spaces whispered into his ear: "Would you not like to be the other tree?" Was it the ever-troublesome Europe, or was it little Richard of the soap-bubbles who, though he surely must now be at the scene of the Italian war, so curiously and shadow-like grew one with young Lothar, the much-too-young son who tried to stifle his sobs at the foot of the bed? Well, at the very last, perhaps this was the question: What was more important, Europe or the soap-bubble? As usual, the question remained unanswered, because he who had put it so astutely and formulated it so cleverly, had at that very moment ceased to breathe.

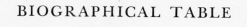

BIOGRAPHICAL TABLE

Biographical Table

ALEXANDER I (1776–1825). Emperor of Russia, grandson of Catherine the Great, autocrat and Jacobin, man of the world and mystic. To Metternich, he was a mad-man to be humored. From 1801 he was a great admirer of Napoleon. He turned against him after several years and was routed at Friedland. For a time the two Emperors were allies but Napoleon turned against him.

BAGRATION, PETER, PRINCE (1765–1812). Russian general, distinguished himself at Austerlitz, Eylau and Friedland. He was killed at the battle of Brodino. His wife was one of Metternich's mistresses.

BALZAC, HONORÉ DE (1799–1850). French novelist. One of the greatest of the 19th century. All of his works are integral parts of what he called The Human Comedy. Balzac was a true child of the Napoleonic era. No writer of the 19th century created such an immense bulk of first-rate creative literature.

BARRAS, PAUL FRANÇOIS NICOLAS, COMTE DE (1755–1829). Member of the French Directory of 1795–1799. Owing to his intimate relations with Josephine de Beauharnais, he helped to facilitate a marriage between her and Bonaparte to the command of the army of Italy in 1796. Overthrown by Bonaparte in the coup d'état of the 18th *Brumaire*.

BAUERNFELD, EDUARD VON (1802–1890). He was for many years in the Austrian civil service. A very clever writer of comedies and farces. He takes high rank among the German writers of the century.

BEAUHARNAIS, EUGÈNE DE (1781–1824). Stepson of Napoleon I

and son of the Empress Josephine. Very valuable to Napoleon at the time of the coup d'état of the 18th *Brumaire* and during the consulate in 1799–1804. In 1806 appointed by Napoleon viceroy of the kingdom of Italy with large administrative powers. Held important commands in the army of France during the wars of Austria, Russia and the coalitions.

BEETHOVEN, LUDWIG VAN (1770–1820). German musical composer. Settled in Vienna in the 1790's. His "Eroica" was written because of his great admiration for the republican general Napoleon. Author of nine classic symphonies. One of the three greatest composers of all times.

BERTHIER, LOUIS ALEXANDER (1753–1815). Marshal of France and chief of staff under Napoleon. One of the most brilliant executive officers of the century who understood and carried out all commands to the minutest details.

BISMARCK, OTTO VON (1815–1898). German statesman. After a long diplomatic career, he became Prussian chancellor in 1862. He was responsible for the dominance of Prussia over the German states, including Austria, and the unification of Germany in 1871.

BLÜCHER, GEBHARD LEBERECHT VON (1742–1819). Prussian field marshal. One of the leaders of the war party in Prussia in 1806, and cavalry commander in the disastrous campaigns of the latter year. One of the officers, chiefly responsible for the decisive defeat of Napoleon at the battle of Leipzig. Commanded the Prussian army in the Waterloo campaign and was important in the crushing defeat of Napoleon at Waterloo.

BONAPARTE, JOSEPH (1768–1844). He was a valuable aid to his brother Napoleon and was made King, first of Naples and then in 1808 king of Spain, but his sovereignty was little more than titular. In 1803 after Wellington's victory at Vittoria Joseph fled from Spain and was disgraced by Napoleon. In 1814, he was restored to Napoleon's favor.

BONAPARTE, LOUIS NAPOLEON (1778–1846). In 1802 Napoleon married him to Hortense Beauharnais, a forced union which led to most deplorable results. In 1806 Napoleon made him King of Holland. In 1808 he offered him the throne of Spain but Louis refused. In 1810 Holland was annexed to France. Louis fled and afterwards he lived chiefly in Rome.

CANNING, GEORGE (1770–1827). British statesman—a follower of Pitt from 1793–1801. From 1801–1809 he was partly in opposition and partly in office fighting for the foremost place. Between 1809–1822 period of comparative eclipse. From 1822 to his death in 1827, he was the most powerful influence in England and one of the most powerful in European politics. His policy was one of non-intervention and the patronage of national and liberal movements in Spain, Portugal, Greece, Italy. Foe of Metternich.

CARLOS, DON (1788–1855). The first of the Carlist claimants to the throne of Spain. When his brother King Ferdinand altered the Salic law of succession in favor of his daughter Isabella, Don Carlos rebelled and on the death of the King he attempted to seize the throne, but failed.

CARNOT, LAZARE (1753–1823). French general. Took part in the campaigns of 1792–1794 and was the victor at Wattignies. He was President-member of the Directory of 1795. In 1800 he was minister of war. His theories were very influential in fortification strategy.

CAROLINE, QUEEN (1768–1821). Queen of George IV of Great Britain. The latter separated from her after a year of marriage. In 1820 King George had a bill brought into the House of Lords to divorce her on the grounds of adultery but the plan failed.

CASTLEREAGH, LORD (1769–1822). Second Marquess of Londonderry. British statesman who with Canning and Pitt, formed a triad of Napoleon's deadliest enemies. In 1812, he became foreign secretary and leader of the House of Commons. This double burden he continued to bear until his suicide in 1822. From March 1812 to July 1822 Castlereagh's biography is in truth the biography of Europe.

CAVOUR, CAMILLO, COUNT (1810–1861). Italian statesman. In 1848 he prevailed upon the King of Piedmont to declare war on Austria, but Piedmont was decisively defeated. In 1851 he was finance minister and after a short retirement he became premier, a post which he held, except for two short periods, until his death. With Mazzini and Garibaldi, he was instrumental in expelling Austria from Italy and unifying Italy.

CHAMPAGNY, JEAN BAPTISTE (1756–1834). French politician. From 1801–1804 he was Ambassador to Vienna and directed with great intelligence the incessant negotiations between the two states. In 1807 he was foreign minister and negotiated the Peace of Vienna (1809) and the marriage of Napoleon.

CHARLES X (1757–1836). King of France 1824–1830. In 1789 he left France and became leader of the *émigrés*. During the reign of his brother Louis XVIII, he was leader of the ultra Royalists. Upon his succession in 1824, it became obvious that he would become a most reactionary king. In 1830, he was overthrown by Louis Philippe, Duke of Orléans.

CONYNGHAM, MARCHIONESS OF (1774–1861). An English mistress of George IV, who had great influence with the King after 1816. She was "The Lady Steward" of his household, and her rapacity and influence added much to his unpopularity. Her influence lasted until his death in 1830.

CUSTINE, ADAM, COMTE DE (1740–1793). French general. General in chief of the army of Vosges. He took Spires, Worms, Mainz, Frankfort in the fall of 1792. In the winter, he was driven back across the Rhine by the Prussians. Was tried in Paris for treason and was executed in 1793.

DALBERG, EMMERICH, DUC DE (1773–1833). After the peace of Schönbrunn in 1809 he entered the service of Napoleon. He was an intimate friend of Talleyrand and attended the Congress of Vienna as one of the three French delegates.

DISRAELI, BENJAMIN. Earl of Beaconfield (1804–1881). British statesman. His career began as a novelist, and he entered Parliament in 1837. He took office as British finance minister in 1852; was prime minister in 1868, 1873–1880 and again in 1886. He was a strong imperialist, and the author of so-called Tory democracy. He was a great admirer of Metternich.

ELSSLER, FANNY (1810–1884). Austrian dancer. One of the great ballet dancers of the 19th century. A remarkably beautiful woman, who inspired the aged statesman Friedrich von Gentz with a remarkable but unrequited passion. In 1845 she retired from the stage.

FERDINAND I (1793–1875). Emperor of Austria. He succeeded his father Franz I. As he was feebleminded, the conduct of affairs was entrusted to a regency council composed of Metternich, Kolowrat, and the Archduke Ludwig. He abdicated in 1848 in favor of his nephew Franz Joseph.

FEUCHTERSLEBEN, ERNST VON (1806–1849). Austrian physician, poet, and philosopher. He was for a time under-secretary of the ministry of education. He was a poet of great ability and the author of the beautiful hymn, *"Es ist bestimmt und Gottes Rat,"* which Mendelssohn set to music.

FICHTE, IMMANUEL VON (1797–1879). German philosopher. His philosophy was an attempt to reconcile monism (Hegel) and individualism (Herbart) by means of theism (Leibnitz). He was a strong partisan of German nationalism.

FOUCHÉ, JOSEPH, DUKE OF OTRANTO (1763–1820). French statesman, whose chief career was spent as a minister of police under Napoleon. He was extremely efficient in suppressing plots against the Emperor. Dismissed in 1810 for secretly negotiating with Britain, he was restored to office when Napoleon returned from Elba, but again turned on his master.

FRANZ I (1768–1835). The last Roman emperor and the first Emperor of Austria. Succeeded to the throne in 1792. From 1806 until the end of his reign he acted as his own prime minister, although in foreign affairs after 1809 he relied exclusively on Metternich.

FRANZ JOSEF (1830–1916). Emperor of Austria. Ascended the throne on the abdication of his uncle Ferdinand in 1848. Until 1852 he was greatly under the influence of Prince Schwarzenberg, but thereafter his personal government began. Under him Austria lost nearly everything Franz and Metternich had gained for her.

FRIEDRICH WILHELM III (1770–1840). King of Prussia. Succeeded to the throne in 1797. Too distrustful to delegate his responsibilities to his ministers, he lacked the ability to carry them out himself. The result was the disaster of Jena. He entrusted the government to Stein later, who was instrumental in the resurrection of Prussia. On Metternich's advice he broke his promise to grant Prussia a constitution.

FRIEDRICH WILHELM IV (1795–1861). King of Prussia. Acceded to the throne in 1840. He refused the German crown in 1848, because he believed the offer to be tainted by revolution.

GENTZ, FRIEDRICH VON (1764–1832). German publicist and statesman. The assistant, confidant, and advisor of Metternich from 1809 to 1822. Gentz was secretary of the Congress of Vienna, and was the most remarkable political writer of the era.

GEORGE III (1738–1820). King of Great Britain. An arbitrary monarch whose policies lost America for Great Britain. From 1801 to 1815 Britain was involved with France in a mortal struggle, though after Trafalgar the danger of direct invasion of England passed. His insanity in 1811 left his son George (later George IV) to act as Regent for nine years.

GEORGE IV (1762–1830). King of Great Britain. His father's insanity caused him to assume the powers of regent for nine years before he ascended the throne in 1820. Perhaps the most unpopular sovereign Britain has had. His notorious divorce suit against his wife after he became king added to this, although other causes were his fantastic extravagance and his mistresses.

GÉRARD, FRANÇOIS, BARON (1770–1837). French painter. From 1799 he was considered the leading portraitist in France. All the most celebrated men and women of the time, including Metternich, sat to Gérard.

GOETHE, JOHANN WOLFGANG VON (1749–1832). Germany's greatest poet and dramatist. The author of "Werther" which had a tremendous influence in stimulating romanticism, of "Wilhelm Meister" which Somerset Maugham called "that wonderful and neglected work" and of the world-famous drama "Faust." His ideas have had an extraordinary influence on European writers.

GRILLPARZER, FRANZ (1791–1872). The greatest dramatic poet

of Austria. He was nearly all his life an Austrian civil servant. His poetry reflects exactly the chafed spirit of his people under the Metternich regime. He expressed the mood of Austria in the epoch of intellectual thralldom that lay between the Napoleonic wars and the revolution of 1848.

GUIZOT, FRANÇOIS PIERRE (1787–1874). French historian, orator and statesman. He advocated the policy of the middle path between absolutism and popular government. After some ten years in French politics, he became in 1840 foreign minister, and several years later, prime minister. He was a bitter antagonist of Palmerston. He fell in the revolution of 1848 and spent the next twenty-six years of his life writing history instead of making it.

HARDENBERG, KARL VON (1750–1822). Prussian statesman. He became chancellor of Prussia after the forced retirement of Stein in 1810. He was chief delegate of Prussia to the Congress of Vienna; he was constantly overmatched by Metternich in the councils of Europe, of Germany, and ultimately of Prussia itself.

HEINE, HEINRICH (1797–1856). German poet. One of the greatest lyric poets of the 19th century. He was of Jewish origin, and his works were suppressed by the German "Bund" for being revolutionary. He bitterly disliked the reaction which set in after the downfall of Napoleon, yet his poems were favorites of Metternich.

HOFER, ANDREAS (1767–1810). Tyrolese patriot. He was an innkeeper originally and was bitterly opposed to the Bavarian rule of the Tyrol. Several times he was able to restore the Tyrol to Austria, but each time France restored it to Bavaria by force of arms. In 1810 Hofer was executed in Mantua for treason.

HÜBNER, JOSEPH (1811–1892). Austrian diplomat. He began his career in 1833 under Metternich whose confidence he soon gained. He filled many diplomatic missions for Austria, and wrote several historical works. He was the last survivor of the Metternich school.

ISABELLA, QUEEN (1830–1904). Queen of Spain. Became queen

on the death of her father, Ferdinand VII, in 1833. Her father had persuaded the Cortes to alter the laws of succession in her favor. Don Carlos, her uncle, who would have become king under the Salic law, rebelled, but due to his lack of ability, and the devotion of the Cortes and the army to the Queen's cause, he never became a serious peril. Metternich espoused Don Carlos' cause. Isabella abdicated in 1868.

JOSEPH, ARCHDUKE, PALATINE OF HUNGARY (1776–1847). He was a brother of Emperor Franz I of Austria, and through Metternich's activity, he was exposed as the romantic lover of the Emperor's wife, Maria Ludovika. This forced his retirement. His daughter married King Leopold II of Belgium.

JOSEPHINE (1763–1814). Empress of the French. The first wife of Napoleon. Josephine's influence as far as it was exerted was nearly always on the side of peace and moderation in internal as well as in foreign affairs. She was opposed to the execution of the Duc d'Enghien and opposed the Spanish adventure. In 1809 she was divorced by Napoleon for reasons of state.

JUNOT, ANDOCHE, DUC D'ABRANTÈS (1771–1813). French general. Best known for his campaigns in Portugal and Spain. Committed suicide in 1813.

KARL, LUDWIG, ARCHDUKE OF AUSTRIA (1771–1841). In 1796 he was in command of the Austrian forces. In his operations against Jourdan and Moreau in 1796 he was brilliantly successful, forcing the French armies out of Germany. He was the only Austrian general capable of defeating the French but after Austria's unsuccessful wars against France in 1809 he retired.

KAUNITZ, WENZEL, PRINCE VON (1711–1792). Austrian chancellor and diplomat. His history from 1750 until 1792 is the history of Austria and even Europe. Grandfather of Metternich's first wife Eleonore.

KLEIST, HEINRICH VON (1771–1811). German poet, dramatist, and novelist. Retired from the Prussian service in 1799 with rank of lieutenant. Studied law and philosophy and in 1800 received a subordinate post in the ministry of finance in Berlin. Traveled about and then returned to his post and was transferred to the department for the administration of crown lands. His work reflects his restless striving after ideal and illusory happiness. Was by far the most important North German dramatist of the romantic movement.

KOLOWRAT, FRANZ ANTON, COUNT (1778–1861). A member of the Regency Council which governed Austria in the reign of Ferdinand, 1835–1848. He was also Minister of the Interior during this time. A rival and bitter antagonist of Metternich.

KRÜDENER, JULIANE, BARONESS VON (1764–1824). Russian religious mystic and author. Creator of "Holy Alliance" which she persuaded Czar Alexander I to sponsor.

LAWRENCE, SIR THOMAS (1769–1830). English painter. In 1794, he became a royal academician and soon was the fashionable portrait painter of the age, having as his sitters all the rank, fashion, and talent of England and ultimately all the crowned heads of Europe.

LIEVEN, CHRISTOPH COUNT (later), PRINCE (1777–1839). Russian diplomat. He was ambassador at the Court of St. James in the 1820's, and took an active part in several of the conferences of the Powers which followed the downfall of Napoleon. He was the husband of the fascinating Dorothy Lieven, who was Metternich's mistress.

LIEVEN, DOROTHY, COUNTESS (later), PRINCESS (1785–1857). Russian ambassadress to London in the 1820's. Her letters to her lover, Metternich, and her journal have been published in the last few years, and revealed her to be a writer of a high order, and to have had great influence in the councils of state of England, Russia, and Austria. She had a true bent for politics.

LENAU, NIKOLAUS (1802–1850). Austrian poet. A friend of Uhland, Kerner and Karl Meyer. He lived for a time in America. He is the greatest modern lyric poet of Austria, and is representative of the Byronic *Weltschmerz* of the period.

LEOPOLD II (1747–1792). Emperor of Austria. In 1765 he became Grand Duke of Tuscany and showed a strong tendency towards liberalism. He succeeded to the throne of Austria at the death of his eldest brother Joseph in 1790. If he had reigned for more than two years it is probable that he would have repeated his successes in Tuscany on a far larger scale. His death was an irreparable blow to Austria.

LIGNE, CHARLES JOSEPH, PRINCE DE (1735–1814). Soldier and writer. He distinguished himself in the Seven Years War. The intimate friend and counsellor of the Emperor Joseph II. His great Brabant estates were captured by the French in 1792. He subsequently devoted himself to literary work.

LOUISE, QUEEN OF PRUSSIA (1776–1810). Wife of King Friedrich Wilhelm III. Commanded universal respect and affection not only in Prussia but in Europe.

LUDWIG, ARCHDUKE (1784–1864). A younger brother of Emperor Franz I, and brother of Emperor Ferdinand. He served in the Austrian Regency council under Ferdinand, from 1835 to 1848. His great dislike for novelty led him to act as a brake on the council, which could accomplish very little. He favored Metternich's downfall in 1848.

MARIE LOUISE (1791–1847). The second wife of Napoleon I. She was the daughter of Franz I, Austrian Emperor. Napoleon married her for reasons of state, the plan having originated with Metternich. There is much reason to believe that Napoleon loved her, probably because she bore him a son, who was heir to his imperial throne. From the time of Napoleon's first abdication in 1814, she never saw him again. The Congress of Vienna created her Duchess of Parma. She lived for years with Count Neipperg while Napoleon was still alive.

MEHEMET ALI (1769–1847). Viceroy of Egypt. The hereditary succession of the Khediviate of Egypt was fixed on Mehemet and his descendants. By using European methods of warfare he made the province of Egypt dominant in Turkey.

METTERNICH, FRANZ GEORG, COUNT VON (1746–1818). Diplomat who passed from the service of the Archbishop Elector of Trier to that of the court of Vienna. At the birth of Clemens Metternich and for some time subsequently was Austrian ambassador to the courts of the three Rhenish electors.

MURAT, CAROLINE, QUEEN OF NAPLES (1782–1839). Youngest sister of Napoleon. Immensely ambitious woman. Mistress of Metternich while he was ambassador at Paris. Deported with

BIOGRAPHICAL TABLE

her two sons to Trieste after the crushing defeat of Murat by the Austrians in 1815. She lived for a number of years after his death in Austria by Metternich's grace.

MURAT, JOACHIM, KING OF NAPLES (1767–1815). One of Napoleon's best cavalry officers. Married Caroline Bonaparte in 1800, youngest sister of Napoleon. Became general in chief of the French armies in Spain, and soon after was appointed by Napoleon to the throne of Naples. His attempt to establish himself as national King of Italy was smashed by Austria.

NAPOLEON BONAPARTE (1769–1821). Emperor of the French, born in Corsica, died in St. Helena, 1821. Metternich was his great adversary and Napoleon was finally overthrown by him.

NEIPPERG, ADAM ADELBERT. (later) PRINCE OF MONTENUEVO. (1775–1829). Austrian cavalry commander. He distinguished himself in the Napoleonic wars, and was assigned by Metternich to act as aide-de-camp to the Empress Marie Louise, after Napoleon's downfall. Even during the latter's life in exile at St. Helena, Neipperg was Marie Louise's lover. They were married, morganatically, in 1821, soon after Napoleon's death.

NESSELRODE, CARL ROBERT, COUNT (1780–1862). Russian statesman and diplomat. From 1812 he directed Russia's foreign policy and was influential in the restoration of the Bourbons. After Waterloo, he was against the imposition of a ruinous war indemnity on France. An advocate of the Metternichian system and of the "Holy Alliance," he retained office under Nicholas I.

NESTROY, JOHANN (1801–1862). Austrian dramatist. He was most popular in Vienna in the Biedermeier era for his folk plays and farces.

NICHOLAS I (1796–1855). Emperor of Russia. Succeeded his brother Alexander I in 1825. The crowning fault of Nicholas was that he would not delegate his authority; in this he resembled his contemporary Franz I. A cordial adherent to the Metternichian system.

DUKE OF ORLÉANS, FERDINAND (1810–1842). A son of Louis Philippe. At the outbreak of the revolution in 1830, which set his father on the throne, he was colonel of a regiment of Hussars.

Appointed Lieutenant General of the army and made several campaigns in Algiers. On his return to France organized the battalions of light infantry known as Chasseurs d'Orléans.

PALMERSTON, HENRY JOHN TEMPLE, VISCOUNT (1774–1865). English statesman. Specialist on foreign affairs, he was a strong adherent of the policies of Canning in the Spanish, Portuguese, Belgian, and Greek questions. On all these issues he was in strong opposition to the policies of Metternich, especially on the Italian question. His chief antagonist was the Emperor Nicholas I.

LOUIS PHILIPPE (1773–1850). King of France. A representative of the Orléanist branch of the Bourbon family. After a long exile during the Napoleonic era he returned to France in 1815. In 1830 Charles X was deposed and he became King.

PICHLER, KAROLINE (1769–1843). Austrian novelist, daughter of a government official. For many years, her salon was a center of the literary life in the Austrian capitol. She made her mark in historical romance.

PITT, WILLIAM (1759–1806). English statesman and youngest prime minister in the history of Great Britain. Mortal enemy of Napoleon. During Napoleon's attempt to invade Great Britain which were crushed by Nelson's victory at Trafalgar, he was prime minister. Died before his dream of removing the Napoleonic threat to Europe could be realized.

RAIMUND, FERDINAND (1790–1836). Austrian actor and dramatist. Raimund was a master of the Viennese farce; his rich humor is seen to the best advantage in his realistic portraits of his fellow citizens.

REICHSTADT, DUKE OF ("KING OF ROME") (1811–1832). Only legitimate son of Napoleon I. In 1814 Napoleon abdicated in favor of his son. The Prince was a pawn in the chess game of European politics but all hopes of his followers were destroyed by his untimely death at the age of twenty-one.

REMUSAT, CLAIRE DE (1780–1824). She was generally recognized as a woman of great intellectual capacity and personal grace. It was not until her grandson published her memoirs long after her death that justice was done to her acid literary talent.

Rossini, Gioachino (1792–1868). Italian musical composer. A prolific writer of opera and orchestral music. After living for a time in Florence he settled in Paris where he was the center of artistic society. The composer of the "Barber of Seville" and "William Tell."

Rostand, Edmond (1868–1918). French dramatist. The production of his heroic comedy "Cyrano" was a great personal triumph for him; it was translated and presented in all the European countries. The author of "L'Aiglon," in which Sarah Bernhardt scored one of her greatest successes.

Rothschild, Solomon (1774–1826). Austrian banker. An intimate friend and associate of Prince Metternich which fact contributed greatly in the success of the firm in its banking negotiations with the allied powers.

Saint-Simon, Louis, Duc de (1675–1755). French soldier, diplomat, and writer. A strong believer in the rule of France by the aristocracy. His greatest fame has come from his philosophic writings.

Schiller, Friedrich von (1750–1805). German poet, dramatist, and philosopher. The premier historical dramatist of Germany. Author of numerous notable plays based on world shaking events in Europe in the 16th and 17th century. First of the great German playwrights.

Schwarzenberg, Karl Philipp, Prince Zu (1771–1820). Austrian field marshal. Served in all the campaigns of the Napoleonic wars in high Austrian command. In 1813 he was in command of the allied grand army of Bohemia and was the senior field commander in the Leipsic campaign.

Semonville, Charles (1759–1839). French diplomat and statesman. Fulfilled numerous diplomatic missions for Napoleon. He was later very influential in the French senate.

Stadion, Johann (1763–1824). Austrian statesman. Rose early to a high position in the diplomatic service. In 1813 he was commissioned to negotiate the convention which finally overthrew Napoleon in the campaigns of 1814.

Stein, Heinrich Friedrich, Baron von (1757–1831). German statesman. After the terrible defeat of Prussia at Jena, Stein became virtually the dictator of the reduced and nearly bankrupt Prussian state. He made far-reaching reforms including the abolition of serfdom, the reorganization of finances, and drastic changes in the army. Metternich check-mated his great plan for the unification of Germany.

STENDHAL (BEYLE, MARIE HENRI) (1783–1842). Great ardent French novelist. An ardent admirer of Napoleon. His fame is based on his novels of which the two greatest were "Le Rouge et Le Noir" and "La Chartreuse de Parme." His work has been most influential in the development of the French novel.

STIFTER, ADELBERT (1805–1868). Austrian author. He was tutor to Richard, the eldest son of Prince Metternich. His sketches of scenery and rural life are among the best and purest examples of German prose.

TAAFFE, EDUARD, VON (1833–1895). Austrian statesman. He had a strong feeling of patriotism for Austria and loyalty to Emperor Franz Josef who maintained him in office as prime minister despite Taaffe's great unpopularity.

TALLEYRAND-PÉRIGORD, CHARLES, DE (1754–1838). French statesman. A unique figure who served in important posts in the *ancien regime,* the Napoleonic era and the restoration. Under Louis XVI he was a Bishop, under Napoleon, Foreign Minister and under Louis XVIII he was chief French delegate to the Congress of Vienna. With Metternich he was important in the downfall of Napoleon.

THIERS, LOUIS ADOLPHE (1797–1877). French statesman and historian. Together with Guizot he alternated in the domination of the French foreign office under Louis Philippe and Napoleon III. The author of the well-known "History of the Consulate and the Empire."

THUGUT, JOHANN, BARON (1736–1818). Austrian statesman. After fulfilling many diplomatic missions he was appointed by Leopold foreign minister and in 1794 he became chancellor. He believed that Prussia was Austria's worst enemy and was a bitter foe of the French Revolution. He retired in 1800 after the Austrian defeat at Hohenlinden.

TICKNOR, GEORGE (1791–1871). American educator and author.

Professor of Belles Lettres at Harvard from 1817. In 1839 he began work on his magnum opus, a great history of Spanish life and literature which is still standing. He traveled extensively in Europe many times.

VARNHAGEN, RAHEL (1771–1833). A woman of remarkable intellectual qualities who exercised a powerful influence on many important figures of her period. After her death much of her memoirs and correspondence were printed and gained for her posthumously a great reputation.

WELLINGTON, ARTHUR WELLESLEY, DUKE OF (1769–1852). British soldier and statesman. His masterly campaign in Portugal and Spain during the Peninsular war 1808–1814 won him lasting military renown to which he added by his smashing defeat of Napoleon at Waterloo. Until his death he exerted tremendous influence in Great Britain.

WINDISCHGRÄTZ, PRINCE ALFRED (1787–1862). Austrian field marshal. He participated in all the wars against Napoleon. A champion of energetic measures against revolution, he was called upon many times to quell various insurrections and uprisings in Austria.

YORK, FREDERICK, DUKE OF (1763–1827). The second son of King George III. Much of his life was spent in the administration of the British army. Although unsuccessful as a field commander in the revolutionary wars of 1799, he was of great importance as an organizer during his long tenure as British commander-in-chief, 1798–1809 and 1811–1827.

INDEX

Index